C0-AOD-329

HARNESSING
Innovative
TECHNOLOGY IN
HIGHER EDUCATION

Access, Equity, Policy, & Instruction

Harnessing Innovative Technology in Higher Education:
Access, Equity, Policy, and Instruction

Edited by Kathleen P. King and Joan K. Griggs

© 2006 Atwood Publishing Madison, WI
www.atwoodpublishing.com
888.247.7101

Cover design by Tamara Dever, TLC Graphics, www.tlcgraphics.com.

Library of Congress Cataloging-in-Publication Data

Harnessing innovative technology in higher education : access, equity, policy, and instruction / edited by Kathleen P. King and Joan K. Griggs.

p. cm.

Includes bibliographical references and index.

ISBN-13: 978-1-891859-63-2 (pbk.)

1. Distance education—United States—Computer-assisted instruction. 2. Educational technology—United States. I. Fund for the Improvement of Postsecondary Education. II. King, Kathleen P., 1958- III. Griggs, Joan Krejci.

LC5803.C65.H37 2006
378.1'758—dc22

2006022989

TABLE OF CONTENTS

PREFACE

Joan Krejci Griggs

This publication is an attempt to capture the evolution of distributed higher education over the last decade by tracing the applications of new technologies funded by the Fund for the Improvement of Postsecondary Education (FIPSE).

Through the mid-1980s and the 1990s, FIPSE's annual grant competition, The Comprehensive Program, received significant numbers of proposals from the field regarding application of the new information technologies to higher education; the competition's priorities in those years usually mentioned technology projects explicitly. Early projects included development of educational databases, such as the Perseus project, and a variety of experiments with hypertext, CD, and other computer-based instruction in many disciplines. In the early 1990s the first proposals appeared that linked the Internet with computer-based approaches. By the mid-1990s FIPSE was already funding such efforts as the development of quality standards for web-based delivery by Western Cooperative for Educational Telecommunications.

In 1998, when Congress held hearings on the re-authorization of the Higher Education Act, the debate centered on concerns about quality (the web-based courses and virtual universities brought back, for many, the ghosts of mail order fraud and abuse), hopes about cost savings, and questions about the "digital divide." The resulting 1998 Amendments to the Higher Education Act of 1965 created several programs related to technology, among them (1) the Distance Demonstration Program—to enable a few institutions to implement changes to federal financial aid policy that were purported barriers to distance education, (2) the Preparing Tomorrow's Teachers to Use Technology grant program (PT3), and (3) the Learning

Anywhere Anytime Partnerships grant program (LAAP). The Education Department asked FIPSE to write LAAP's guidelines and administer the program.

As FIPSE surveyed the current state of distance/distributed education, we saw an opportunity to help postsecondary education make the transition to a new generation of distance education made possible by the explosive growth of the Internet and other new technologies. Instead of relying on closed networks—such as broadcast satellites—to deliver courses on fixed schedules to students within limited geographic boundaries, postsecondary institutions now had the capacity to reach students regardless of where they were located, at any time of day. The technologies created the potential for students to access learning that was interactive, customized, and self-paced; to more easily merge lifelong learning with the demands of careers and families; and to expand their choice of institutions and programs. To fulfill its potential, however, this new generation of distance education would require systemic reforms of institutional practice and policy, and new relationships among postsecondary institutions, employers, technology companies, and other important stakeholders.

At that time there were several problems as higher education rushed into the dot.com revolution, creating web-based courses and contemplating revenue streams; FIPSE's LAAP program was designed to address those problems directly.

Most institutions were still trying to serve only those students within close geographic proximity and could afford to offer only those programs that would easily generate large enrollments. At the same time, other institutions were beginning to market courses nationally, causing program redundancy and competition over the same students instead of focusing on unmet needs. Typically, institutions were still "going it alone."

LAAP sought to encourage consortia of institutions within and across state lines. The emerging regional or statewide virtual university consortia were potentially good mechanisms to reach more students for existing courses, but generally they did not lead to the development of new and different instructional formats, or the delivery of needed specialized programs, nor did they prevent the competition for student or funding allocations among their members. If learning anytime, anywhere was going to be achieved, and if students were going to have the options they needed, educational providers would have to find new ways to leverage their investments, to build economies of scale, and to share courses and programs through partnerships. It was expected that such consortia would also facilitate seamless educational transitions between programs, whether certificate, two-year or four-year degrees, or graduate/continuing education. Partnerships, for example, could include collaborative web-based portfolios of student work, transcripts, and other records.

LAAP also sought partnerships linking academic institutions with commercial enterprises. The hope was that these relationships would expand the development and distribution of web-based tools and academic content. The projects would explore how these complex relationships could be formalized in arrangements for licensing, royalties, and other financial agreements; and how to do so within the context of differing institutional policies on intellectual property.

The rush to put courses online in the late 1990s had paid little attention to the provision of comprehensive online student support services—including everything from enrollment and financial aid systems to counseling, assessment, remediation, library access, bookstore services, career placement, technical support, and other services. A survey by the Western Cooperative for Educational Telecommunications concluded that very few comprehensive models existed, and that institutions would likely have to undergo rather significant changes to reform the usual delivery of services to "one-stop shopping" with integrated systems. Consortial arrangements, of course, complicated the delivery of such services.

At this time, FIPSE also noted that there were insufficient mechanisms in place to assure the quality of distance/distributed education and the accountability of higher education. Existing accreditation and licensing organizations were under pressure to adapt or change their practices to accommodate new types of distance education. Assuring the quality of programs and courses that were offered outside the traditional academic calendar or delivered across state and regional borders presented challenges to the usual peer review. LAAP partnerships were formed to encourage the educational provider, professional associations, and the accreditation community to rethink quality assurance and accountability in order to ensure that credentials were meaningful, providers were accountable, and courses met at least the same high standards demanded of traditional means of delivery. But how could higher education measure quality and achievement when the traditional parameters of seat time and credit hours were irrelevant?

The anytime, anywhere paradigm challenged higher education's assumptions about quality assurance and measurement of achievement. LAAP asked applicants to consider whole new ways to evaluate web-based learning, looking at how different types of learners learn more effectively and how different approaches differ in costs. We had moved beyond the question of whether online courses produced learning equal to that of traditional classes. New models and methodologies were needed to take advantage of the data captured easily by the new technologies to assess learning outcomes. Rather than taking for granted that learning is a function of time spent in the classroom, LAAP encouraged competency-based curriculum and assessment. We envisioned courses or modules of content that could be mapped to specific learning competencies to facilitate analysis of transcripts, credit transfer, and student advisement.

While LAAP urged applicants to consider new ways of clearing educational pathways, "packaging content," and credentialing students, we were well aware of the likely difficulties as students assembled their program or degree from multiple providers:

> The problem with assembling offerings from multiple providers is three-fold. First is the question of what is included in a course and whether an institution will have assurances both of its content and of its fit with other offerings. Second is the question of control over the shape of a program. Student may in many ways be served by a broader menu of choices, but will they select a coherent collection? Finally, what is the meaning of a credential? Who grants the credential, and who determines how it will be comprised? (Learning Anytime Anywhere Partnerships: Information and Application Materials, FY 1999, U.S. Department of Education)

Another aspect of the quality issue was only too evident at this time. Although there had been a proliferation of web-based courses in the couple of years prior, these online courses were often simply electronic conversions of text and lectures and did not use the full interactive potential of the technology or adapt instructional methods to the new medium.

FIPSE urged not only computer-mediated interactivity, but experimentation with greater interactivity between the student and the instructor, peers, mentors, and communities of learners. We contended that online learning needn't mean learning in isolation. We were interested that projects balanced interactivity and the use of multi-media with reasonable costs.

This quality issue was related to another characteristic of the late 1990s. The so-called "cottage industry" of instructional and administrative software development utilized individuals or small groups that worked to meet local needs, but were usually unable to meet commercial standards for portability and quality. Institutions generally were relying on the traditional curriculum development model—one instructor designing "his" course—rather than a more systematic courseware development process grounded in expert instructional design principles and applying a range of media or technical features. Private courseware developers were often reluctant to enter the postsecondary education market, unsure of how to recoup their investments in a fragmented marketplace whose culture valued the individual faculty shaping individual courses and resisting products created by others.

True to its mission, FIPSE was as concerned about access as about improving quality with the new technologies. In the late 1990s, institutions involved in online learning were likely to offer courses rather than full programs. Thus, their efforts were only marginally successful in opening access to higher education beyond the traditional learners. Some programs that were sorely needed in many areas of the country were particularly difficult to mount online, because they required "hands-on" activity—lab science courses, experiential learning, or clinical courses, for example. Several projects funded by LAAP and The Comprehensive Program experimented with approaches to teaching the most difficult subjects online.

In other ways, too, we found online learning was not fulfilling its potential for opening doors to non-traditional learners. FIPSE recognized that the learners who were traditionally underserved by postsecondary education had much to gain from anytime, anywhere learning, but they were precisely those who faced special barriers to accessing programs delivered online. Individuals with disabilities, individuals who had lost their jobs, individuals trying to enter the workforce from welfare, individuals seeking basic or technical skills, ethnic minorities with no personal or family college experience, learners with limited English or English as a second language: we hoped to demonstrate how online learning could be effective for these populations. We challenged applicants to look beyond the self-directed, highly motivated, experienced adults who had often comprised distance education's clientele, recognizing that hybrid models of distributed learning could result in greater numbers benefitting from postsecondary education.

From 1999 to 2001, 50 LAAP projects were funded. Running for three, four, or five years, almost all have been completed at this writing, and almost all of the projects are continuing after FIPSE funding ended. Within this same time span, FIPSE also funded a number of technology projects through The Comprehensive Program. The idea for this publication evolved in discussions among FIPSE project directors at their annual meetings, and the conceptual framework crystallized in Education Department staff conversations—meetings of Brian Lekander, Lavona Grow, Kay Gilcher, Karen

Levitan, and myself. Former LAAP project directors Kathleen King and Vickie Freeman took the seed and brought it to fruition.

Although the above issues have been addressed by FIPSE grantees and by higher education generally in the past several years, few of the problems have been universally solved and many challenges remain. While various partnerships and consortia have found ways of overcoming many policy obstacles, higher education is still far from embracing credentialing based on competency rather than seat time and Carnegie units. Similarly, courses are generally more engaging and interactive—utilizing discussion boards, desktop cameras, simulations, online mentors, to name a few features—and faculty are more accustomed to guiding learning rather than lecturing. But we haven't yet tapped the new technology's capability to provide customized—even personalized—instruction. We've refined our ideas about storing, organizing, and using metadata—those vast amounts of academic information—in ways that are standardized and much more efficient. Even so, there are few examples of course development processes in which these common databases of content can be accessed for students at different levels, or for professional development, or for community and public information. More institutions have courseware development processes that are standardized and scalable, using modular formats, IMS, or other standards, and new distribution mechanisms. We still lack knowledge about how different types of learners learn most effectively and how different approaches, including hybrid approaches, differ in costs.

In the area of teacher education and professional development, the new technologies make it easier to deliver pre-service and in-service education together. We need to explore methods of combining this delivery with teacher development approaches such as professional development schools in order to make those models more labor and cost efficient. Finally, in the area of assessment and workforce development, higher education has rarely joined employers in the effort to create systems of continuous work-related competency assessment and development that are accessible to the individual worker, the employer, and the education providers.

Looking at what had been recognized by the Department of Education at the beginning of this "journey," the emerging vision, and the pathways that the FIPSE and LAAP RFPs and funded projects took, there still lies ahead much more to be discovered in the areas of distance and distributed learning. It is our sincere hope that the advance made through these innovative projects, supported through the FIPSE and LAAP grants, will be of great assistance to future developments in the field. In addition, the work represented in this publication incorporates not only these grant projects, but also the synthesis of their evaluation studies in the context of distance learning, then and now. Embarking on distance and distributed learning with the knowledge of what dedicated, innovative higher education professionals have learned provides many advantages. Our primary hope is that future endeavors will be able to take the field of postsecondary education much further in terms of matching and serving the changing needs of our learners, institutions, organizations, and the potential of innovation.

ACKNOWLEDGMENTS

Since this publication was inspired by a large number of technology projects spawned by the Learning Anytime Anywhere Partnerships (LAAP) and the Comprehensive Program grants, we are indebted to the Directors of the Fund for the Improvement of Postsecondary Education (FIPSE) during this time period, roughly 1994-2004—Charles "Buddy" Karelis, Kenneth Tolo, and Leonard Haynes.

The LAAP program, which funded a majority of the projects in this volume and became a catalyst in the burgeoning field of online learning in the late nineties, was coordinated by FIPSE Program Officer Brian Lekander. The guidelines he authored for LAAP provided a vision for many applicants and resulted in projects that were nurtured by a team of FIPSE Program Officers—Joan Krejci Griggs, Lorraine Kleinwaks, Karen Levitan, and Joan Stramanis.

As it became clear that there were many lessons to be learned from this varied body of projects, several colleagues from the U.S. Department of Education's Office of Postsecondary Education developed what became the conceptual framework for this book: Brian Lekander, Joan Krejci Griggs, Karen Levitan, Kay Gilcher, and Lavona Grow.

It was more than a year later that Dr. Griggs found the opportunity to award a supplemental grant to Dr. Vicki Freeman, University of Texas Medical Branch, and Dr. Kathleen King, Director of the Regional Educational Technology Center at Fordham University. Both had been successful FIPSE Project Directors and joined forces to make this publication possible. While Dr. Freeman provided administrative support, Dr. King was the heart and soul of the collaborative process. She worked with authors and wove together the disparate strands of these stories. Dr. Griggs offered editorial counsel, FIPSE project documentation, and feedback on drafts throughout.

We are indebted, of course, to the several authors who used the projects to focus their own expertise in distributive education.

We'd also like to acknowledge the contribution of Dr. Susan Biro of Fordham University who collaborated in copy editing and research assistance in preparation of this publication. Her expertise in distance education, research, and academic publications has been invaluable.

Another Fordham colleague, Dr. Barbara Heuer, collaborated on continuing research for this effort and other distance education projects at Fordham.

Finally, but most of all, we greatly appreciate those project directors who invested themselves so deeply in their funded FIPSE projects. For those who have done so, we know that writing a grant is no small task, but it pales in comparison to implementation and sustainability. Thank you for your vision, commitment, and labors in a difficult and long task. The future of innovative educational developments depends on minds and lives like yours.

Kathleen P. King
Joan K. Griggs
Editors

INTRODUCTION

Kathleen P. King

Looking at distance education for the last 20 years, one can't help but realize that the field has expanded dramatically. We have lived through a time of great advances in technology, policy, educational readiness, and societal technology adoption, but at the same time we have also struggled with great challenges in these same areas. This chapter provides an introduction to this volume about United States Department of Education Fund for the Improvement of Postsecondary Education (FIPSE) distance education grants. In particular, we aim to paint a picture of the context in which these projects were conducted. For instance, what was happening in distance education and related trends during this time? Within this context, we then introduce the projects in the following chapters to produce a one-of-a-kind publication. The FIPSE-funded distance education projects have provided substantial bases of theory, research, and practice for the field to build upon, and yet the results of these projects have seldom been widely disseminated to the general academic communities. The main goal of this publication is to present substantial, thought-provoking, and well-written lessons that will bring the experience and findings from over 40 grant projects to you and your colleagues. We sincerely hope this book will encourage you to continue or begin your work in distance education with strong evaluation and research roots so that you may continually reflect upon and improve the work we all do in providing educational experiences.

DEFINING DISTANCE EDUCATION

You would think that offering a definition of your topic would not be drastically difficult, but in the case of distance education, you step into not only a widely elastic scope of definitions, but one which is related to rapidly changing technologies. Therefore, crafting a definition is not for the fainthearted! Distance education is:

- the working mother in rural Nebraska completing her bachelor's degree online through her local state university while her children sleep at night.

- the single young man in New York City studying for the GED exam via public television and telephone tutoring.

- the mid-career business woman executive pursuing her doctorate in education via a hybrid online and residency program in order to change careers.

- the retired bus driver engaged in a collaborative webinar for his class through a University of Beijing class on the Eastern perspective of global issues.

Defining distance education by varying degrees of physical separation between the teacher and learner is no longer an effective strategy (Boettcher 2004). The reason for this is that many people are taking "distance education courses" that are at a close proximity to one another. Indeed, the field began by accommodating and bridging learners and educators who were substantial distances apart, but current adoption patterns indicate that convenience is the primary determinate in selecting a "distance education" course. One way to conceptualize distance education is to examine it across three dimensions: technology, time, and focus (King 2005). Using the dimensions of technology, time, and instruction, one can construct a multi-layered definition of distance education that accounts for the varied options included in this very broad field.

Technology

As technology in everyday life, business, industry, and science has advanced, so has the availability for education also progressed, albeit not as quickly. Detailed surveys such as The Campus Computing Project document this shift in technology focus, use, and spending in higher education over recent years (Foster 2005; Green 2004). Often forgotten today, early distance education initiatives included postal mail (beginning in the 1840s), radio, television, audiocassettes, and videos. Even today, many of these technologies are still the major forms of distance learning. In the 1960s and 1970s, there were a few major endeavors in higher education that used several technologies and instructional designs, including television, telephone, audiocassettes, radio, correspondence, and tutors (Moore and Kearsley 1996). The intended audience of these endeavors were similar to today's target population: working adults seeking additional credentialing for career advancement, who sought part-time and independent learning opportunities, who could not come to campus, and who needed flexible offerings (Cantelon 1995; Holmberg 1986).

In the 1980s and 1990s most people thought "videoconferencing" when one said distance education, but in the 2000s "online learning" (web-based) is the mainstream image and understanding. The widespread adoption and availability of the Internet in some developed countries has made distance education a major delivery interest and popular option (Cahoon 1998). Further from the mainstream, in more experienced circles of distance education, "hybrid" or "blended" formats are seen as forerunners in design (Boettcher 2004; King 2001; Wallace 2003). Hybrids use multiple technologies or traditional formats to create courses and learning experiences that can be richer experiences. For example, an online class might be combined with face-to-face learning or an iPod terminal.

Since 2002, we have seen the "mobile device" movement take such roots that it is no longer dominated by cell phone use by business people and teenagers. The "movement" has swept ahead to include PDAs, MP3 players, convergence devices that combine cell phone and PDA, and brand names or product lines such as iPod, Smartphone, BlackBerry, and Treo. With this social trend of widespread technological availability and use educators, educational organizations, and technology companies are examining ways in which mobile devices may be used to deliver or support instruction (Alexander 2004; Northrup and Harrison 2005; Shih 2005), while colleges and universities are devoting greater IT resources each year for wireless technologies (Green 2004). Will "m-learning" (mobile-learning) be the new wave of distance learning? We have to wait and see the leveling out of innovation, outcomes, benefits, and adoption in order to have a reliable answer to that question. Time will tell if it is a "flash" of excitement or an enduring pathway of distance education's future. But the mobile device experience demonstrates how innovation, technology, and adoption impact distance education.

Time

Time is another effective way to examine distance education. Distance educators refer to "synchronous" and "asynchronous" learning to distinguish between when students and educator are interacting simultaneously or at dif - ferent times, respectively. Chat rooms and videoconferencing are usually synchronous formats and have definite limitations regarding scheduling, not only for rooms (videoconferencing), equipment, and other time schedules, but also time zone differences, technical support, and high cost. One of the benefits of the less intensive, older technologies, and many web-based applications, is that teachers and learners can sign in anytime 24 hours a day, seven days a week—whenever it fits their schedule. With greater convenience, however, comes greater responsibility! Without the structure of established meeting times learners now shoulder the responsibility of keeping up with their classes and assignments more independently. Depending on personality types, learning styles, and work habits, this can be a benefit or a significant obstacle without the familiar structure, accountability, and safety net of traditional, face-to-face meetings (Desanctis and Sheppard 1997).

Instruction

Examining distance education according to the criteria of instruction leads us to differentiate between learning experiences that are independent, self-study, or learner engagement with instructor and/or classmates. While classes that are pursued independently can be very valuable for gaining knowledge, technical information, and informal learning, when learners and instructors dialogue there is the opportunity for greater depths of reflection, analysis, debate, and understanding (King 2002; Palloff and Pratt 1999; Wallace 2003). Indeed, it is when we are called upon to explain ourselves to others that we often come to better understand ourselves. Skilled distance education facilitation through technology can provide powerful dialogue among participants across small and great distances. Online learning does not have to be an isolated affair.

Building upon this concept, several national and international collaboratives, including FIPSE-funded projects, have further developed the instructional dimensions of distance education through learning objects and distributed learning. Realizing the expense and duplication of effort and resources that are involved in developing online courses, groups such as Advanced Distributed Learning (ADL), Co-Lab (http://www.academiccolab. org/index.html), and MERLOT (www.MERLOT.org) have led coordinated efforts to design, articulate, and support the development of parallel, reusable, cross-platform, "learning objects" (Boettcher 2004; Tozman 2004). IEEE Learning Technology Standards Committee (LTSC) (http://ltsc.ieee .org) has been the leading technical group that has supported the development of the technical standards for the projects (Hodgins and Conner 2000). For instance, in the simplest sense, a PowerPoint presentation on Biology 101 is created within a specified standard or template. Then the designer could upload the presentation, or learning object into a shared online database that other designers, professors, and cooperating organizations could access and incorporate into their own presentations, classes, and courses.

Combining the power and economy of learning objects in instructional design, the result is a distributed learning environment. Resources no longer need to be located in one room, building, or even university. Not only is time a continuum, but distributed learning allows space to become a continuum—and, through learning objects, instructional modules can become elements that can be manipulated, obtained, and moved about through a continuum as well. The power is fundamentally found in breaking through two-dimensional design, financial constraints, and physical limitations. Instruction can be conceived of, prepared, and delivered in a new conception of space through distributed learning.

Learning objects and the related sharing system of distributed education provides a powerful learning design, articulation, and improvement system, and reduces costs since it is no longer necessary for everyone to recreate the same materials (Tozman 2004). This consolidation of resources frees up time and finances to pursue the development of additional materials and innovation. Instead of redundancy, this distance education instructional model provides for scalability and development.

So what definition do we come to? Distance education is technology-assisted education that is always conducted when the teachers and learners are separated by a distance, small or great, but not always by time or space. This technology-assisted education may use a variety of technologies singly or in combination to develop or combine teaching and learning.

FIPSE CONTEXT OF DISTANCE EDUCATION

Today, if I were asked, "If you had to pick one, to which animal would you compare distance education?" I would have to say a *tiger*—lively, spirited, powerful, and ready to spring ahead when unleashed. Higher education has the tremendous challenge of continually discovering and creating the best ways to harness the raw energy, brawn, and independence of that instructional dynamo, *distance education.* Over the last 30 years, distance education has experienced a torrent of technological change. From mainframes to 300 baud dial-up modems to DSL and POD casts, distance education has traversed the massive to the micro, the egghead to the masses. The field of distance education has been shaped by administrators, educators, technologists, educational institutions, corporations, and community organizations —all seeking to discover the ways to harness the power of the spirited tiger and utilize its previously untamed characteristics to extend our understanding, practice, and reach of teaching and learning.

Through the U.S. government, FIPSE, a division of the U.S. Department of Education's Office of Postsecondary Education, has funded a wide range of projects that use web-based distance learning. This volume particularly focuses on The Comprehensive Program and the Learning Anytime Anywhere Partnerships (LAAP). These programs also benefitted from the oversight and support of an assigned FIPSE program officer to guide program directors, and hopefully help avoid common pitfalls, as well as increase completion rates, accountability, sustainability, and the involvement and reporting of external evaluators. Through these competitively funded programs, FIPSE has funded scores of distance learning projects to advance the field in developing a base of understanding, practice, and data on distance learning.

PURPOSE OF THE BOOK

This book aims to be a valuable resource for understanding current practice in distance education. In addition, it seeks to highlight a wide variety of innovative and high-need projects funded by FIPSE since the mid-1990s. While some books on distance education share the knowledge and experience gained from developing and directing a distance education program, this book is unique in that it has the powerful vantage point of having its authors draw upon, analyze, consolidate, and present practices that could inform the education field for many years to come. Additionally, by having multiple expert researchers conduct the analysis, this book provides a variety of perspectives of promising practices examined across the distance education topics. Therefore we benefit from a close analysis across programs within the topic areas. In the concluding chapter of the book, comprehensive themes across the chapters are identified in order to guide further thought and exploration for the field.

Until now, information about these grant-funded distance education projects has often been only available in program evaluations, individual sources, or conference papers that are not always available on an enduring basis. Atwood Publishing has partnered with the two FIPSE grantees to provide this book in print, and also allow it to be provided in portable document format (PDF) in order to maximize the preservation and dissemination of the information.

CRITICAL EVALUATION

Distance education is not just about what is in this book and what we have today. Really, if you are going to be working in the field of distance education you need one eye on today and one or two on the future at all times. I encourage you to read through these chapters over and over again, mull over the programs and findings, discuss them with your colleagues, and see what you can develop by building upon them! How can you use this information in the context of your program needs and these resources, to take hold of that spirited *tiger of distance education*? How can your organizations harness the unbridled energy and use it to develop new technology solutions for education? We encourage you to capture the tremendous power that distance education has to change teaching and learning.

POTENTIAL, PROMISES, CONSIDERATIONS, AND CAUTIONS

In recent years distance education was frequently held forth as the panacea for fiscal and enrollment shortfalls of postsecondary education. Indeed, distance education was going to make it possible to schedule classes that were not restricted to size because they were not restricted to the number of seats available, and the potential student pool for every college would be boundless as they would be able to reach and enroll students from every corner of the earth. As we know now, such grandiose expectations were not to be realized and institutions suffered varying degrees of loss. Indeed, some major institutions withdrew from their eager "for-profit" distance education ventures when it became apparent that it was too costly (Blumenstyk 2001; Carr 2001).

A few of the benefits we have realized are that distance education has been found to have great potential and promise to provide new ways of learning, new forms of access, more convenience, and flexibility for learners, great possibilities for student and expert communication, and collaboration locally and globally.

At the same time we have understood in very significant ways the financial, personnel, time, and physical resource costs that need to be continually invested in developing, supporting, and upgrading technology-based distance education. Distance education that is "done on the cheap" may suffice for some specific purposes, but as technology advances quickly such approaches frequently fall behind in meeting the expectations and needs of the general public, who include even our less technologically savvy learners. Just the cost of technical support and upgrades for current distance education can be a sizeable budget. Nonetheless, many administrators still hold the misconception that distance education is a *vastly* inexpensive way to provide education, and students expect to pay deeply discounted tuition for it! Financial models that include the true costs for providing these services over an extended period of time indicate a very different picture.

Even with these sobering budgetary and operational realities, distance education still offers profound opportunities for innovation, advancement, and service for teaching and learning organizations. This book provides examples of extensive programs that have explored some of these possibilities and what has been learned about them. Some examples include online writing clinics, competency-based learning, teacher online professional development, collaboratives to reduce barriers to higher education for underserved populations, nursing education online, and virtual postsecondary consortia.

In light of the potentials and concerns regarding distance education, administrators and educators must consider the following when planning:

- PURPOSE: Determine why your institution is pursuing distance education.

- EXPERTISE: What could your institution provide that will be unique to the field?

- RESOURCES: Do you have available, or can you attain, the needed resources to fully support the curriculum and technical needs of a distance education program?

- MARKET: Is there is a viable demand for distance education among current or prospective students?

- COST–BENEFIT: After a careful analysis of costs and income for the endeavor, can the fiscal requirements of the institution be met? (Does your endeavor need to break even or make a profit?)

As we learn about the many distance education programs available, these are a few of the questions to keep in mind as you think of applications to your programs and institutions. The real excitement is that this is not a "how-to" book of how to tame the powerful tiger of distance education; instead, this book provides program overviews, resources, and insights that you and your colleagues can use to develop the best approaches for your educational contexts. You have the opportunity to become creators and innovators and join us as contributors to this dynamic field.

How the Chapters Fit Together

As previously stated, in the design of this book topics and projects were chosen that would demonstrate critical best practice in distance education in areas that are not always given a great deal of focus or discussion. The layout of the book has the **Preface** as an introduction to the history of the project and of FIPSE while this **Introduction** offers a more comprehensive view of the framing context of distance education and the plan and details of the book. The individual chapters have been ordered to provide two major categories: organizational issues and instructional issues addressing student and instructor.

Policy is the first chapter of project analyses for a distinct purpose. In evaluating our experience, the field, and the manuscripts prepared for this book, we found the policy environment—whether institutional, state, or federal—can have enormous impact on distributed or distance education. Even though entirely committed to students, teaching and learning, and instructional design, if distance education professionals do not successfully deal with policy within and beyond their organizations, it appears that they will be held at a standstill in the technological waves of change. This chapter provides insight into many significant and difficult issues that organizations must address, including but not limited to: (1) faculty rewards, support, technology education, intellectual property; (2) student support, advising, readiness for the environment; (3) transferability of distance education courses; and (4) student tuition and fees, collaboration, programming/curricula, and delivery.

As postsecondary organizations pursue distance education and engage in developing, revising, and resolving policy issues, very often issues and dynamics of "partnerships" emerge. Since **partnerships** (chapter 2) were a central focus of the LAAP grant program, virtually every funded project had extensive experience with collaborative arrangements of all sorts; therefore the chapter on this subject offers much insight. These partnerships may include formal partnerships (or consortia) among colleges and universities, businesses, associations, and any other relevant organizations. A major purpose for many of these partnerships was specifically how they might create new learning opportunities and access for students that would not have been possible if postsecondary institutions were acting individually. In this chapter, readers will find recommendations and insights regarding how partnerships have shared resources to enable delivery of programs that would not otherwise be feasible because of economic, resource, or expertise limitations. The collaborations also fostered greater scalability to enable larger enrollments for programs and increased program reach.

In the U.S. educational system creating a simple and transparent continuum of learning from the K–12 system to higher education and beyond continues to be a challenge. For this reason the concept of educational *pathways* has been an important theme for FIPSE projects and increasingly important in distance and distributed education initiatives. The **pathways** chapter (chapter 3) in this book provides an overview of a few funded projects identifying online strategies to increase access to higher education, facilitate the movement of students from one level to the next, and provide flexibility to address individual educational needs. These are critical issues for today's youth, adults, and traditionally under-served learners in order to encourage and support them to complete their courses of study leading to associate or bachelor's degrees and continued professional development. For some readers "pathways" may be an unfamiliar phrase in the education context. However, the concept and possibilities should be familiar, and, as they are developed in this chapter, it is exciting to see the empowerment of learners and the dynamic possibilities for programs, even while acknowledging the great distance we have yet to travel.

Dealing with the more organizational issues up to this point, the following chapters focus on teaching and learning issues. While the distance education literature appears to have a plethora of publications on the effectiveness of instruction, many of the deeper, critical issues seem to have been avoided. In the chapter on **instructional effectiveness** (chapter 4), an insightful analysis of the field is provided and explores the ways a number of projects can best take advantage of the potential of new distance delivery technologies. Particular focus is given to a discussion of competency-based learning as an example of how to explore and study an innovative approach, as well as, how to learn its specific benefits. Here you will find discussions about techniques that effectively build an online community of learners, the role of instructional design in moving to learner-centered instruction, projects that help students measure their competency in multiple domains, and how new communities of practice are being formed through the use of technology.

However, even with the most powerful instructional strategies learners need support, and distance learning provides distinct challenges in this respect; hence the next chapter of our book becomes very important for instructional success.

Support (chapter 5) via distance learning is still an emerging area of activity, and there are few institutions that have a comprehensive or cost-effective set of services. A variety of projects intended to provide counseling, assessment, mentoring, and many other services to learners enrolled in distance education programs have been funded by FIPSE over the years. This chapter provides insights into what has been learned about best practice regarding (1) how to support admission, registration, tuition, and textbook ordering via a student's desktop or laptop; (2) what services best support student retention in the distance learning environment and program completion; (3) how the delivery of writing assistance may be achieved via online methods and collaborations within and between institutions; and (4) the utilization of consortia relationships to create a set of services that support student retention in the distance education environment. Providing support services via distance technologies is a great challenge, and postsecondary organizations have invested tremendous time and resources in designing and providing these services for the largest constituencies. However, it is also critical to consider special populations and how to serve their distinctive support, learning, and access needs.

Reaching target populations under-served by higher education is a challenge that we have reason to believe can be effectively addressed by distance technologies. The chapter on **special populations** (chapter 6) provides insight into a variety of projects that have explored effective ways to serve students by overcoming barriers such as lack of proficiency in English, lack of proficiency in information technology, and lack of access to technology through designing learning environments that enable these students to succeed academically. Again, this is a distance education topic not frequently discussed in the literature, so this chapter will be a valuable resource for programs which need to, or are, proactively addressing innovative solutions. In concert with programmatic planning, distance education administrators and instructors must also be knowledgeable in addressing the needs of special populations in educational settings in general, and in distance education in particular.

Several FIPSE funded programs have developed or delivered professional development for teachers, faculty members, and administrators electronically, as well as broadening access to professional development for a variety of other nontraditional learners through the use of web-based courses and curricula. **Professional development** (chapter 7) via distance technology has many benefits and capabilities that are delineated in this chapter, but one which repeatedly emerges is that of convenience. Like other distance education learners, educators identify convenience as a major benefit in their lives of "maxed out" work, family, and recreation schedules. This chapter's analysis focuses on programs that develop innovative tools, strategies, or curricula to reach rural or otherwise isolated educators; programs that meet individual needs for self-determined, self-paced, interactive professional development; and programs that are standards-based with strong accountability components.

From the organizational perspective of policy and partnerships, to the teaching and learning focus of instructional effectiveness and faculty professional development, the **integrated conclusion** (chapter 8) of this book identifies the major themes that traverse these chapters. As each chapter has identified its topic's patterns across the specific programs, now across all the *topics* (chapters) we offer a perspective of the themes that emerged. The final chapter of the book provides the *themes* that emerge across the topics; then *principles* of practice are identified to guide faculty, administrators, program directors, and those designing new projects and courses; finally, *recommendations* are provided as we look at what is indicated for the future.

In many ways distance education seems to be a tiger which is constantly running, never resting, seeking the next trail, running ahead on the path of innovation. Because of this dynamic trait, broad strokes of characterization and anticipation are offered. These themes, principles, and recommendations are based on the details of the information provided in these chapters, and our authors' and practitioners' knowledge of, and experience of, distance education. We anticipate that our observations and suggestions will not be the final word. Instead we desire them to be a new beginning as they provide direction for much greater innovation, new directions, and great accomplishments for the future.

OUR AUTHORS

One of the great challenges of taking on this project was identifying the right people to author the chapters. We believe we have been fortunate to gather an amazing group of experts who not only know the field of distance education, but have lived it as program managers, project directors, and project evaluators. In addition they are all skilled researchers and accomplished academic authors. As a team we gathered in the fall of 2004 at Educause in order to collaborate on the book as a whole and each of the chapters individually. It was our vision as editors that this book would be more than a series of chapters joined together on a common topic, but that the purpose of the book, the philosophy of the project, and the joint expertise and knowledge of distance education be further explored, shared, and developed together into a collaborative whole. Our grant project director is *Vickie S. Freeman*, chair and professor of the CLS Department at The University of Texas Medical Branch, who brings experience with online learning, distance education, and community collaborations to this project.

While there are more complete biographical sketches available at the back of the back, a brief word of introduction to our authors is appropriate in order for the reader to understand the expertise that has been gathered. In the order of appearance of their chapters, *Joan Krejci Griggs* is a former coordinator of the FIPSE Comprehensive Program and LAAP program evaluator and FIPSE program officer, while also having extensive experience as an administrator in adult and higher education and author. *Kathleen P. King* is a professor of adult education and director of the Regional Educational Technology Center at Fordham University in New York City; she has directed several grants including a LAAP grant and authored several books and publications on distance learning, adult learning, and professional development.

Harvey Blustain, president of Act IV Consulting, Inc., is a specialist in business and organizational needs for higher education; prior positions have included academia, international development, market research—including serving as director of the Pricewaterhouse Coopers National Higher Education Consulting Practice. *Raymond J. Lewis* has over 25 years experience in higher education and distance learning as a program officer for the Fund for the Improvement of Postsecondary Education (FIPSE), as the director of Oregon's statewide distance learning network (Oregon ED-NET), and as a higher education consultant. *Marianne R. Phelps* is a higher education consultant in distance education, accreditation, and institutional assessment. Dr. Phelps has extensive experience in University administration and academic policy, having held a number of posts in the U.S. Department of Education and at George Washington University, including University Planning Officer and Associate Provost.

Gary Brown has written and presented extensively on undergraduate learning, assessment, and technology; he directs the Center for Teaching, Learning, and Technology at Washington State University and the CTLT Silhouette Project, which hosts Flashlight Online for the TLT-Group. *Julie Porosky Hamlin* is executive director of MarylandOnline, a consortium of colleges and universities engaged in collaborations in online learning; Dr. Hamlin has been senior vice president of statewide programs for University System of Maryland central office.

Chère Campbell Gibson, professor emerita at the University of Wisconsin–Madison, founded The Certificate of Professional Development in Distance Education. Her research focuses on learners and learning at a distance, with specific emphasis on persistence and learner support. Most recently this research has included serving learners with disabilities and their transition to college, and the issues facing tribal colleges and migrant families. *Darcy W. Hardy* is Assistant Vice Chancellor and Director of the UT TeleCampus, the virtual university of The University of Texas System that supports online delivery of system-wide collaborative academic programs from UT institutions. Dr. Hardy is a nationally recognized leader in distance education management, virtual university issues, and collaborative program development. *Susan C. Biro* is an administrator and researcher at Fordham University's Regional Educational Technology Center in New York City. She is also the former director of distance learning at University College, Widener University, where she was responsible for delivering online and hybrid degree-completion programs to adult students, improving online student services, and designing professional development that supports faculty who teach with technology.

CONCLUSION

As we consider the tremendous daily demands and needs for learning, coupled with rapidly changing technologies, we see the exciting, churning vortex that is the context in which the FIPSE distance education grants have sought to develop, explore, and innovate new solutions. Much like grabbing the tail of that proverbial tiger, it has been a wild ride. Distance education grant projects tend not to be docile affairs. They are challenging, unpredictable, and exciting. In distance education, every day comes with new challenges and new possibilities, new problems, and new creations.

It is our sincere hope that this book captures the impact and meaning of the lessons learned from the remarkable people who have charted the last 10 years of this field. We hope it will inspire more of our colleagues to master the challenge of harnessing the power and possibilities of distance education. We look forward to seeing how each of you will rein in that potential and shape the path of that spirited tiger along with us.

@

Special thanks are due to *Vicki S. Freeman*, chair and professor of the CLS Department at The University of Texas Medical Branch, who has worked with online learning, distance education, and community collaborations during the last 15 years.

Chapter One

POLICY AFFECTING
DISTANCE EDUCATION
PROGRAM DEVELOPMENT AND DELIVERY

by Harvey Blustain

OVERVIEW

The framers of the original 1998 LAAP program guidelines were prescient in identifying the policy issues that would surface. They assessed correctly that institutions would need to confront challenges ranging from the financial (e.g., distribution of costs and revenues), to the academic (e.g., fixed academic schedules and credit hours), to the "cultural" (e.g., overcoming the objections of the professorate). Some projects did indeed find that they had to meet these issues head-on just to move forward with their primary agenda. For others, such as SREB's Policy Laboratory, such policies themselves were the focus of the project. This chapter discusses several of the projects that had a heavy focus on policy and identifies some of the major policy lessons from these LAAP initiatives. [See the proliferation of position papers and publications from higher education organizations such as American Association of University Professors (1999), Educause (n.d.), and now American Council on Education (2003) to see the accuracy of this prediction of need.]

POLICY AND CHANGE

An analysis of policy is instructive because (among other reasons) it can tell us much about what is important to people. Policies about uncontroversial things are routinely followed, seldom discussed, and sometimes not even written down. Policies that prove controversial or difficult to implement, on the other hand, throw into relief the clashing interests, the challenges to tradition, and the conflict over new behaviors that get lumped under the generic heading of "resistance to change." A large uproar or high noncompliance indicates that the policy has hit a nerve. This is especially true in higher education, where institutions are sensitive to, and protective of, their prerogatives, autonomy, and "traditions." Of a policy's many functions, therefore, one of the most potent is its role in the change process and policy study can be invaluable in distance education planning and administration within higher education [Timpane and White 1998, Western Interstate Commission on Higher education (n.d.)]. In addition to serving as a barometer of attitudes, an analysis of policy can inform us how well behaviors are (or are not) aligned with new strategies, directions, or technologies. The fact that so many LAAP projects needed to revise policies in so many areas provided an excellent indication of the disparity between the practices of "traditional" higher education and the demands of anytime, anywhere learning.

This chapter examines five projects that paid high levels of attention to policy issues:

- SOUTHERN REGIONAL EDUCATION BOARD: "The Distance Learning Policy Laboratory"

- OREGON NETWORK FOR EDUCATION: "The Oregon Network for Education (OregonONE)"

- OREGON UNIVERSITY SYSTEM: "Second-Generation University System Distance Education Model via Public/Private Partnerships"

- THE GREAT PLAINS INTERACTIVE DISTANCE EDUCATION ALLIANCE (GPIDEA): "A National Model for Inter-institutional Postbaccalaureate Distance Education Programs"

- PRINCE GEORGE'S COMMUNITY COLLEGE: "Quality Matters: Inter-Institutional Quality Assurance in Online Learning"

Significantly, all five of these projects involved large consortial arrangements that created a rich medium for cultivating policy issues. Focusing on these more complex projects is instructive not only for the range of issues they offer, but also because both technology and market forces are driving virtually all institutions of higher education toward greater numbers and types of partnerships; in that regard, these projects are a sign of things to come.

PROJECT SNAPSHOTS

SOUTHERN REGIONAL EDUCATION BOARD

Due to increasing enrollments and activity in e-learning, the Southern Regional Education Board (SREB) created the Distance Learning Policy Laboratory in 1999. The Laboratory was intended as a vehicle for assessing, developing, and promoting policies that encourage distance learning in the South. Partners included commissions, boards, and consortia from Alabama, Arkansas, Delaware, Florida, Georgia, Kentucky, Louisiana, Maryland, Missouri, North Carolina, Oklahoma, South Carolina, Tennessee, Texas, Virginia, and West Virginia. The perceived need for the Lab arose from SREB's success with its Electronic Campus, a regional marketplace of more than 5,000 electronic courses and 250 degree programs from more than 375 colleges and universities.

OREGONONE

OregonONE is an initiative to establish a virtual postsecondary consortium in the state. Funded with a three-year grant in 1998, the Oregon Network for Education (ONE) developed a one-stop website with a searchable database of distance education courses, certificate/degree programs, and other information for students interested in electronic delivery modes. Nine Oregon community colleges, eight Oregon universities, and four independent higher education institutions participated in ONE, with several K–12 providers of distance education courses joining in 2002. There are typically 1,200 to 2,400 courses in the database (courses vary by terms) and 75 college level degree and certificate programs at OregonONE.org. Among the perceived advantages of having information consolidated at a common site were an increase in student access to quality courses, a reduction of course duplication across institutions, and useful information and cost-effective services to faculty and staff. The project was also seen as a means of facilitating planning among distance education staffs and policymakers.

OREGON UNIVERSITY SYSTEM

For more than a decade, the eight universities of the Oregon University System (OUS) had offered degrees using the state's "first-generation" satellite interactive video network. Seeking to expedite the transition to delivery over high-speed broadband terrestrial Internet (the "second generation"), OUS received a LAAP grant for the "Second Generation Distance Education Partnership Project." The "meat" of the project was the redesign of 238 courses from 20 programs across the state, preparing them for the "second generation" of delivery systems. More broadly, however, OUS sought a model that would address all salient elements of the model.

GREAT PLAINS INTERACTIVE DISTANCE EDUCATION ALLIANCE

Ten public universities (Kansas State University, Michigan State University, Iowa State, Montana State, Nebraska, North Dakota State, Oklahoma State, South Dakota State, Texas Tech, and, later, Colorado State) created the Great Plains Interactive Distance Education Alliance (GPIDEA) to offer inter-institutional post-baccalaureate distance education programs in specific areas. Representing a wide diversity of administrative cultures and policy environments, the members recognized that being competitive and cost-effective would require them to alter their institutional policies and practices as well as to develop sound programs. Over 60 academic leaders —representing graduate faculty, academic administrators, graduate deans, chief financial officers, registrars, and continuing education directors—participated in teams to revamp policy, simplify partnership arrangements, and provide for academic and fiscal accountability.

PRINCE GEORGE'S COMMUNITY COLLEGE

Recognizing that a concern with quality is a primary barrier to the sharing of courses between institutions, Prince George's Community College in Maryland took the lead in "Quality Matters," a project designed to certify the quality of online courses and course components. The key was to establish a set of objective standards for identifying and demonstrating quality. Nineteen institutions from Maryland and eight other states have participated in the Quality Matters consortium. To date, Quality Matters has reviewed 14 courses and certified 65 peer course reviewers. The Maryland Distance Learning Association (MDLA) recognized Quality Matters as the Best Distance Learning Program for 2005.

THE RANGE OF POLICY ISSUES

When universities initiate online learning activities, many find that their policies need to be either substantially revised or created de novo. What course management system should we use? Who is qualified to teach a graduate course? How do revenues and costs get distributed? How do we reward faculty for their e-learning contributions? What do residency requirements mean when students can be anywhere? Some of these issues are easily anticipated, while others seem to emerge from the woodwork. Some colleges and universities, as their first step, try to catalog the issues as a way to get their arms around the looming effort; others plunge in and take the problems as they present themselves. There are any number of ways to organize the diversity of policy issues engendered by distance learning. James King and others (2000) at the University of Nebraska, for example, building on the work of others, developed a "three-tiered policy analysis framework" based on:

- Faculty (rewards, support, technology education, intellectual property)
- Students/participants (support, advising, requirements and records, transfers)
- Management and organization (tuition and fees, funding, collaboration, financial support, programming/curricula, delivery)

This division is as serviceable as any, and each institution will need to develop its own taxonomy to reflect its own situation and needs. In some cases, as the LAAP projects demonstrated, institutions will have to contend with a smaller set of policy challenges. The 16 two-year colleges of the Wisconsin Technical College System, for example, created the Wisconsin Online Resource Center (Wisc-Online), a digital repository of more than 500 learning objects created by 122 faculty. Their primary policy issue, not surprisingly, was ownership, with two-thirds of the colleges expressing "serious questions" about intellectual property issues.

Established to "define and reduce barriers to electronic learning" across 16 states, the SREB Policy Laboratory organized its main committees around seven federal, state, and institutional practices. These "barriers to distance learning" were credit transfer, faculty concerns, financial aid, finance, quality assurance, student services, and the under-served. Each committee had four deliverables: guiding principles, specific policy goals and recommendations, a set of illustrative or "promising" practices, and pilot projects. In some areas, so many policies were involved that some committees found themselves with a broad and diffuse scope. The SREB's Student Services committee, for example, saw their purview as "not as clearly defined as other committee areas" because student services "cover a wide array of services that encompasses a variety of professional interests" among members of the committee.

The primary goal of the Oregon University System project was to develop a "new model for second-generation distance education" to succeed interactive video (Oregon University System 2001). To launch the model, the project sought to redesign 238 courses from 20 programs across the state.

Although course redesign to accommodate new technologies sounds relatively straightforward, OUS found itself in 2001 issuing policy guidelines in 53 areas within five general categories (see Table 1).

This framework forms a rich checklist of the policy issues that can surface when developing a comprehensive new distance learning model. Again, each project and institution needs to identify and look after its own policy agenda. The OUS list illustrates the deep and broad implications of anytime, anywhere learning, and reminds us once again why multi-institutional change is so hard.

THREE CORE POLICY AREAS

We cannot address here all of the policy issues raised by distance learning. Instead, three broad policy areas will serve to illustrate the dimensions and difficulties involved with defining and applying policies in a learn-anytime-anywhere environment. These three areas are not only central to the success of LAAP projects—and of virtually any distance learning initiative —but they also demonstrate the range of creative solutions that have been applied:

- ACADEMIC: How do institutions address the varied concerns of the faculty?
- GOVERNANCE: How do many institutions work with each other?
- FINANCE: How do institutions divide up costs and revenues?

Academic Policies

Ultimately, all LAAP projects are about "academics": not only the pedagogy, courses, and programs, but also the credit articulation, rewards and recognition, intellectual property, and other facets of the academy that have to do with teaching and learning. Within any particular project, the specific policy areas needing to be addressed depended, of course, on what the project was trying to accomplish. For the Oregon University System, for example, partnering with private course management system vendors on a second-generation distance learning technology initially raised concerns about the vendors assuming ownership of courses and content. As we noted earlier, the Wisconsin Online Resource Center's repository of more than 500 learning objects from 122 faculty elevated the issue of intellectual property.

With a goal of program transferability among its member states, the SREB Policy Lab was especially concerned with academic policies. Some of these issues are discussed below.

A. PLANNING, QUALITY, AND
    PROGRAMS/COURSES

1. Statewide planning
2. Needs assessment
3. Program scheduling priority
4. Lead institutions
5. Home institution arrangements
6. Inter-institutional communication and change, reducing barriers
7. Learning centers/models
8. Quality criteria, guiding pedagogical principles
9. Addressing student diversity
10. Selection of instructional technologies
11. Accreditation
12. Program review and approval
13. Academic integrity/student conduct
14. Program/course support services
15. Program continuation
16. Shared courses and programs
17. Academic residence
18. Evaluation of courses/programs
19. System data collection/analysis
20. Student transfer and articulation
21. Academic calendar

B. STUDENT SERVICES

22. Student services
23. Orientation and technical requirements
24. Admissions
25. Financial aid
26. Transcription
27. Academic advising
28. Library, textbooks/learning packets, media
29. Copyright
30. Technical support services
31. Counseling
32. Other campus services/privileges
33. Information clearinghouses, one-stop services

C. FACULTY ISSUES

34. Faculty compensation and recognition
35. Faculty responsibility/role
36. Faculty training and support
37. Intellectual property rights

D. TUITION/FEES AND STUDENT
    ENROLLMENTS

38. Tuition
39. Electronic payment of tuition and fees
40. Provision of programs for business/industry
41. Delivery cost fees and waiver of unused fees
42. Use of general fund monies
43. Revenue sharing
44. Infrastructure support
45. Student enrollments
46. Identification in databases

E. TECHNICAL STANDARDS,
    INFRASTRUCTURE

47. OUS inter-institutional committee's role in setting technical standards
48. Minimum standards for user hardware/software for online courses
49. Technical production guidelines for courses; courseware management system for online courses
50. Security
51. Technical standards for reliability, consistency
52. Send and receive site technical standards
53. Universities and commercial entities

Table 1. Oregon University System policy guidelines for distance education

CREDIT TRANSFER

Within all states, residency requirements demanded that a certain percentage of coursework be completed at the degree-granting institution. The committee recommended a multi-state agreement that would recognize as fully transferable to four-year institutions the Associate of Arts degree and general education credits earned from any regionally accredited community college. This was a critical priority for SREB and exemplifies how online technologies run head-on into the protectionist practices easily established in an on-site learning environment. SREB recommended that residency requirements be waived for any student earning three-quarters or more of degree requirements through distance learning. Two years after the end of the project, this issue has still not been resolved.

FACULTY

The faculty committee identified three policy goals: to improve effectiveness of teaching and learning, to support new roles and reward structure, and to establish equitable intellectual property and access policies. Specific recommendations to meet these goals included, among others, strengthening financial commitments to human resources development, establishing start-up funds for program start-ups, recognizing e-learning contributions in promotion and tenure, and creating intellectual property policies that provide financial incentives.

QUALITY ASSURANCE

This committee sought to alleviate fears about distance learning lowering the quality of courses and programs. It began its work by reviewing current policies used by accrediting agencies, state-level organizations, and institutions to ensure quality. It then sought to institute mechanisms for deregulating program review and for disseminating information to potential students about program quality, both of which would enhance the market flexibility of programs.

Not all of the recommendations involved policy in the strict sense of the term; strengthening local tutorial support of distance education students, for example, could be viewed as more of a "best practice." Still, the array of issues demonstrates once again the wide-ranging impact that anytime, anywhere learning has on the institutions' business-as-usual practices.

The equivalency and transfer issue is not just a barrier to policy changes across states. For OregonONE, the academic issues swirled around the goal of developing a Common Course Marketplace (CCM), in which "a CCM course will be able to be taken for credit at participating Oregon institutions for residency credit." The goal was to create transparency across institutions with respect to courses. This vision foundered over establishing equivalence across the nine community colleges, eight universities, and four independent higher education institutions.

As the final project evaluation report stated, "One reason the common course marketplace could not move forward was because of faculty concern about quality and equivalency of coursework." The report further noted that this issue "remains foremost in the minds of faculty" for all forms of education, not just distance learning. Beyond the obvious issue of differences over learning standards, there were differences in the definition of the term "common" related to the student experience, the acceptability of courses to faculty, and the transferability of instruction across institutions. In the end, the full CCM was deferred in favor of pilot projects, pending the development of clear, shared definitions of such terms as "common," "acceptability," "residency," and "transferability."

The Great Plains Alliance (GPIDEA) confronted many of these same academic policy issues as they sought to establish an inter-institutional, post-baccalaureate Family Financial Planning program (Moxley and Maes 2003). Academic involvement was vital to promoting success. GPIDEA was started and developed by academic deans, and the faculty had a critical role in identifying areas for policy change. Curricula were developed by inter-institutional faculty teams, but academic credit and degrees are awarded by each member institution. The contentiousness over specific policies was also ameliorated by adopting policy principles that recognized that the GPIDEA is an alliance of independent institutions:

- Although the curriculum is the same, the program name, course titles, and course numbers are similar, but may be unique to each member institution.
- All courses and curricula receive full institutional review prior to implementation and must meet institutional academic standards.
- Students seek admission to the institution of their choice and institutional admissions standards and processes prevail.
- Assessment of instructional program quality and student learning outcomes are institutional responsibilities.

As shown below, high levels of trust between GPIDEA institutions further greased the skids on a lot of these issues.

Prince George's Community College (Maryland) took another approach to the question of inter-institutional quality assurance. Its "Quality Matters" project developed a "faculty-centered, peer review-based, consortium-wide" process to certify the quality of online courses. Forty elements, distributed across eight broad standards (e.g., resources and materials, learner interaction, assessment, and measurement) were identified as having a strong impact on student learning. By fully articulating these success factors, the project gave faculty specific, objective, and verifiable criteria through which to evaluate courses. More importantly, faculty themselves were brought into the process in two significant ways. First, they were trained as reviewers so that the courses would be assessed—and, just as important, be perceived by other faculty to be assessed—by peers. Second, faculty were strengthened in their ability to design and deliver effective courses through training and instructional design support. Through this approach, the project designers cleverly avoided having to address the issue in a "thou shalt" policy sort of way; by bringing faculty into the process, they created the conditions for the faculty themselves to promote the needed policies and processes.

Faculty were brought into the process in two significant ways: (1) as peer reviewers for course assessment; and (2) as recipients of instructional design support to strengthen their ability to design and deliver effective courses.

Faculty are often viewed as obstacles to distance learning initiatives because they raise any number of objections over intellectual property, course equivalency, quality assurance, compensation, and other issues. Their intent (in most cases) is not to be obstructionist, but to allay their genuine concerns about the impact of the new technologies, practices, and policies on their profession. There is no silver bullet to make these issues go away, but as GPIDEA and Prince George's demonstrated, they can be addressed.

Governance Policies

For most of their history, institutions of higher education have prided themselves on being individual cloisters of learning. This is clearly changing as colleges and universities cooperate on a variety of fronts, including libraries, information technology, and academic programs. Still, as the SREB report noted, the fact that institutions "take pride in their individuality and uniqueness" can be a deterrent to adopting joint ventures and policies related to distance learning. The consortia involved in these LAAP projects, therefore, were forced to confront important questions about how they would work together. How would they navigate between autonomy and co-operation? How strongly would they push for uniformity of practice and policy among member institutions? How could they work together while respecting the sovereignty of each member institution? As with most of the policy areas, each project developed its own approach.

When SREB personnel examined the situation with each of its 16 member states, they found four models of distance learning employed by their state systems:

- Centralized, in which the consortium offers courses and services through a central portal;
- Decentralized, in which each institution offers courses, sometimes with financial and other support from the state;
- Free-standing, in which each university grants its own degrees and provides its own services; and
- Mixed, in which critical programs and services are established at the state level, with everything else left to the individual institution.

The range of governance structures and decision-making mechanisms within the states made it difficult for the Policy Laboratory to promote a single mechanism for promoting change. And as a regional think tank, SREB would not likely have had the authority to enforce a decision in any case. Accordingly, it was decided that "the Policy Laboratory should not try to affect policy on whole systems, but encourage individual institutions to participate if they wish." As a result, this placed greater responsibility on the SREB representatives from the constituent institutions to spend more time on education to secure executive-buy-in. For example, Florida Gulf Coast University and the SREB President launched a "Presidents to Presidents" initiative designed to expose college and university executives to distance learning policy issues. Similarly, the Louisiana Board of Regents instituted an Executive Seminar Series to educate the leaders of higher education institutions about the costs of learning technologies. This approach takes time, and is not as emotionally satisfying as formulating extensive policy recommendations. But as SREB noted in a LAAP progress report, "Fundamental policy changes, the real objective of this project, can only be measured in the long term."

The Great Plains IDEA was also careful to acknowledge and respect the integrity of each institution. From the beginning, the alliance adopted several principles that highlighted how they want to work together:

- Behave as equals
- Share leadership
- Respect and accommodate institutional differences
- Simplify student access
- See the compelling elegance of simplicity

The alliance culture is egalitarian and participatory, and accommodates differences in institutional cultures. The program alliance is led by an inter-institutional board of college-level academic administrators who elect officers from among their members. Operational policies and procedures are recommended by experts representing registration, finance, continuing education, and graduate schools at member institutions. Each of the central functions for the alliance—such as financial and data transaction oversight, alliance website maintenance, communications, governance, and program management support—are managed by a lead institution. As issues and work have arisen, individual institutions have assumed responsibility for getting things done. Oklahoma State, for example, conducted the market research for the Family Financial Planning (FFP) program; Montana State took the lead on the business plan and the policy handbook; and Iowa State created the student information database. Because the work is distributed across institutions, alliance overhead is kept to a minimum.

GPIDEA's decentralized approach was given further impetus by the complexity of the policy environment. As they were gearing up the program, the numerous teams found that there was an

> overwhelming, overlapping, and ever-expanding list of administrative/policy issues to address. Emergency FFP program implementation issues needed to be addressed immediately. Several teams were working on the same issues. Too many issues were identified as requiring immediate attention. (Moxley and Maes 2003)

After creating a project master plan, the program directors and coordinators decided to focus the teams' attention on alliance issues, leaving the institutions to initiate changes in their own policies and procedures. As long as the alliance strategy on online programs was clear, they believed, the individual universities could find their own way to accommodate the overall direction. For example, while the alliance adopted the principle that faculty teaching web-based courses should be treated equitably in their evaluation, workload, promotion, tenure, and compensation, they left it to each institution to review its own policies and procedures.

Trust was central to the success of the GPIDEA approach. An issue that trips up many consortia, for example, is equivalency: How can I be assured that the courses offered at Institution A are as good as mine? For GPIDEA's FFP program, that issue presented itself in terms of the instructors for graduate courses. The solution demonstrated an openness that does not come readily to institutions of higher education: If a person is considered qualified to teach a graduate course at his/her home institution, then he/she should be considered qualified to teach at all institutions. A further manifestation of the trust issue was the fact that, for the program's early stages, the institutions had based their involvement on "good faith" agreements. Over time, the universities decided to formalize their understandings into a Memorandum of Agreement. Tellingly, the process got bogged down by the lawyers from the 10 institutions, who were not party to the spirit of the alliance.

Related to governance, of course, is leadership, and strong, involved leadership was no less important in LAAP projects than anywhere else. The Wisconsin Online Resource Center had the task of rounding up 16 institutions, many of which had reservations about the intellectual property policies. In that project, "the colleges with the greatest participation in the project activities were those colleges with the strongest administrative support" (Moxley and Maes 2003). Similarly, at the Oregon University System project, the System office played a crucial role in coordination and planning. "Without the System office playing such a role," the final report noted, "it is unlikely that any of the universities—and certainly not a partnership of ten universities spanning some 20 disciplines—would have developed a systematic approach, and assembled/kept together the partnership during the project" (Oregon University System 2001). Whatever structures are established, it still takes committed leaders to make them work.

Financial Policy

For an industry that is not supposed to be concerned with the bottom line, financial considerations were an ever-present and difficult issue. How should the participating institutions divide up the costs? How should they split the revenues?

For the 16 state partners in SREB's Policy Lab, the "pricing barrier" became a substantial obstacle to student access across state lines. Nonresident students were being asked to pay up to three times the in-state rate for courses delivered electronically, a practice that potentially negated the technical promise of anytime, anywhere. These protectionist barriers reduce student choice, and also prevent institutions from expanding their market, utilizing available capacity, and avoiding duplication of courses. Midway through the project, the SREB partners had instituted a single rate policy for only about 20% of the courses in the Electronic Campus, a regional market-place of more than 5,000 electronic courses and 250 degree programs from more than 375 colleges and universities. To lower the barriers still farther, SREB has promoted an "Electronic Tuition Rate" by marrying the Electronic Campus with the Academic Common Market, a program that since 1974 allowed in-state rates to be applied to on-site courses in other SREB states. This new initiative made selected programs available at in-state tuition rates and through distance learning. Over time, SREB expects to expand the courses and programs offered at the Electronic Tuition Rate. The main challenge has been getting the states to lower the barriers at a time when those states' education budgets have been experiencing severe cuts.

OregonONE encountered difficulties over financial issues when, midway through the project, the community colleges raised questions about the financial formulae used to apportion revenue between the host (which receives the state subsidy) and the provider (which receives the student tuition) institutions. Even after formulating other financial arrangements, agreement could not be reached and OregonONE decided to slow down this part of the project in favor of pilots in selected areas. As the OregonONE example shows, operating with a common state framework is no assurance that resolution of the financial issues will be easy.

One of the most successful projects at resolving financial policies was GPIDEA, which creatively solved the problem by avoiding the baggage of existing concepts and applying a neutral term—the "common price"—to create the alliance Common Course Price and Revenue Distribution model. Students pay a negotiated common price per credit hour to the institution at which they matriculate. Initial disagreement over the price (the $400 per credit hour charged at some institutions seemed too high at the others) was resolved through market research and consensus reached around a $350 charge. Of this price, 75% goes to the teaching institution, 12.5% supports costs at the admitting and enrolling institution, and 12.5% goes to the alliance. To avoid perceptions that it is draining money from other institutional needs, the alliance imposes no membership fees and holds no property. Financial support comes from student enrollments in courses and from in-kind contributions from partner institutions. Part of the rationale for the 12.5% going to the alliance was also to provide ongoing maintenance of the program when the LAAP grant ended. Course development and delivery costs and faculty workload assignments are institutional responsibilities. It is probably no coincidence that GPIDEA, as we saw in a previous section, was established on the basis of mutual trust and respect.

LESSONS LEARNED

Each LAAP project contains a wealth of lessons specific to that initiative's goals and activities. Some of the lessons will be transferable to other situations, others will not. Taken together, however, the projects reconfirm the fundamentals about effecting large-scale change.

It's about Behavior

In the popular mind, policies are declarations of the "shalt" or "shalt not" variety, usually issued by a higher authority, frequently expressed in mind-numbing language, and seemingly intended to make things more difficult. But interpreted more broadly, policies are developed for the purpose of guiding decisions and actions. As statements of intent, they are goals that serve to set expectations and define responsibilities. They are, in effect, descriptions of how people should behave. Long-standing policies that have become part of our behavioral repertoire are acknowledged as "normal," and accepted with little thought and no protest. But when circumstances change —and learning anywhere and anytime is a big change—there can be a large gap between current practices and the expected behaviors. Policies bridge that gap by portraying a different set of behaviors. For new policies to be effective, people need to behave differently, whether it be students registering for classes, faculty advisors steering students to courses at other institutions, or CFOs dividing up the financial pie.

As noted, behavior tends to become entrenched, which is why policy change is so difficult and why, as the LAAP project reports continually emphasized, sustained change takes time. The OregonONE project reported that, "When we initiated the project, we underestimated the challenge the community colleges and universities would face working on the concept of a Common Course Marketplace, and also financial course-sharing when they are in different sectors with different budget approaches." GPIDEA noted simply and directly that, "This grant is a policy and cultural change project." The second annual progress report of the SREB Distance Learning Policy Laboratory noted that "The real challenge of changing public policy ... is still to be tackled. Policy change does not come quickly or easily." To be sure, framing new policies and getting them accepted can be arduous. But the real victory comes when people change what they do.

Policies Operate at Multiple Levels

Another reason why policy change is so difficult is that, inelegantly but ap-appropriately phrased, everything is connected with everything else. A new program has implications for the recruitment of students and faculty. A decision on credit transfer has an impact on finance and marketing. A recommendation made by a consortial steering committee must be reviewed by institutional bodies. GPIDEA developed a chart (Figure 1) to illustrate the interrelationship between the key dimensions of their project.

Administrative and policy changes need to occur simultaneously in several areas. First and foremost, there must be a specific program (Family Financial Planning, in GPIDEA's case) that motivates people to participate; in the absence of a worthy program, there is little point in trying to capture resources or attention. At the same time, programs must be supported by structures and processes at both the alliance/consortium and the individual institutions. As we have seen in several of the projects, the consortium's directions and goals must be aligned with an institution's willingness and capacity to actually make things happen. The inner circle on Figure 1 reminds us that without effective means to support faculty, to support students, and to be financially viable, programs and alliances, however good the concept, are likely to collapse.

To be complete, of course, Figure 1—and this chapter—would have included federal and state policies as well. Their exclusion has not been intended to minimize their importance, and e-learning efforts everywhere have realized that government policies can trump efforts to institute policies that improve access to distance education. Within SREB, for example, the Financial Aid Subcommittee concluded early on in their deliberations that Title IV (especially the rule that requires students to be enrolled at least 12 hours per week to receive federal aid) was a barrier since most states follow or avoid conflict with federal regulations. SREB has also sought to work with both state legislatures and university administrations to achieve a unified vision of educational reform. But while federal policies are central to the overall success of online learning in this country, they cannot become an excuse for inaction. There is still much that can be done, and the most significant barriers often lie at the local level.

Be Pragmatic

Given the extraordinary range of issues (policy and otherwise) involved in launching a distance education program, institutions are advised to be ag-

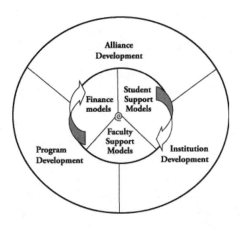

Figure 1. Interrelationships between key dimensions of GPIDEA project

gressive but to bite off only what they can chew. SREB recognized that it could not change legislation pertaining to entire systems, and so focused on specific areas of policy, such as encouraging institutions to function as degree completers for students who have earned distance learning credits from multiple institutions. A more pronounced example is the OregonONE project. When project leadership realized that they would not be able to move as quickly as they had hoped, they refocused their efforts on specific demonstration projects between some of the campuses, such as:

- National Guard Pathways Project, to identify degree pathway options for Guard soldiers using alternative delivery methods.
- OregonONE Writing, major gap analysis and plan, to investigate the feasibility of a multi-institutional distance-delivered writing major and/or minor.
- College Headstart, intended to develop three collegiate mixed delivery mode courses for high school students.
- Course-sharing in personal finance, to develop two, two-credit courses acceptable at multiple institutions.
- Design of a common template for degree pathways, information for prototyping in nursing, agriculture, and liberal studies.

Incremental change is often less appealing than radical transformation, but slow and steady does, in fact, win more races.

FUTURE DIRECTIONS

With a full decade of e-learning experience, colleges and universities have come to appreciate the broad range of policy issues engendered by students' ability to learn anywhere and anytime. The process is unending. New programs and new initiatives will foster the need for new policies, of course, and new technologies will require that institutions revisit their policies on, say, privacy or fair use. But online learning is not the culprit. As several of the LAAP projects demonstrated, the need for policy reviews are not uniquely triggered by distance education. Concerns about course equivalency and faculty competence across institutions, for example, are made more visible by online programs, but they will arise increasingly even in the off-line world as students continue to be more mobile, shop for the best courses, and exhibit other "nontraditional" behaviors. The policy challenge will always be with us.

For colleges and universities, the challenge will continue to be getting it done. Innovation will demand that institutions swim against the current of the traditional behaviors that assume a captive student population, institutional isolation, and program uniqueness. The LAAP projects were pioneers in demonstrating how radically the educational world has changed, and, like all pioneers, they had to create a vision of a different world, overcome skepticism, push forward, and clear the underbrush. A hundred years hence, the policies which the LAAP projects identified and fought for may be the new business-as-usual, and may in fact become obstacles to yet another, unimagined educational frontier. But for now, the policy environment remains a formidable thicket, and those wanting to move forward face a long, hard slog.

Chapter Two

EXTENDING THE REACH
OF DISTANCE EDUCATION THROUGH
PARTNERSHIPS

by Raymond J. Lewis

OVERVIEW

This chapter explores how some higher education institutions have combined two strategies—information technologies and partnerships—to accomplish outcomes that otherwise would not have been possible. By sharing resources with other organizations and using information technologies to deliver services to students, these partners have been able to pursue mutually beneficial goals.

The primary focus here is not so much on how they use information technologies because much already has been written about that. Instead, the emphasis is on what happens when autonomous organizations decide they can achieve more with better results by committing to working together. This chapter draws on lessons emerging from the experiences of a group of ambitious partnership projects funded by the Fund for the Improvement of Postsecondary Education (FIPSE) in its Learning Anytime Anywhere Partnerships (LAAP) program and its Comprehensive Program.

NEED

Most of the projects discussed in this chapter were designed in the 1990–2000 timeframe to respond to a number of needs that are even more acute today than they were then. The rapid pace of change in the economy was making it increasingly difficult for colleges and universities to meet the nation's education and training needs. In addition, demands for educational services were coming from a growing, and increasingly diverse, student population, most of whom had special needs because of, among other issues, their ethnicity, geographical location, health, job, or family obligations.

At the same time most colleges and universities were coping with financial constraints imposed by policymakers and compounded by competitors. There was also pressure from business and policymakers to increase the relevance, accessibility, and quality of educational services. Many critics and supporters alike were urging higher education to make more effective use of new information technology tools as one way to address these challenges.

Essentially the message to colleges and universities at the time these projects were conceived was an earlier version of the same, but even louder, message we hear today: "find new ways to do more with less." The persistence of this message is one of reasons why it's important to learn from the lessons that emerged from these FIPSE-sponsored partnership projects.

COLLABORATION AND PARTNERSHIP

The idea of higher education institutions entering into collaborations with other organizations is certainly not new. But historically, such collaborations have most often focused on activities that were somewhat peripheral to the academic core of the institutions (e.g., facilities, technology, professional development). More ambitious collaborations that involved sharing curriculum, credits, or tuition were rare and usually limited to campuses in close geographical proximity to one another.

As long as political and financial support for higher education was abundant, there was little incentive for individual campuses to enter into collaborations that might limit their autonomy or impinge on their academic prerogatives. By the late 1990s both the political and financial support had waned to such an extent that colleges and universities had new incentives to consider collaborative arrangements, like partnerships, as viable strategies for changing the way they conducted their core business.

At the same time, the rapid expansion of Internet access and the development of online course development software made it more feasible for higher education institutions to extend their reach beyond the campus. These new tools also made it easier to envision groups of colleges and universities increasing their effectiveness by offering collaborative courses and programs without regard to geography. However, there was a dearth of large-scale collaborative efforts that were taking full advantage of the new technological advancements.

In the late 1990s, the staff at the Fund for the Improvement of Post-secondary Education (FIPSE) recognized this convergence of unmet societal needs and new opportunities afforded by information technologies. Their response was to create the LAAP program with its incentives to apply the newer technologies within the context of multi-organizational partnerships.

When FIPSE initiated the Learning Anytime Anywhere Partnerships (LAAP) program in 1999, it required that proposal applications involve two or more independent organizations or institutions. FIPSE used the term "partnership" to convey that prospective projects needed to involve a high level of commitment and resources from two or more organizations in order to be funded.

For purposes of this chapter, we use the term "collaboration" to refer to a broad class of shared activities that organizations voluntarily undertake together, with or without formal written agreements. However, the term "partnership" conveys a greater level of commitment and formality. In this chapter we use a definition for partnership that was devised to refer to a high-level "collaboration" by the Wilder Research Group as part of their review of the literature on collaboration. Their definition of what we refer to here as a "partnership" is "a mutually beneficial and well-defined relationship entered into by two or more organizations to achieve common goals. The relationship includes commitment to mutual relationships and goals; a jointly developed structure and shared responsibility; mutual authority and accountability for success and sharing of resources and rewards" (Mattessich, Murray-Close, and Monsey 2004, 4). In this chapter, we sometimes use the term "alliance" as a synonym for "partnership."

Because they combine the expertise and resources of two or more organizations, partnerships "enable people and organizations to support each other by leveraging, combining, and capitalizing on their complementary strengths and capabilities, thereby achieving more than either partner working alone" (Baer and Duin 2004, 1). Given these advantages, it seems that we should see more examples of partnerships in the higher education community than we do today.

One reason for the dearth of large-scale partnerships is that building, maintaining, and sustaining partnerships is very challenging. Both this essay and an earlier study of the FIPSE LAAP program testify to the fact that a significant portion of the time and effort of an alliance's leadership has to be spent building and nurturing the partnership itself. In an earlier study of LAAP projects, the authors found that when project directors reported being frustrated, "their frustration most often related to the partnership itself rather than the outcomes of the project (e.g., the distance learning program or resource developed)" (Baer and Duin 2004, 6).

The purpose of this chapter is to extract some of the lessons learned from a sub-set of nine FIPSE-funded projects—seven from the FIPSE LAAP program and two from the FIPSE Comprehensive Program. This examination is undertaken against the backdrop of some of the current literature on the partnership process. In spite of the wide diversity among these nine projects, each sought, in one way or another, to expand access to online educational or training opportunities to groups of learners with special needs or requirements.

The nine FIPSE projects referred to in this chapter are the following:

CPB/WGBH NATIONAL CENTER FOR ACCESSIBLE MEDIA (NCAM). Specifications for Accessible Learning Technologies (SALT). The SALT project is a collaboration with IMS Global Learning Consortium's members and experts on distance learning and accessibility to develop and promote technical specifications for the open accessibility of software applications for the e-learning industry. IMS is a non-profit organization that includes more than 50 contributing international members and affiliates representing hardware and software vendors, educational institutions, publishers, government agencies, systems integrators, and multimedia content providers.

EDUCATIONAL COMMUNICATIONS FOUNDATION (ECF). National Community College Asynchronous Learning Network for the AV Industry: A Partnership Between a National Trade Association and Seven Community Colleges. The AV-ALN is the result of a national partnership committed to educating the current and future workforce of the audiovisual communications industry. The project will develop eight courses and offer certificate or degree programs for the incumbent workforce, as well as those seeking careers in the AV industry.

GOVERNORS STATE UNIVERSITY (GSU). Foster Pride Digital Curriculum. The Foster Pride Digital Curriculum has a two-fold mission: to address issues of training and education for foster parents confronted with logistical challenges in accessing the traditional classroom, and to develop multiple asynchronous delivery systems to provide Foster Pride curriculum to homebound foster parents seeking continuing education for relicensure or professional development in specialized areas. Governors State University is leading the project in partnership with the Child Welfare League of America, the Illinois Department of Children and Family Services, and child welfare agencies in six states (California, Illinois, Kentucky, Michigan, North Dakota, and Texas).

HISPANIC EDUCATIONAL TELECOMMUNICATIONS SYSTEM (HETS). Forging Partnerships and Networking Skills with the Virtual Learning and Support Plaza. Founded in 1993, HETS is the first bilingual distance learning consortium dedicated to serving the higher education needs of our fast-growing Hispanic communities. HETS comprises a membership of colleges and universities in the mainland United States, Puerto Rico, and Latin America, and provides an opportunity for affiliated institutions to deliver training programs, courses, and conferences to geographically distributed Hispanic communities.

KANSAS STATE UNIVERSITY. Great Plains Interactive Distance Education Alliance project (KSU, GPIDEA). The mission is to serve the faculty and administrators of member institutions by offering workshops, recommending standards, sharing practices, and disseminating policy issues and recommendations to offer educational programs with other institutions more easily, giving students and professionals access to more educational experiences.

KANSAS STATE UNIVERSITY. Institute for Academic Alliances (IAA), Advancing the Efficiency of Diverse Higher Education Academic Alliances (KSU, IAA). The higher vision of this collaboration involves creating inter-institutional teams of faculty, administrators, and peers to share resources in order to develop curricula, implement programs, and resolve program, financial, and procedural issues to ensure that academic programs are financially viable and sustainable.

KIRKWOOD COMMUNITY COLLEGE. Environmental Technologies Online (ET-Online). ET-Online features Internet-supported instruction, coupled with hands-on training and workshops across the nation, to provide flexible training for workers in the hazardous materials, wastewater, water, and solid waste fields. It is being developed by Hazardous Materials Training and Research Institute (Davenport, Iowa) and Kirkwood Community College (Cedar Rapids, Iowa).

UNIVERSITY OF MARYLAND. Consortium for ITS Training and Education (CITE). The purpose of this consortium is to create an integrated advanced transportation training and education program open to anyone pursuing a career in advanced transportation. CITE will offer graduate and undergraduate courses, skills-based training, and technology transfer while facilitating networking and communication among universities and other CITE members.

PUGET SOUND EDUCATIONAL SERVICE DISTRICT (PSESD). Early Literacy Outreach Project (ELOP). This project in Washington state focuses on creating partnerships throughout the region to offer training, resource connections, and opportunities to learn more about early literacy development of children ages birth through eight years old.

ECONOMIC FEASIBILITY

One of the key reasons why educators partner with other organizations is to achieve outcomes that otherwise would not be possible for their own campus to accomplish by itself. Genuine partnership is too complicated, time-consuming, and risky to undertake unless the leadership at the participating organizations are convinced there is no way they can accomplish the desired outcomes alone. In their review of the literature on partnerships, Deborah Merrill-Sands and Bridgette Sheridan concluded that "alliances appear to be more likely to succeed when they are formed to address problems that no single member can do on its own" (Merrill-Sands and Sheridan 1996, 16).

That description certainly fits all the FIPSE projects mentioned above. But it is particularly apparent in four of the LAAP projects that linked educational organizations with industry-based organizations that possessed specialized content knowledge and/or technical skills otherwise unavailable and yet essential to achieving the goals of the projects. In each of these four cases, the project director was emphatic in his or her assertion that it would never have been possible to successfully tackle such a complex set of tasks without the respective contributions of all partners.

In the case of the University of Maryland, the industry partner brought specialized expertise in the relatively narrow niche of intelligent transportation systems while the UM staff contributed its extensive experience in placing educational content on the web. For the Governors State University project the networks of foster care professionals in the participating states provided specialized knowledge, training materials, and field testing while the university contributed project management skills and high-quality digital video production capability. In another project, the Educational Communications Foundation benefitted from the expertise of numerous industry-association businesses specializing in audio and video technologies and the instructional expertise of numerous community colleges. In the case of CPB/WGBH project, the industry members of the IMS Global Learning Consortium added their software and hardware expertise to WGBH's expertise in making digital resources more accessible to users with various disabilities.

Even for projects in which the primary partners all were educational organizations, there is plenty of evidence that without the particular combination of skills and resources brought by various partners, the projects, and the innovations they produced, would not have been possible. The Great Plains IDEA project was the direct outgrowth of a shared recognition among Human Sciences deans at ten Mid-Western campuses that none of them, on their own, had the resources to offer a new graduate degree in Family Financial Planning. Because of this collaboration, all the partner universities can now not only offer a new M.A. degree, but their students and faculty benefit immensely from the unique mix of expertise available at different partner campuses. Since their initial success with Family Financial Planning, the GPIDEA has added three more online master's degrees.

Another example of how FIPSE-funded partnerships combine strengths to achieve new and important outcomes can be found in the Seattle area where Puget Sound Educational Service District (PSESD) uses its strong expertise in early childhood education (training content, outreach services, etc.) to help public and private colleges train low-income early childhood educators. The colleges work with PSESD to devise flexible learning opportunities that hopefully will serve as the initial steps in a career pathway for adults who may never have considered themselves "college material." Some colleges have been so pleased with the ways PSESD helps them to better access this special population that they have been willing to lower tuition or fees for specific early childhood classes.

Nearly all the proposed activities of these projects required resources and expertise that went far beyond the capacity of any single organization to accomplish on its own. Through their sharing of resources and expertise, these FIPSE projects have made it possible for institutions to deliver programs that would not otherwise have been economically feasible.

ECONOMIES OF SCALE

Since its inception, FIPSE has actively encouraged its funded projects to achieve economies of scale that increase the number of learners and geographical areas served. The LAAP program, in particular, had a strong focus on using partnerships to expand the scale of innovative projects in order to increase their impact.

Some organizations view partnering merely as a way to achieve cost efficiencies by offering the same unimproved services to more people. FIPSE's approach to "scaling up" emphasizes combining organizational strengths as a strategy for reaching more students with high quality programs that are appropriate to their needs. The literature on partnerships supports this position by pointing out that financial efficiency should not be the central focus because when it is, the likelihood that the alliance will fail is much higher (Merrill-Sands and Sheridan 1996).

As it turns out, it's difficult to assess the extent to which complex partnerships like those in the LAAP program foster economies of scale that enable larger enrollments and extend the reach of educational services. A review of the nine projects listed above suggests that most of these larger scale and more complex partnerships take much more time to move beyond the capacity-building stage to the service-delivery stage than anyone involved originally envisioned.

This pattern is perhaps most obvious in the case of the HETS, Governors State University, and Educational Communications Foundation projects where, by the end of the grant period, they had succeeded in building substantial new capacity, but had not yet demonstrated the full extent to which the services eventually can be scaled up. And in each case, the potential number of students who could be served is very large. Whether they can achieve greater economies of scale will depend on what they do in the postgrant phase of the projects. It's worth noting that there are other FIPSE projects—not included in this chapter—that fit the same pattern.

Kirkwood Community College's Environmental Training Online project is one of the LAAP projects that managed to achieve impressive economies of scale. Working in cooperation with the Hazardous Materials Training and Research Institute and its 118 community college partners in 46 states, the ET-Online project delivered courses to more than 2,300 students during the five years of the grant. Since then the program has continued to serve growing numbers of students.

The Early Literacy Outreach Project (ELOP), based at Puget Sound Educational Service District, is another example of how the funding of a partnership can significantly increase the number of learners served. By developing or adapting new training curricula and sharing it with multiple college partners and childcare delivery agencies, the ELOP has greatly increased the number of childcare workers who are taking college-level courses; many are taking them for the very first time.

LESSONS ABOUT PARTNERSHIPS

The staff members of these FIPSE-funded projects can attest to the fact that building and maintaining a partnership can be extremely challenging. It isn't easy to convince the leaders of autonomous organizations that they have more to gain by joining, and then staying with, an alliance where the decision-making and responsibility are shared. As Virginia Moxley and Sue Maes (2003, 5) of the Great Plains IDEA put it, "Alliance building is an intellectually and emotionally intense endeavor of great complexity. Each partner is expected to give a little with the hope of getting a lot."

Given the difficulties inherent in building and managing partnerships, it's worth examining some of lessons emerging from FIPSE-funded collaborative projects. Hopefully some the observations gleaned from these projects will help make life easier for others who engage in alliances. The following discussion is divided into lessons about institutions, individuals, and the partnership process.

LESSONS ABOUT INSTITUTIONS

Having History Helps

Given the choice, when undertaking a complicated task, most of us prefer to work with a long-standing friend or trusted colleague rather than risk working with a new person. So it shouldn't be surprising that when it comes to partnerships between organizations, those with a prior history often have a distinct advantage over those that are newly formed.

In their 2004 study of LAAP projects, Linda L. Bear and Ann Hill Duin, made the following observation:

> Successful projects—i.e., those that met their goals and were continuing to evolve and become sustainable—were in most cases those that had been built by partners who were part of a consortium or alliance prior to the LAAP project. The presence of this pre-existing trust and relationship proved extremely valuable. Partners were able to get started more quickly, were less likely to encounter unforeseen political and philosophical obstacles, and were more likely to remain committed to the LAAP project because of the consortia foundation. (Baer and Duin 2004, 6)

This conclusion is certainly born out by the experiences of the nine FIPSE projects covered in this chapter, each of which benefitted from prior informal professional relationships and/or formal partnerships. The leaders of the Great Plains IDEA project, based at Kansas State University, are the first to admit that the long-standing professional relationships among the deans of Human Science programs at the respective campuses was a key element in their extraordinary success of getting 10 Mid-West land-grant universities to agree to jointly offer an online M.A. in Family Financial Planning with common curriculum, pricing, and transfer policies.

In the case of Governors State University, two formal, long-term partnership relationships were key to their success. In their effort to adapt a print-based curriculum for foster parents into a multiple-media digital form, Governors State University benefitted immensely from its long-term working relationship with the Illinois Department of Child and Family Services (DCFS). And in turn, the project was able to involve at least 14 states because of the ten-year working relationship between the Illinois DCFC and the Child Welfare League of America (CWLA). The Project Director, Charles Nolley of GSU, credits these historical relationships with helping the project persevere through some very difficult challenges (personal communication, January 19, 2005).

Likewise, the CPB/WGBH National Center for Accessible Media (NCAM) was able to successfully impact the learning technology industry largely because of its long-term involvement with the IMS Global Learning Consortium. IMS itself is an alliance of education and industry organizations that have been working together for years to increase the interoperability and accessibility of online learning software. Similarly, Kirkwood Community College's Environmental Technology Online project had a head start on building its partnership of 118 colleges because of its historical relationship with other community colleges in the waste management and environmental fields.

Even though the FIPSE projects discussed in this chapter involved partners with relatively long histories of either formal or informal relationships, some of the other LAAP projects did involve more recently-formed partnerships. In their studies of LAAP projects and other partnerships, Baer and Duin (2004) found that those partnerships which were not based on existing alliances were more likely to encounter competitive or passive aggressive behavior on the part of some partners.

Compatibility Matters

What criteria should project leaders use when selecting partners? A review of the projects discussed in this chapter suggests there are reasons for choosing partners that are at various points along a continuum from similar to different. One of the advantages of partnering with organizations that "look like ours" is that it can reduce the possibilities of serious culture clashes. Of course, institutions that are very similar can also be competitors.

The Great Plains IDEA project (KSU, GPIDEA) is an example of how the similarities—in this case among Human Sciences programs at the ten Mid-Western, public, land-grant universities—can increase the likelihood of a project solving very challenging problems. Key stakeholders in that project are very aware that the online academic degree program model they developed would have been much more difficult to achieve if there had been a more diverse mix of institution types and if the inter-personal relationships had not been so strong. Not only did the institutions and programs share many similarities, but the key players had a history of professional and personal relationships. As Virginia Moxley of KSU put it, "Alliances between institutions are only as strong as the relationships between the people who represent the institutions in the alliance. Relationships built on friendship over time, trust in each other's integrity, and confidence in each other's talents foster good relationships" (personal communication, March 7, 2005).

As it turns out, the number of partners in an alliance can be an important factor as well. A previous study which included all LAAP project directors found that those who had early on indicated a need to "find more partners" later indicated that they had too many partners (Baer and Duin 2004, 10). Adding partners has the potential of enhancing the project, but each additional partner also adds complexity and time demands, not to mention potential for conflicts.

When the purpose of the project is to build bridges between different sectors of society (e.g., higher education and business), there are compelling reasons to select partners based on differences that lend complementarity to the project. The Educational Communications Foundation, University of Maryland, and the CPB/WGBH projects obviously looked for industry partners that could provide complimentary skills and resources to the projects.

One of the lessons that is emerging from the HETS project and the KSU (Institute for Academic Alliances) project is that for projects involving activities that are very close to the core of the academic enterprise (e.g., joint online academic certificate or degree programs), too many differences can be paralyzing. If the mix of institutional partners is too diverse (e.g., public, private, 2-year, 4-year, multi-campus systems, individual institutions, multiple states), the probability of arriving at mutually acceptable policies and procedures is vastly diminished and, at best, the process is likely to more difficult and time consuming. If partnering across such diverse boundaries is the goal of a project, it's advisable to keep the number of partners small and, if possible, avoid going across system or state lines, at least in the initial phase.

Organizational Cultures Count

As it turns out, not even long-term partnerships are always a guarantee that project leadership will be able to overcome differences of organizational culture. Prior to its LAAP grant, the leadership of the Educational Communications Foundation (ECF) had a long history of working with the leading community colleges in distance learning and they also had a close relationship with the international audio-visual industry association (ICIA). However, the project was unable to overcome some significant negative impacts growing out of the clash of cultural perspectives between its business and education partners, each with sharply contrasting assumptions about the proper pace at which project decisions and actions should take place.

The ECF project's experience illustrates Rosabeth Moss Kanter's observation that operational and cultural differences often emerge after a collaboration is underway. "Differences in authority, reporting, and decision-making styles become noticeable at this stage in the new alliance; what people get involved in decisions; how quickly decisions are made; how much reporting and documentation are expected; what authority comes with a position; and which functions work together" (Kanter 1994, 104).

Partner Relationships Are Challenging

All the project directors contacted for this chapter agreed the process of building and maintaining the partnership was much more challenging than they had anticipated. In their study of all LAAP projects, Baer and Duin found the partnering process was one of the most difficult challenges that project managers faced:

> It was clear from the interviews that the partnerships evolved over time and for the most part, the partnerships matured. Many project directors found that they were overly enthusiastic or ambitious in their initial expectations. This was often due to the fact that developing or nurturing the partnership took longer than anticipated, and most concluded that building and maintaining partnerships was not easy. As one project director commented, "No one helped us with partnering. Everyone assumed that we just knew how to partner." (Baer and Duin 2004, 6)

In the best of all possible worlds, all the partners in a funded project would be on board from the beginning and stay actively involved up to and beyond the closing date. In fact, one of the lessons learned from the LAAP projects was that some partners do drop out along the way, requiring the project staff to adjust the original plan or to pursue replacement partners. For example, when the Educational Communications Foundation project ran into problems related to the pace at which project decisions and activities were progressing, some of the industry partners withdrew from the project or lost interest.

Unforeseen external events can also impact partnership projects. The CPB/WGBH project was impacted early on in its life when some of its industry partners dropped out due to the bursting of the "dot-com bubble." Fortunately for the project staff, their lead partner was the industry association IMS which continued its support even when some of its member companies left or diminished their role in the project. The lesson that the project director, Madeleine Rothberg, drew from this experience was that educators can reduce the risks of partnering with individual businesses by working with industry associations.

Because FIPSE projects involve innovative approaches to significant educational challenges, they sometimes attract new partners after the project is underway. For example, the University of Maryland project managed to attract key business partners after project activities were underway and publicized. And in its second year, the HETS project attracted two major corporate partners—IBM and Banco Popular—that volunteered employees to serve as online mentors for Hispanic students.

Structure Is Important

The LAAP projects reviewed for this chapter employed a variety of governance and advisory mechanisms to represent the interests of the respective partners; some merely relied on informal communication. One of the lessons that emerged was that while it is critical to have the support of college or university presidents, they are not necessarily the group that is most able to help the project staff solve some of the complex problems faced by large-scale partnerships such as the LAAP projects.

Both the HETS project and the Educational Communications Foundation project found that, in spite of the presidents' good intentions, they were unable, or poorly positioned, to impact some policy barriers (e.g., tuition rates, registration, credit transfer) that prevented collaborative online academic programs from crossing state boundaries or, in some cases, system or even institutional boundaries.

Both projects also found that when institutional presidents return to their campuses from partnership project meetings they rarely communicate to their key staff and faculty about the project's activities or needs. The lesson some have drawn from observing this phenomenon is that partnership efforts involving complex issues such as cross-institutional sharing of academic programs must have the active involvement, at some level, of key academic leaders (e.g., provosts, deans, department chairs) and key administrative leaders (e.g., business officers, registrars).

Presidential support and advocacy has been shown to help persuade external and internal campus policymakers to consider removing barriers to collaboration, but relying heavily on presidential-level involvement in project governance and communication does not appear to be a wise use of anyone's time. In contrast, the Great Plains IDEA project staff attributes much of their success to the active involvement of key academic and administrative leaders (e.g., deans, finance officers) in working sessions with their peers from other campuses and as members of campus teams that can look for solutions acceptable to their institutional colleagues.

For projects that involve a small number of partner organizations —even those where the partners represent a large membership—when it comes to solving important issues, the appropriate motto might well be "less is more." The Governors State University project found that it could not meet its timelines when it relied on the consensus decision-making model of one of its key partners that represented many member organizations. Eighteen months into the project, it became necessary to drastically shrink the size of the group that could review and approve the educational modules they were producing for foster parents. This major cultural shift was painful to implement, but it was necessary to enable the project to produce its products within the timeframe of the grant; and, as it turned out, the smaller group was so sensitive to the concerns of the constituent member organizations that they earned the trust and acceptance of the members for the digital curriculum modules they produced.

Unlike the GSU example, projects that involve many partner organizations that can't, or don't need to be, centrally involved in day-to-day management may want to adopt the motto "more is better." For example, the Puget Sound Educational Service District project provides educational resources to many childcare agencies (public and private) as well as to colleges and universities in the Seattle area. Project staff members use multiple strategies to interactively engage their numerous partners in sharing information and shaping project policies. (e.g., an informal advisory committee, regular involvement in various early childhood community planning groups, conferences, and an extensive web site). However, the PSESD project staff members do the bulk of project decision-making.

LESSONS LEARNED ABOUT PEOPLE

Leadership

It's impossible to look at the FIPSE projects covered in this chapter without noticing the significant roles that individual leaders play in envisioning, championing, and managing these ambitious partnerships. All of these projects had the benefit of multi-talented project directors who were able to successfully guide their projects. Even so, these directors will be the first to admit that they and their staff could never have shepherded their projects without the commitment and effort of key stakeholders in each of the partner organizations.

Serving as the leader of an alliance is an extremely demanding job. "The nature and complexity of the problems brought about by inter-institutional efforts force leaders to be savvy, flexible, and creative. Alliance leaders have to learn to compromise and balance collective needs and preferences with those of their individual institution. They have to recognize ideas that will best benefit the alliance" (American Council on Education 2003, 11).

Vision

Based on his experience directing the Governors State University LAAP project, Charles Nolley believes that having a clear vision for the project from the beginning is critical to keeping the partners working on the same track even in the face of major challenges and distractions. While the project directors didn't know exactly how they were going implement the vision that they documented in their proposal, they often returned to that vision statement to "help them get off of many rocks" (personal communication, January 19, 2005).

Nolley feels strongly that partners in a potential collaborative project should pay special attention to the vision statement they include in their grant proposal because they will have to rely on it as their compass when they encounter challenges. His advice to those who may be developing a partnership project is "the proposal is not just about getting the grant" (personal communication, January 19, 2005).

Some of the project directors are convinced that the nobility of their LAAP project's vision (innovative ways to serve groups with special needs) helped motivate partners to stick with the project through difficulties that might otherwise have prompted them to leave or diminish their role. This has been the experience of the CPB/WGBH, Governors State University, Puget Sound ESD, and HETS projects that served, respectively, the interests of the disabled, foster parents, childcare providers, and Hispanic students.

Trust and Generosity

Trust in the other partners plays a very critical role in any successful alliance; this is obvious from conversations with these LAAP project partners and in the literature on partnerships. Unfortunately, there is no predictable formula for creating a sense of trust among partners, but honest and open communication is certainly one essential ingredient.

In the absence of trust, partnerships can fall far short of their potential, regardless of how attractive their mix of expertise and resources appears. "Without mutual trust, respect, and commitment, partners rarely take the risks needed to make the partnership investment successful" (Baer and Duin 2004, 7).

Along with trust, Virginia Moxley, Chair of the Board of Directors of the Great Plains Interactive Distance Education Alliance (IDEA) firmly believes that to be successful, partners in an alliance should bring with them a "spirit of generosity." And while a generous spirit may facilitate compromise, Moxley believes that "alliance partners must work beyond compromise (which is generally the outcome everyone can agree on, but also the outcome that doesn't advance much of anything) to find a compelling shared vision that informs and inspires the work together" (personal communication, March 7, 2005).

Even though traits like trust, generosity, and a willingness to move beyond mere compromise are difficult to quantify—much less engineer—their presence or absence clearly impacted the outcomes of many of the LAAP projects. The quality of human relationships are often a better predictor of success in partnerships than how the arrangement is structured or who is in charge.

LESSONS LEARNED ABOUT THE PARTNERSHIP PROCESS

Guiding Principles

As voluntary associations, partnerships must rely on the good will and perceived mutual self-interest of their member organizations. And because partnerships rely more on consensus than on hierarchical rules, the members need general guidelines about how to work effectively in the collaborative framework. One of the useful lessons coming out of the Great Plains IDEA project is that partnerships can operate very effectively by agreeing to a simple set of guiding principles. In their case the principles are as follows:

- behave as equals
- share leadership
- respect and accommodate institutional differences
- simplify student access (Moxley and Maes 2003, 6)

Communications

The one lesson on which alliance observers and practitioners alike agree is that communication among the partners is the most critical factor in determining the success or failure of partnerships. While the patterns and modes of communication may vary from project to project, having a commitment to regular, open, and responsive communication among all participants is absolutely essential. The lesson about communications that Charles Nolley, project director of the Governors State University project, learned was never to minimize the importance of listening, communicating, and facing the hard issues (personal communication, January 19, 2005).

The LAAP projects bear witness to the unavoidable reality that communication in partnership projects is far more challenging than it is in any single organization for a number of reasons:

- Project participants' first obligations are to their home organizations.
- Participants are usually scattered over large geographical areas.
- The priority participants give to decisions and commitments made at partner meetings can easily slip many notches in the face of home-organization demands.
- All too often some or all of the roles project participants play in partnerships is an add-on to their normal responsibilities rather than a compensated or release-time commitment (regardless of what is promised as in-kind contribution).
- Partnership project staff generally have limited rewards or incentives to offer participants in alliance activities.
- Partnership project staff generally have to depend on designated representatives to communicate messages to important players within each partner organization.

Because of these last two points, it's particularly difficult for partnership project staff to establish and maintain the kind of communication links they need between different levels (e.g., administrative leadership, academic leadership, operational staff, faculty) within individual participant organizations. This is a particularly frustrating challenge for projects implementing collaborative online academic programs projects (e.g., HETS, KSU, IAA).

For all of the reasons cited above, one of the clearest lessons emerging from the review of these partnership projects is that having a written communication plan from the outset is just as important as having an evaluation, dissemination, or institutionalization plan. Ideally, all key partners should participate in developing, refining, and periodically revisiting the communication plan to assure a strong sense of ownership and compliance. Ultimately, it is the project director's responsibility to implement the communications plan and to assure that the other partners are satisfied with the quality, frequency, and modes of communication in the project.

Most of the projects cited here relied on a combination of face-to-face meetings, telephone conference calls, and email. All the projects had web sites to disseminate information and some also used their site to obtain interactive input from partners.

Communication Suggestions from Project Directors

The project directors interviewed for this chapter suggested some approaches to communicating in partnership projects that may prove helpful to others:

- Commit to holding regularly scheduled telephone conference calls, even if they are short, in order to keep partners' attention focused on the project and its timetable.

- Take minutes of all meetings and, within a week, send copies to participants highlighting decisions, commitments, and timelines.

- Use travel funds to enable key project participants to meet in a face-to-face mode when critical agreements or products need to be produced or when it's critical to develop rapport and trust that will enable people to conduct subsequent work via phone or email.

- Use regularly scheduled conference calls to help keep stakeholders focused on the collaborative agenda while minimizing the negative impact on their busy schedules at their home organizations. (The project directors report that this works best after project participants have meet face-to-face and have established rapport with one another.)

- Do not assume that communication has actually occurred when you send an email to partners.

- Strive to strike a comfortable balance between too little and too much communication with partners, but when in doubt, it's advisable to err on the side of more rather than fewer messages.

- When dealing with boards or steering committees of presidents, prepare letters for them to sign that will go to their respective academic leadership summarizing the outcomes of the meeting.

- Supplement regular email and telephone communication with a project newsletter to keep project participants and colleagues at their institutions informed and involved.

Communication Suggestions from Literature on Collaboration

Based on their 2001 review of the literature, a team from the Wilder Research Center made a list of recommendations (paraphrased below) to people who participate in collaborative group endeavors (Mattessich, Murray-Close, and Monsey 2004, 23):

- Interact often, update one another, discuss issues openly, and convey all necessary information to one another and to people outside the group.

- Set up a system of communication at the beginning of a collaborative effort and identify the responsibilities each member has for communication.

- Consider setting up a staff function with specific responsibility for communication.

- Provide incentives to encourage effective communication and discourage ineffective communication.

- Establish communications strategies that reflect the diverse communication styles of the partners.

- Acknowledge that problems will occur and that they must be communicated.

- Avoid selective distribution of oral and written communication that may splinter the group.

Management

Even if a partnership project is fortunate enough to have the kind of leadership, shared vision, high level of trust, and excellent communication strategies described above, it is unlikely to achieve its collaborative goals if it is not well managed. Just as universities have historically assumed that people who earn a Ph.D. automatically know how to teach, there is a similar tendency to assume that anyone with academic credentials knows how to successfully manage a collaborative project involving colleges and universities. Most experienced FIPSE project directors would heartily disagree with this assumption because they learned much of what they now know about project management on the job.

Involving Multiple Levels at Partner Organizations

Partnership projects pose a particularly difficult management challenge because generally only a handful of people (and sometimes only one person) are directly assigned to represent their organization in the alliance, yet the attention, time, and energies of other colleagues at each organization are needed to achieve the partnership goals. The leaders of the FIPSE projects reviewed in this chapter have been creative in devising management strategies designed to actively involve multiple layers of administrators, faculty, and operational staff in the work of the partnership.

Both of the Kansas State University projects (KSU, GPIDEA and KSU, IAA) as well as the HETS project have used similar strategies to reach into the institutions to involve various layers of administrators and academics. Through the strategic use of travel funds, they have covered the costs of bringing faculty and administrators together into face-to-face meetings with groups of their peers from other partner campuses. These peer group meetings are used to accomplish specific project tasks (e.g., curriculum development, credit transfer policies).

Bringing such groups together in these meetings is no guarantee of good results but, more often than not, this is where the major breakthroughs are made. Debbie Haynes, a faculty member involved in the Great Plains IDEA project made the following observation: "It was amazing how that peer pressure of fellow professionals from other campuses changed people's minds from 'We have never done it that way' to 'Well, maybe we could try this' to 'We could change our rules'" (Eckel, Harley, and Affolter-Caine 2004, 13).

These structured face-to-face sessions often yield added benefits for the partnership. Most participants in such meetings not only report that they come away more committed to the partnership project, but they also say they greatly appreciate the unique professional development experience of problem-solving with other professionals in their field. Correspondingly, if the purpose of the meetings is not well defined and the group lacks effective facilitation, these meetings have the potential to generate a great deal of confusion and ill-will for the project. The risks are high, but the rewards can be impressive.

In addition to sponsoring similar face-to-face meetings with working groups from partner organizations, the HETS LAAP project also used internal RFP competitions to attract the attention and the best efforts of key administrative and academic personnel at their member institutions. Even though the amounts involved were modest, the project staff was able to engage a wider range of participation than they had through more conventional means such as publicity and working through campus representatives.

Decision-making

Because partnerships lack a hierarchical structure, they rely primarily on consensus. Charles Nolley of Governors State University notes that, in the absence of hierarchy, projects have to find a balance between traditional management and collaboration that suits the partners. Because partnerships place greater reliance on consensus than the exercise of authority, they tend to generate levels of ambiguity that make some participants uncomfortable (personal communication, January 19, 2005).

This situation can be further complicated when consensus-based decision-making is much more central to the culture of one or more of the partner organizations. In the case of the Educational Communications Foundations project, it was the community college faculty and administrators who highly valued a consensus approach more than did their industry partners. In the Governors State University project it was the professionals in the Child Welfare League of America (CWLA) who were more accustomed to operating within a consensus model than were the faculty and staff of the Communications Department at GSU. In both cases, the differences in decision-making styles caused serious problems for the projects.

Nevertheless, alliance projects do need to make decisions; eventually someone has to make the final call. "Processes need to be designed which allow for active participation and consensus-building, but at the same time promote efficient decision-making" (Merrill-Sands and Sheridan 1996, 12).

Once they arrive at agreements, most partnership projects rely on memorandums of agreement (MOA) or memorandums of understanding (MOU) to document important policies and procedures. In the Great Plains IDEA project, "the notion of shared governance is so pervasive in this alliance that formal memoranda of agreement about program and alliance participation were initiated only after effective working agreements were informally arranged and tested. In this alliance, agreement on principles precedes agreement on policies" (Moxley and Maes 2003, 4). A sample Memorandum of Agreement is included at the end of this chapter.

This lesson from the Great Plains IDEA is worthy of consideration by all partnership projects. However, being willing to rely on informal agreements until the formal MOAs or MOUs can be worked out requires a level of trust among the partners that may be difficult for some partnerships to achieve initially, or ever.

Task Management

Once a decision is made in a partnership context, the next most likely challenge will be motivating well-intentioned partners to follow through in a timely fashion on their commitments. In their survey of the literature on collaborative alliances, Merrill-Sands and Sheridan (1996, 12) observed the following: "Perhaps the most vexing problem for public sector collaborative alliances is establishing accountability mechanisms to ensure that members perform their roles and fulfill their commitments."

For many alliance projects it turns out that the most effective accountability mechanism is the project director and/or his or her staff. Through a combination of persuasion and prodding, it seems that many project directors have learned how to apply their own version of "tough love" to keep the work flowing on, or near, schedule. For the project director this means learning to walk a thin line between reminding and harassing colleagues through the judicious use of emails, phone messages, newsletters, web pages, and face-to-face meetings.

When the inevitable surprises and obstacles arise, the lesson many project directors rely on is the need to be flexible. Linda Hoover from Texas Tech University expressed this well in a video produced by the Great Plains IDEA and conveyed in writing by Moxley and Maes (2003, 2-3):

> As we've worked through trying to develop policies and procedures for the alliance, we found that from university to university, everyone is pretty flexible until you get to their 'sacred' policy or

procedures. But if a real alliance is going to be created, you have to trust each other, you have to be flexible, you have to move toward truly realizing that flexibility, and putting away some of those sacred policies and procedures.

Margorie Kostelnik, Dean of the College of Education and Human Services, University of Nebraska–Lincoln summarized the benefits that can be derived when an academic partnership is successfully implemented. Referring to her experience with the Great Plains IDEA, she said the following:

> There is a cooperative spirit within the alliance. People sometimes think of that as being simply a group of people being nice to each other. This is more than nice. It's good business, because through this collective effort, we're...able to offer degrees that we couldn't offer otherwise. We're able to give the students who are enrolled in our programs access to students from all over the world and to faculty from all over the region, and as a result we are able to produce a higher quality product. (Moxley and Maes 2003, 9)

Intellectual Property Rights

While most colleges and universities have adopted policies regarding ownership of intellectual property rights for online courses, in an alliance setting it can be much more difficult to arrive at a workable arrangement. If the alliance merely facilitates the creation of shared online courses by supporting faculty travel to development meetings, it is likely that the ownership will reside with the faculty member or their institution. This was the case with the HETS project that also was unable to obtain from its members intellectual property rights to courses it directly funded at its member campuses. Some alliances like the GPIDEA have a general policy that in all cases the rights reside with the campus that developed the course.

When the alliance fully supports the development of a course that is then shared by partner organizations, they are in a stronger position to retain ownership. This approach, taken by the Kirkwood Community College hazardous materials training project, enabled the alliance to retain control over courses that needed to meet national safety standards while at the same time being flexible enough to be adopted by over a hundred partner colleges.

FUTURE DIRECTIONS

There is little doubt that American higher education is in for some unprecedented changes in the not too distant future. The cumulative effects of changing public policies, ongoing funding constraints, growing demands for services (both current and new), as well as growing competition from the private sector and abroad will require changes in the way higher education conducts its business. The real question is, to what extent will it be educators who shape those changes?

Partnership models, like those discussed in this chapter, offer educators powerful tools for coping with major challenges on their own terms. Unlike change strategies that may be hierarchically imposed, alliances can be shaped to address the specific needs and cultures of the organizations involved. Partnerships also have the advantage of allowing the partners to reach over or around bureaucratic structures such as higher education systems, state governments, or national boundaries.

Because partnerships are voluntary associations, institutions get to choose their partners. Through carefully crafted MOAs and MOUs, it's possible to structure partnerships to maximize predictable outcomes and reduce potential risks. As evidenced in these FIPSE-funded projects, there are a variety of ways to structure the working relationships within a partnership. And, as the Great Plains IDEA model illustrates, it's even possible to finance alliances in ways that do not require partner institutions to cover the operational costs of managing the alliance.

One of the lasting legacies of the FIPSE LAAP program to higher education is its contribution to our knowledge about partnerships—their possibilities and their limitations. We now know about partnering strategies that work very well in certain circumstances (e.g., collaborative online degrees offered by campuses with similar cultures). We also know more about situations where partnering is more difficult, but still possible (e.g., business–education partnerships). In addition, we have learned about problem areas that need more experimentation by alliance practitioners and investigation by researchers.

Some examples of partnership issues that still need more attention from practitioners and researchers include the following:

- Adapting proven partnership models to groups of diverse institutions. (The KSU, IAA project is currently working to adapt the Great Plains IDEA model to four very different partnership groups.)

- Overcoming cultural barriers between diverse organizations (e.g., business–education partnerships).
- Devising model agreements and guidelines for use by business–education alliances.
- Developing better models for actively involving various participants from partner organizations in alliance activities —especially individuals from multiple functional areas and different levels of authority within partner organizations.
- Handling intellectual property rights issues within the context of an alliance.
- Documenting alternative communication models for partnerships (e.g., suggested patterns of communication, use of technology and print resources).
- Devising escalation procedures that can be implemented in the event partner representatives, or alliance staff, fail to follow through on communications or commitments. (Identifying higher level positions within the respective organizations that agree to be accessible, responsible, and responsive, if needed.)
- Devising financial models for resolving tuition differentials —especially across diverse institution types (e.g., two-year, four-year, public, private, perhaps involving multiple states).
- Refining survey instruments used to assess partner needs and resources for use with partnerships with diverse membership. (The Institute for Academic Alliances and the Great Plains IDEA have made substantial progress developing such tools for shared academic programs.)

CONCLUSION

As noted earlier, colleges and universities are increasingly being asked to "find new ways to do more with less." While partnerships are not new to everyone in higher education, they remain underutilized tools. This is in spite of the fact that partnerships, like those described in this chapter, are powerful and flexible tools that allow educators to shape their responses to their changing environment. In a period where political, financial, and market forces are increasingly impacting the range of options available to higher education institutions, partnerships are one of the most effective tools available.

The knowledge and experience emerging from the many FIPSE-funded partnership projects constitute a unique resource for practitioners and researchers interested in helping higher education adapt to change. The lessons we are learning from these projects are invaluable to those who want to build and sustain effective partnerships that permit thoughtful experimentation and innovation in higher education.

Appendix

Sample Memorandum of Agreement for an Alliance Program

Great Plains Interactive Distance Education Alliance Program Memorandum of Agreement for the Masters Program and Certificate

The Great Plains Interactive Distance Education Alliance (hereinafter called the "Great Plains IDEA") is comprised of academic colleges offering baccalaureate and higher degree programs.

This Memorandum of Agreement is entered into by _____ _____University, College of _____ regarding the creation of the Great Plains IDEA inter-institutional post baccalaureate distance education program in _____ _____.

The Alliance Members and/or Institutional Affiliates initiating this memorandum and agreeing to these terms and conditions include:

_____

_____

It is understood that additional parties may be invited to join this cooperative effort either as Alliance Members or Institutional Affiliates as outlined in the Great Plains IDEA Policies and Procedures Manual.

_____University will participate in this inter-institutional program by granting a Master's Degree and/or a post baccalaureate certificate in _____ to students who successfully complete the inter-institutional program.

_____ University agrees to provide distance education courses for students admitted to the program by other Alliance Members, to incorporate approved courses offered by other Alliance Members or Institutional Affiliates into its appropriate degree and certificate, to admit fully qualified program applicants and to advise graduate students in the inter-institutional program.

_____University agrees to respect the academic standards and quality of the academic departments involved in this joint program. Faculty members of the Alliance Members who provide instruction in this program must meet qualifications for teaching graduate courses at their employing institution; further documentation or approval will not be required by the other Alliance Members.

_____University retains the right to:

1. Uphold its established University admission processes and admission standards for students entering the inter-institutional program as _____ University students.

2. Monitor academic performance, enforce standards, including disciplinary policies and procedures, and adherence to all other graduate school policies for students admitted to study at the institution.

3. Conduct graduation audits to assure compliance with University requirements.

4. Follow its established University review processes for approval of and modification to the curriculum.

5. Implement its University processes for course and program assessment.

6. Assign to the student's graduate committee approval oversight for courses applied to the student's program of study.

Institutional Courses designated as "Alliance courses" will be:

1. Taught by faculty members approved by the Alliance Member that provides the instruction.

2. Taught according to the published schedule and at the enrollment capacity agreed upon by the inter-institutional program faculty.

3. Priced to all students enrolled in the Alliance section of the course at the current Alliance credit hour price for the program as recommended by the financial officers at each institution and approved by the Alliance Board of Directors.

4. Open to other qualified students on a space-available basis.

Each Alliance Member has the following responsibilities related to the Inter-institutional program:

1. Support the development and delivery of courses taught by its faculty.

2. Provide student services and Internet based program information to support the Alliance Program.

3. Provide web-based information about the Alliance Program and maintain links to the Alliance website for purposes of marketing the program and providing information to students and the public.

4. Support faculty participation in inter-institutional program faculty meetings and faculty development workshops.

5. Offer the courses it is assigned to teach according to the published schedule and provide the agreed-upon enrollment capacity for each course.

6. Comply with the pricing and fee sharing agreements negotiated for Great Plains IDEA inter-institutional programs.

7. Notify the Great Plains IDEA board if it wishes to withdraw from the program. Such intent must be announced to the Great Plains IDEA Board a full twelve months in advance of the date of withdrawal and provisions made to allow admitted students to complete program requirements.

If the decision is made to discontinue the program, every effort will be made, in accordance to the Alliance Member's policies, to allow Alliance students who are currently admitted to the program to complete the program within four years and no students will be allowed to take more than five years from the dissolution date to complete their program.

By affixing the appropriate signatures to this document, the College of _____ at _____ University indicates its *intent or desire* to participate in the _____ Inter-Institutional Distance Education Program of the Great Plains Interactive Distance Education Alliance and to adhere to the terms of the Memorandum of Agreement.

Signed the _____ day of _____, _____.

_____

Signature of Unit Chair

_____

Signature of College Administrator

_____

Signature of Distance Education Officer

_____

Signature of Graduate School Administrator

_____

Signature of University Academic Officer

Chapter Three

USING DISTANCE EDUCATION TO INCREASE HIGHER EDUCATION OPPORTUNITIES

by Marianne R. Phelps

OVERVIEW

The pathways developed by the projects discussed in this chapter clearly point the way to improving access to higher education and relating education to the world of work. They suggest that the availability of information and student support and articulation among the various levels of education can be effective in increasing access to higher education for minority and lower-income students. Creative uses of technology and partnerships can extend the reach of programs to serve new groups of students and address workforce shortages. The development of competencies makes explicit the standards that are used to evaluate performance and should help students and parents monitor performance. Finally, experimentation with modifying what is the rather rigid organization of higher education in the United States around courses and semesters can enable better access for adult students and perhaps improve learning as well.

INTRODUCTION

Pathways to education are designed to surmount barriers to access to higher education. Some of these barriers are caused by the disjointed, decentralized "system" of education in the United States. Decentralization of responsibility for education has its value, of course, and is often cited as one of the strengths of the higher education system in the United States. The disadvantage is that the differences in curriculum and policy that naturally occur in such a system also constitute barriers to student access. In addition, workforce education and training is often not efficient, requiring students who wish to advance through the various levels of training in many fields to repeat work. Although there has been some change, very little work has been done to define pathways that allow students to move seamlessly through the various levels of training required to advance in their fields.

Minority and low-income students face another kind of barrier. Many of these students have not grown up with the expectation that they would be able to participate in higher education. This means few such students have developed goals for higher education. They also have very little idea of what high school course work is required, how to navigate the admissions process, or to access the resources available to help them finance a college education.

An additional barrier to access has been that the primary focus of higher education has been on students 18 to 25 years of age. As a result, despite the efforts of continuing educators, access to higher education has often been difficult for adults who face barriers related to the time and place education is offered. Pathways can help make higher education more available to adult students.

The concept underlying pathways is not a new one. Many programs were developed in the last quarter of the 20th century as increasing access to higher education was recognized as a critical goal for American society. Technology, particularly the Internet, began to transform the options for creating clear pathways in the mid-1990s. The availability of instruction "any time, any place" has made higher education more accessible to adults and individuals living in remote locations. In a very short period of time e-learning has gained wide acceptance as a legitimate form of education. Still, educators have yet to exploit fully the application of new technologies to expand and enrich opportunities for increasing access to higher education. This chapter explores various ways that educators are experimenting with the application of technology to develop and support pathways. These new approaches can expand opportunities for higher education development and reach new populations.

NEED

Providing opportunity and access for higher education have been major factors in shaping the history of higher education in the United States ever since its founding. The early establishment of colleges in the colonies, the spread of small denominational colleges during the early 19th century, the

Morrill Land Grant Act of 1862, the GI bill passed after World War II, the Higher Education Act of 1965, large scale development of community colleges, and laws prohibiting discrimination on the basis of race, sex, religion, disability, and age clearly illustrate how important the question of opportunity and access have been to Americans (Rudolph 1962).

Still, many factors continue to limit individuals from advancing their education. As mentioned above, the lack of curriculum and assessment linkages make transitions from high school to college, and from one level of higher education to another, difficult. Institutional policies that preclude recognition of skills and knowledge obtained at other schools clearly are part of the problem. Many senior colleges are still reluctant to grant credit for courses completed at other institutions, and even when credit is granted, it is often not applied to program or major requirements. While e-learning has increased access, students may not be able to complete entire programs at a distance. A large number of institutions offer courses online; fewer offer entire programs. Other factors are poverty, inadequate academic preparation, lack of knowledge and role models, and cultural barriers. These limit opportunities significantly for minority and low-income students (National Center for Education Statistics 1995, 2002).

Considerable efforts have been made over time to address these problems. Collaborative efforts at articulation of course content, for example, are helping students to move more efficiently from community colleges to four-year institutions, although the transitions are still far from seamless. E-learning is increasing access for adult students although this mode of delivery has considerably more potential to broaden access. There have been numerous programs aimed at addressing the barriers many minority and low-income students face. Government programs such as Upward Bound and Gear Up, and the various programs provided by individual colleges and universities, have addressed these barriers in making the transition from high school to college, but these barriers are persistent (Cavanagh 2004, Venezia, Kirst, and Antonio 2003). There is more that needs to be done to expand access.

At the time the Learning Anytime Anywhere Partnership (LAAP) program was authorized in 1998, few institutions or programs had explored the use of technology comprehensively to enrich the services provided or scale programs to benefit larger populations of students. Over the course of the past seven years, LAAP and other FIPSE grants have supported projects that have utilized technology to add new dimensions to pathways programs. They have also supported innovative projects that use technology to make workforce training available to individuals in areas distant from the training site. These projects have the potential to address workforce shortages in the health care and other fields by reaching these new student populations.

EVOLVING PRACTICE

As discussed earlier, pathways that facilitate access to higher education and help individuals reach their goals are not a new phenomenon. What is new about the projects discussed in this chapter is that they use innovative strategies to alleviate the problems people face in making education transitions, to reach new and larger audiences of students, and to address workforce needs. Technology is also integral to each of these pathways. All rely on technology in some way as the means of delivering their programs and/or for communication and transfer of information. Technology makes the program design possible.

The information included in the project descriptions was derived from a number of sources. These include project abstracts, reports prepared for FIPSE, project websites, emails from project directors, and telephone interviews.

PATHWAYS TO ADMISSION AND TRANSFER

LADDER K–16, OREGON UNIVERSITY SYSTEM

The project the Oregon University System has initiated is certainly the most comprehensive among the projects selected for this chapter. The project grew out of a larger effort initiated by the state legislature in 1991 to improve student performance at the K–12 level by regular assessments of student knowledge and skills. Now that the assessments are in place, Oregon is revamping its state university admissions criteria by replacing traditional measures as the primary means of determining admissibility with assessments of student competencies or proficiencies. This change in admissions policy is scheduled to begin in 2006.

During the first stage of this project, OSU developed new college admissions standards and aligned these with the competencies required for high school graduation. The second stage, currently underway, is to align high school assessment data with college admission. The goal is to create a more transparent pathway to college admission that will enable students and parents to assess progress toward meeting admissions requirements.

Given the scale of this project, technology is essential to achieve project goals. In the initial stage, web-based communications enabled the many stakeholders distributed across the state to provide feedback. The reform also depends upon the development of a student data transfer system, currently underway, that can collect and transmit a massive amount of individual student performance data to admissions offices.

On a somewhat smaller scale, a common goal of many pathways projects has been to increase the representation of minority and low-income students in higher education and to facilitate their success. While the goal of many pathways is academic remediation, there are other barriers to address. Many minority and low-income students are simply not aware that attending college is a possibility. The projects discussed below focus on the importance of the student developing goals for higher education, obtaining the knowledge and skills necessary to be successful in the admissions process, and finding the right fit between the students and the college(s) where they are applying.

These programs also provide support to students in various ways as they go through the admissions or transfer process. Many minority and low-income students lack the confidence that they can be successful, and support is an important ingredient of success.

COLLEGE SUMMIT, A COLLABORATIVE SOLUTION TO INCREASE COLLEGE ACCESS FOR AND RETENTION OF LOW-INCOME YOUTH

College Summit (CS) is the most extensive of these projects in terms of its scope. As of the 2004–2005 school year, the project is serving 3,600 students in 39 high schools in five locations across the country as compared to 900 students in 2002–2003. The CS protocol is designed to build low-income students' confidence that attending college is a feasible goal both academically and financially, and to help students identify colleges where they are likely to succeed, manage the application process, and present themselves effectively in college applications and portfolios supplementary to the application.

Initially, the program served a limited group of rising seniors who had been selected by participating high schools on factors, other than their academic records, that signaled they possessed characteristics that would enable them to be successful in higher education. These students were invited along with teachers in their schools to participate in four-day workshops, conducted on a host college or university campus, during which they worked through the CS protocol. This program has been very successful. Since 1993,

79% of the students who participated in the workshops enrolled in college as compared to 46 % of low-income students nationally (College Summit 2004, abstract).

These invitational workshops remain an important part of the CS program. However, for the 2003–2004 school year, the program was expanded to serve all seniors in participating high schools, and the approach was modified to accommodate these larger populations. During the school year, time is set aside for students to work through the CS program in classrooms guided by teachers and peer advisors who have been trained by attending one of the workshops.

By the end of the program students will have selected the colleges to which they will apply, completed their applications, and developed a portfolio that can be used to provide colleges with additional information about their qualifications. While the emphasis of the CS program remains on helping students work through the steps that will help them be successful in college, it also serves as a pathway for students who are not college bound to make other post-high-school plans.

Technology is essential to the scalability of the program, and CS is now in the process of developing the technology (CSNet) that will support administration of the program as it expands. Also, with the completion of CSNet, students will have online access to the CS training modules and teachers will be able to comment on student work and track student progress online. CSNet will also provide the capability to forward student portfolios electronically to colleges and universities. With the technology in place, CS projects the program will be able to serve 55,000 students by the year 2009.

ETRANSFER, LAGUARDIA COMMUNITY COLLEGE

LaGuardia Community College has developed a transfer preparation program that is designed to assist students in developing career goals and preparing for transfer to senior colleges. Virtual Interest Groups (VIGs) are the centerpiece of the program. These are essentially asynchronous online five-week mini-courses which lead students to explore possible career fields and issues relating to transfer. The VIGs are embedded in key courses such as the clusters required of all liberal arts students (P. Arcario, personal communication, March 2, 2005). Participation in a VIG is a course requirement and is included in the course grade. The groups are led by faculty members and former LaGuardia students currently attending senior colleges.

eTransfer also has an e-portfolio component. The portfolio is an "online locker" for students to store the information gathered in completing the VIG requirements and to refine and further reflect upon the career and transfer goals they began to formulate in this program. The plan is that students will ultimately use these portfolios as supplements to their applications to senior colleges and as electronic resumes.

NATIONAL ARTICULATION AND TRANSFER NETWORK

The innovative and challenging goal of the National Articulation and Transfer Network (NATN) is to develop a pathway for students generally under-represented in the college population to access colleges and universities whose missions include education of minority and low-income students. The network is made up of community and senior colleges, most of them minority-serving institutions and urban high schools. The project is large in scale. At one time the membership included 61 colleges and universities and 46 high schools (A. Zinn, personal communication, February 16, 2005).

The project has several facets, perhaps the most ambitious being the development of articulation agreements between the community colleges and senior institutions of higher education that are part of the network. A "General Articulation Agreement" guarantees that senior institutions will admit community college students graduating with an associate's degree who meet certain conditions such as a GPA of at least 2.5. Under study is the feasibility of an agreement that would involve the senior institutions accepting all credits in the general education core earned at a community college and applying them to departmental and program as well as institutional requirements. The project also addresses non-uniform needs as it facilitates specific articulation agreements among institutions to handle individual situations and programs.

Collegestepsz.net, a website developed by the network, makes the college articulation agreements available to students enrolled in participating community colleges and high schools. In addition to the information on transfer and articulation, the site leads students to a powerful array of resources to assist them in preparing for college or for transfer. A particularly interesting feature of the Collegestepsz.net website is that it matches the information students provide in personal profiles with institutions that meet their criteria. This is an example of how technology can be used to empower people who previously have often been marginalized or held distant from information.

HERITAGE UNIVERSITY: A PATHWAY FOR ADDRESSING CULTURAL
BARRIERS TO PARTICIPATION IN HIGHER EDUCATION

The Heritage University project entailed the development of pre-college courses in mathematics and English specifically designed to serve the surrounding population of Native American and Latino students. The need for the project was the extensive amount of remedial work that entering students from these populations required before they were ready for college level mathematics and English. What is unusual about these courses is that they were designed to be culturally relevant to the student populations.

The first phase of the project was the development of standardized assessments in mathematics and English, both of which are available in Spanish. The assessments themselves use situations and vocabulary that would be familiar to the populations to be served, thus removing some of the cultural barriers to performance. The pathway consists of online college preparation courses in mathematics and English reading, writing, and comprehension that address deficiencies identified in the assessments. The reading, writing, and comprehension course is designed to increase communication skills of Native Americans and Hispanic students for whom English is a second language.

Assessments are conducted electronically, and the courses are delivered via the Internet in order to reach widely dispersed populations. The project uses Adaptex multimedia software, which enables the incorporation of multimedia files that are important to establishing a familiar context for students. The mathematics course utilizes film clips that use situations that Native Americans and Hispanics would commonly encounter to illustrate mathematical concepts. The English course, still in development, will also use materials that are culturally relevant.

PATHWAYS TO EDUCATION FOR WORK

The projects summarized above provide pathways that help students make transitions between different levels of education. Pathways that are designed to assist students in obtaining the training required for a career enable transitions as well, but address different barriers. Perhaps most important are the barriers relating to the place where training is available and the time it is offered. Place and time constraints particularly limit the participation of adult students. However, barriers presented by the lack of articulation of the training required to advance upward through a career path are sometimes equally daunting. To move from one career level to another often requires repeating considerable amounts of coursework. This is discouraging to students and sometimes prohibitive in terms of cost. The following programs developed innovative programs to address these needs.

E-LINE, TEXAS A&M–CORPUS CHRISTI: ELECTRONIC LEARNING IN NURSING EDUCATION

The e-Line nursing education program developed by Texas A&M and Delmar College was designed to remove these barriers, enabling students to complete an entire Associate Degree in Nursing (AND) or Bachelor of Science degree (BSN) curriculum online and at their own pace. The clinical component of the program is provided in locations convenient for the students by preceptors who are required to complete extensive online training.

Developing the online nursing curriculum required working around a host of obstacles posed by the traditional organization of education in courses and terms. A first step was to move from a content-oriented curriculum to one based on the nursing competencies as defined by the Board of Nurse Examiners for the State of Texas. The second was to develop instructional modules that provide students with the knowledge and skills needed to achieve the competencies and to organize the modules into courses. Project staff describe this process as unpacking the nursing curricula at the two schools to their "basic competencies," and repacking them into the existing course numbers for "purposes of crediting and transcripting."

Offering the curriculum in modules provides considerable flexibility to students in completing their work. Students can move through the program as quickly as they are able to complete the modules—or if the time they have for study is limited, they can stretch the work out over a longer period of time as long as they complete the program within four years, an accreditation requirement. The program structure also allows a student to stop during a semester and still retain credit for any modules completed.

Another important advantage of the program is that it enables a more efficient articulation between the AND and BSN. Students do not have to repeat modules they completed while enrolled in the AND program if they choose to continue on to a BSN degree. Conversely, students enrolled in the BSN program who decide to transfer to the AND program do not have to repeat modules they completed as BSN students. The information concerning the modules required to complete each program is available on the e-Line website so that students can plan their course of study.

MILES COMMUNITY COLLEGE:
BRIDGING HEALTH CONNECTIONS IN MONTANA

Part of the impetus for the Texas A&M/Delmar College partnership was the need to address serious shortages in the nursing workforce. The Miles Community College program is designed to address the shortage of nurses as well. A first step in the project was to develop career pathways to advancement from Certified Nursing Assistant (CNA) to Associate Degree in Nursing (AND), Licensed Practical Nurse (LPN) to AND, and AND to Bachelor of Science (BSN). A second was to provide the programs at a distance to students throughout Eastern Montana. All of the nursing courses required to move through the career pathways are available through a combination of online and videoconferencing technologies in this project. The college offers the AND degree both onsite and via ITV at several educational partner sites. The LPN to RN program is also offered via ITV. Clinical training is provided by partner hospitals and other health care facilities.

In addition to providing clear and accessible pathways to advancement in the nursing profession, the program is reaching out to high school students to generate the interest of students at this level in pursuing careers in the health professions. The college offers two courses to high school students. These are Fundamentals for Health Professions, which is an introduction to careers and issues in the health area, and the Certified Nurse Assistant (CNA) Preparatory Course. This latter course prepares students for state certification and employment in long-term care. Students earn both high school and college credits for the courses. The courses are currently delivered online to 11 high schools with further expansion expected (interview with K. K. Wankel, Project Director, March 2, 2005).

PATHWAYS FOR TRAINING AND CERTIFICATION

COLORADO STATE UNIVERSITY:
DEVELOPING AN ONLINE CREDENTIALING SYSTEM FOR CAREER AND TECHNICAL TEACHERS

Colorado State University (CSU) developed a pathway for career and technical teachers to obtain State of Colorado certification. A shortage of certified teachers trained in this field has required the state to issue emergency credentials to meet instructional needs. Once employed, constraints of time and location within the state have made it difficult for teachers to participate in the training needed for certification.

CSU and its partners, Northeastern Junior College and the Colorado Community College System, the credentialing office, addressed these problems by creating an online training and certification process. The first step in its development was the identification and validation of the competencies required for certification. Once this step was completed, content from previous courses was selected and new material necessary for students to meet each competency requirement developed and organized into instructional modules. In a particularly varied and integrated model, the content for each module is delivered in a variety of formats that include narrative, links to Web-based resources, PowerPoint presentations, video-taped interviews, samples of work, and experts online. Each module also contains pre- and post-assessments. All modules have three levels of content, which means they can benefit educators interested in professional development as well as those seeking entry level certification. The use of online modules allows students to enroll anytime that is convenient for them.

The second phase of the project was the development of the Colorado Credentialing Website. The website, providing both information and services, is a one-stop credentialing center for career and technical education teachers. The information concerning credentialing requirements, previously dispersed and difficult to locate, is readily available on the website. A planning tool helps credential applicants assess the training they need to meet the requirements and to develop a plan for completing the training that meets their individual needs. Once an application for certification is made, the system tracks the plan as the teacher progresses through the requirements. The website also provides links to the training modules and information concerning how teachers might develop a portfolio documenting their learning and experience that would meet some of the certification requirements.

Oregon University System: The PK–16 Digital Learning Environment

One of the challenges of the state of Oregon in implementing the plan to assess student performance at various points in K–12 education was the need to train teachers to evaluate student proficiencies (see LADDER K–16, another Oregon University System pathway, described earlier in the chapter.) A digital learning environment was developed to meet this need. The learning environment has three parts: a training laboratory where teachers can learn about teaching and assessment in a competency-based environment; a scoring laboratory where teachers review and assess student work; and a "calibration" laboratory where teachers can compare their judgments of student work with that of their colleagues' throughout the state. The training is critical to developing a level of commonality among teacher judgments such that colleges can confidently rely on their evaluations in making admissions decisions. The Digital Learning Environment makes this training in a multiple dimension, robust model of evaluating student proficiencies readily available to all teachers in the state, a task that would be almost impossible without the technical solution the Oregon University System devised.

IMPLICATIONS FOR THE FUTURE

The pathways described in this chapter are designed to innovatively and effectively address challenges that higher education is facing today. While it is too early to gauge the success of most of the projects, they clearly suggest directions that are worthy of further exploration. The challenges include:

- Providing a more seamless educational system that would enable students to move efficiently from high school through to graduation from a senior college and also through the various levels of career or professional education.
- Increasing the representation of minorities and low-income students in higher education.
- Providing education and training that will alleviate critical shortages in the workforce and better meet student needs.

The principal approach to a more seamless educational system has two dimensions addressed by technology. The first is making the requirements for admission more transparent. The second is the development of articulation agreements between junior and senior colleges. The two significant advances brought to these strategies by technology are scalability and widespread partnering.

Transparency

The Oregon PASS program has led to the development of competencies students are expected to achieve at various levels of their progression through the K–12 system. The Oregon University System has, in turn, developed admissions standards that are aligned with these competencies. In theory this would lead to transparency in the admissions process. In practice, a preliminary study of the concept showed a correlation between achievement of competencies at the end of 10th grade with success in first year of college. However, the theory has yet to be tested since the new admissions requirements will not be implemented until 2006, and there remain significant administrative barriers to implementation. Despite the obstacles, Oregon's ambitious reforms could point a way to much greater clarity concerning the standards students need to meet for admission to college.

Articulation Agreements

Articulation agreements between community colleges and senior institutions of higher education are another means of providing transparency. The idea, of course, is not new. What is new is the significant expansion in the number of these agreements and the work being done between individual senior and community colleges to articulate curriculum that NATN is facilitating. The agreement among senior college network members to accept all credits earned by students who have received associate degrees at member community college schools, given certain conditions, is groundbreaking. The LaGuardia College eTransfer pathway also provides students with information concerning articulation agreements to CUNY and SUNY system institutions and other selected public and private colleges and universities. Articulation agreements are probably the most effective pathway to removing barriers to transfer. They also promote efficiencies in that students do not have to repeat coursework already completed.

The Texas A&M–Corpus Christi/Delmar College, and the Miles Community College projects also address the problem of articulation. Disjunctures in requirements between certificate, associate degree, and bachelor's degree program requirements often mean that students need to repeat courses as they move from one level in a profession to another. Both projects involve the development of pathways that enable students to move easily from one level of the profession to the next. Miles Community College also has a LPN to AND program that takes into account the clinical experience gained practicing as an LPN.

FACTORS CRITICAL TO PERFORMANCE

The pathways developed by College Summit, LaGuardia College, and NATN are designed to provide students with the skills and support they need to be successful in seeking admission to college or transfer. The question is whether or not such programs will be successful in increasing the numbers of minority and low-income students who enter college and complete their education. This is a particularly challenging goal since high school graduation rates have declined significantly, making the pool of potential applicants smaller than it may have been in the past (Orfield et al. 2004).

The data concerning the admission and persistence of students who participated in the College Summit workshops is certainly very positive. Seventy-nine percent of the participants enrolled in college, and approximately 80% persisted (College Summit 2004, abstract). The students, however, elected to participate in pathways programs, and this may have influenced the rate of success. Generally, participation in pathways is voluntary. It is interesting that participation in the CS program at member high schools and in the LaGuardia College eTransfer program is required. This means that more students will be exposed to programs that support transitions from one level to another. Neither program yet has data concerning the effect of requiring participation. Conceivably, the programs could increase the pool of minority and low-income students who make the transition from one level of education to the next. These could be important experiments.

The Heritage University pathway addresses the challenge of the preparation of minority and low-income students for college level work. Remediation is commonly one goal of pathways programs. The Heritage University approach is unusual in that it focuses on cultural differences as a barrier to preparation. Heritage University serves Native American and Latino student populations who have often required up to two years of remedial work before beginning college courses. The project involved the development of remedial courses in math and English that use words and examples that they would commonly encounter in their cultures.

Project activities are still in development, but the evidence thus far is that the courses are reducing the amount of time these students spend in remedial courses once they begin work at the College. The Heritage University project is small in scope, but it points to one way to reach low-income students who are part of minority cultures and better prepare them for college work. Given the increasing cultural diversity in our society, pathways that acknowledge and address cultural barriers to help students succeed will be important.

Scalability

While program design is important in addressing current challenges to higher education, the scalability of the pathways may be even more important to the impact they will have. Replicating pathways such as the LaGuardia Community College Virtual Interest Groups and the Heritage

College culturally relevant remedial courses at other institutions could expand the impact of the experiments at these institutions. However, scalability is the more likely vehicle that will enable large numbers of students and professionals to benefit from the innovative solutions to problems of access represented in the projects.

In many respects the approaches to the pathways to admission and transfer represented in the projects are not new. Pathways for minority and low-income students commonly include information, counseling, opportunities to develop educational and career goals, assistance in developing applications, and, sometimes, academic preparation. Articulation agreements are a relatively common means of facilitating transfer. All of these elements may be found in one or more of the pathways described. What is unique is the marriage of these familiar strategies with technology to expand their reach.

Technology will support the infrastructure needed for College Summit to expand its reach up to 18,000 high school students. The information and services NATN provides to students are totally web-based thus allowing students at an expanding number of high schools and colleges to benefit from the information and services the network provides. Technology also enables LaGuardia College to offer virtual interest groups to large numbers of first year students.

Miles Community College nursing courses can be delivered to any location where ITV reception is available, and the availability of the nursing programs to students in Eastern Montana communities is already helping to meet the needs for trained nurses in this area. The online nursing programs developed by the Texas A&M and Delmar College nursing programs could potentially reach very large numbers of students interested in a career in nursing.

Similarly, creative uses of technology enable the Colorado credentialing system for career and technical teachers to reach a population distributed throughout the state. Online training modules enable teachers to access the training they need, and the website guides the teachers in developing a pathway to certification that meets their own individual needs. The program to train teachers in evaluating competencies developed by the Oregon University system is also web-based. Among other functionalities, it enables teachers across the state to interact with each other and compare their evaluations of student work, thus helping to meet the goal of the OSU system project to increase the validity and reliability of teacher evaluations.

Both of these projects illustrate that digital learning environments are especially effective in meeting needs for training. The director of the Oregon University System project indicated that participation in the program they developed to train teachers in evaluating competencies was far greater than expected (M. Endsley, personal communication, February 16, 2005). The approach to resolving the barriers to credentialing for career and technical teachers used in Colorado could be adapted to other fields. Simplifying the process of credentialing and licensure and providing the training needed anytime, anywhere would be helpful to individuals in many career and professional fields.

Of course, technology cannot solve all problems. Scalability of the Texas A&M project, for example, will require new ways of providing for instruction. The Program Director for the Texas A&M–Corpus Christi/ Delmar College project estimates that their program could be scaled to produce 10,000 new nurses by 2010, but for the shortage of Ph.D.-qualified nursing faculty available for teaching full-time. Solutions to this problem may prove difficult.

Partnerships

In addition to technology, partnerships have also been critical to the success of several of the projects. The Colorado credentialing service is an example of how assembling partners who each have a stake in solving a problem can lead to a creative solution. Miles Community College is on track to increase the supply of RN's in Eastern Montana because of the partnerships it has established with other educational institutions and health care providers. The program can expand to the extent that there are educational partners that have the equipment required to receive ITV and heath care providers that are willing to support the instructors required for the clinical components of the programs.

The key to the scalability of NATN is the addition of new partners. NATN extends its services to new groups of students each time it adds a new partner school, college, or university. The partnerships CS has developed with colleges and universities, high schools, and community groups are the key to the project's success. CS can scale its program simply by adding new partners in different parts of the country. The partnerships persist over time because the program serves the interests of each of the partners. CS provides college and university partners access to an expanded pool of qualified low-income applicants. School districts benefit because a greater percentage of their students attend college and because CS provides training to teachers.

Community partners that help support the program benefit because it helps provide a larger pool of college educated minorities in the workforce.

Organization of Instruction and Content

The discussion thus far has focused more on issues related to access than to pedagogy. The Heritage University project to incorporate materials into assessments and courses that are relevant to students' cultural background is one example of how instruction might be adapted to meet students' needs more effectively. Modularization of course content is another. Abandoning the semester-long course as the organizing principle of the curriculum, Texas A&M–Corpus Christi/Delmar College developed competency-based modules that can be completed at the students own pace. This accommodates adult students' needs for flexibility and enables the program to reach a larger population of students. Project staff also believe the modularization of the curriculum is better in accommodating student learning styles since the objectives of modules are clearer to the student and the work is more manageable.

The training Colorado State University provides to career and technical teachers is also organized in competency-based modules providing advantages similar to those of the nursing program. The modules are self-paced and enrollment is open, meaning the teachers can begin and end a module at any time that is convenient to them. Used in such situations, modularization has advantages that are probably yet to be exploited in higher education.

LESSONS LEARNED

Expect the Unexpected

Implementing innovations as complex as those described in this chapter is difficult. Even when projects are carefully designed, there are often unexpected problems encountered in the course of implementation. LaGuardia Community College, for example, encountered delays in the development of the technology needed to support the e-portfolios that are an integral part of their eTransfer program. To provide another example, Miles Community College staff did not anticipate that some high school students would need scholarships to cover the tuition the College charged for them to participate in the health courses. Taking stock of the progress of the project on a regular basis and exercising creativity in addressing problems as they arise, as these colleges have done, are the best antidotes for the unexpected.

Identify Stakeholders

Another challenge in project planning is anticipating all of the stakeholders that will be needed to play a role in project implementation. An example is that program staff at Texas A&M University–Corpus Christi and Delmar College found that the enrollment management systems used by their campuses would not accommodate their plans for rolling enrollments. The problem was solved by working with enrollment management staff at each school, but not without extensive conversation (e-Line FY2003 Annual Report, 6). Miles Community College faced a similar problem in that the college had not developed the online services required to support the nursing students studying at a distance (K. Wankel, personal communication, March 2, 2005). The College is now responding to the need. However, anticipating the potential demands the project might make on the various administrative functions of an institution would help to insure that project stakeholders are consulted and prepared to help in project implementation.

The Digital Divide

Technology has been important in the development of each of the projects. In designing projects that rely on technology for delivery, it is important to keep in mind that many minority and low-income students still do not have ready access to technology. The Heritage University project director reported that 40% of the students their project serves do not have ready access to technology (R. Landvoy, personal communication, February 15, 2005). Similarly, the tool College Summit has developed for students to use to work through their program will continue to be available on paper (K. O'Shaughnessey, personal communication, February 15, 2005). High schools, particularly in urban areas, simply do not have the technology to offer the program online. The digital divide still is a barrier in developing pathways that rely on technology for the delivery of their programs.

External Barriers

Clearly, pathways to careers can be effective in reducing workforce shortages. Several of the projects illustrate ways that education can be organized to address this problem. However, the standards and policies of accrediting and other agencies may limit the options institutions have to provide the flexibility that students may need to participate and complete the programs. Developing some consensus among educators, professional organizations, and accrediting bodies around best practices in e-learning in fields where there are shortages or imbalances in distribution could be of assistance to institutions interested in adapting their own programs to reach larger populations of students.

Accreditation requirements, in particular, may present unnecessary barriers to expansion of e-learning. Nursing accreditation agencies, for example, have rigid timeframes for the completion of nursing programs, which would seem to be a barrier for some adult students. These constraints are evident in both the Texas A&M–Corpus Christi/Delmar College and the Miles Community College programs. It would also be important to examine how licensing requirements might limit how programs are delivered. The health care and teacher preparation fields, for example, would benefit from examining the impact licensing and accrediting requirements have on efforts to make education and training accessible to these students at a distance.

The Challenges of Transformation

Major transformative projects such as that undertaken by the Oregon University System (OUS) are extremely difficult to implement. The idea behind establishing competencies as benchmarks for performance, as opposed to grades, is an attractive one for educators interested in raising the level of performance in elementary and high schools. However, it may not be realistic to replace courses completed with achievement of competencies as a requirement for graduation. The issue raised is where to set the required standard. Currently, there is debate in the State of Oregon concerning the extent to which the competencies present an unrealistic barrier to high school graduation for many students. The result may be that the requirements for graduation will continue to be the completion of the courses required, with the 12th grade competencies considered as evidence of achievement (M. Endsley, personal communication, February 16, 2005).

The use of e-portfolios to transform the college admissions process is an idea embedded in several of the projects. The Oregon University System developed a prototype, but according to the OUS project director, no one has really taken advantage of the option (M. Endsley, personal communication, February 16, 2005). LaGuardia Community College plans that e-portfolios will be an integral part of its eTransfer program as a means of helping students evaluate their learning and prepare goals for transfer. As part of their eTransfer project, one senior college has agreed to evaluate e-portfolios on an experimental basis (P. Arcario, personal communication, February 14, 2005). However, the college has found it difficult and expensive to develop the technical capacity required to incorporate this into the project and, thus, has no experience with senior colleges using e-portfolios as part of their admissions process.

Further, while the idea that portfolios could be an important means of providing admissions officers with key information concerning students' qualifications that are not apparent in test scores and grades is attractive, the question remains as to whether senior colleges have the capacity to evaluate e-portfolios. The number of applications reviewed is such that it would be difficult to evaluate the kind of information found in an e-portfolio, perhaps leading to a role supporting student development rather than college admission.

Conclusion

While there may be some aspects of the pathways projects that will not become part of the mainstream of higher education, the experiments clearly identify innovative and successful approaches to removing barriers to access and simplifying transitions, particularly through the use of technology to scale programs. The partnerships forged for purposes of the projects were also very important and, in some instances, critical to their implementation. This organizational element may be the most important of the lessons learned. It may also be one of the most difficult to emulate. Working across organizational boundaries is always difficult. It is particularly difficult for higher education institutions because the culture discourages collaboration. It can be done, however, as many of the pathways projects illustrate, and perhaps their examples will cause others to look to partnerships as a solution for addressing some of the many challenges facing higher education today.

Chapter Four

NEW PERSPECTIVES
ON INSTRUCTIONAL EFFECTIVENESS
THROUGH DISTANCE EDUCATION

by Gary Brown

OVERVIEW

Persistent doubts about the effectiveness of distributed and technology enhanced instruction rest mostly on assumptions about an imperative of real-time, face-to-face interaction with students. Critics assert that online learning and even classroom-based technology enhanced instruction either misses or somehow compromises this essential human interaction. This chapter on instructional effectiveness addresses how a number of projects have belied the assumptions that such doubts are based upon. This chapter describes the instructional strategies and effectiveness of a sample of FIPSE-sponsored projects in particular, and how those projects have been implemented to demonstrate effective practice. These FIPSE-funded projects and other examples illustrate how effective technologies and their use have countered criticism that has dogged early efforts in online learning, and, in particular, how new models of software and their implementation can be used effectively to improve students' learning even in math, science, and clinical science courses—frequently accepted as the last bastion of traditional instructional models.

The case studies in this report provide examples that illustrate how online, technology-based and blended learning, when situated in good learning designs and facilitated in alignment with research-based principles, can improve student attitudes and student retention, and foster inquiry, self-direction, and improved learning. Finally, this chapter examines these results in the context of a new emphasis on assessment and the importance of using outcomes-driven models not only to meet the expectations generally attributed to traditional models, but to expand those expectations in sustainable, extensible, and efficient ways.

NEED

The advent of new technologies somehow introduced a virulent strain of amnesia of a fundamental but hard-learned educational lesson. Before the Internet, educators generally understood there was as much difference in the outcomes between two instructors who took the same approach with the same material in two different classes as there was between two instructors who used different approaches (Worthen, Sanders, and Fitzpatrick 1997). Now, as educators explore instructional strategies required to implement new media and the Internet, to move instruction partly (hybrid) and fully (distributed) online, legislators, taxpayers, and even educators are asking, *does it work?* Unfortunately, they are increasingly impatient with complex answers even as the answers grow increasingly complex. And perhaps the most complex response is the need to recognize that *does it work* is not the real or even a good question. The better question is: HOW can we best use new technologies to improve student learning outcomes. This chapter examines the way a selection of FIPSE-sponsored and other projects started in the late 1990s and early 2000s have successfully addressed this question and, at the same time, surfaced new ones.

INSTRUCTIONAL EFFECTIVENESS AND THE OUTCOMES CONTEXT

For many reasonable and perhaps a few problematic reasons, there is a new emphasis in higher education on accountability. Critics and supporters both want evidence that investments in education and, increasingly, technologies are producing improvements in student learning outcomes. Central to concerns about investments in technologies are expectations that investments will help meet access demands and keep costs down, but even those concerns are subordinate to recognition that increasingly competitive and complex global culture requires an increasingly educated population. The call for outcomes assessment is reminiscent of the objectives movement in educational assessment in the 1930s and 1940s. The objectives-based efforts then, as now, were based on good intentions to improve education and to respond to reasonable calls for accountability and efficiency. As it turned out, however, the mapping of measurement techniques to the cultural forces of the

1930s and 1940s produced a proliferation of objectives that tended to be so narrowly defined that they fostered curricula characterized by outcomes rendered to the recall of atomized, often inert facts (House 1993).

In some respects, little has changed. The reasons are complex. Meaningful outcomes are hard to assess because meaningful learning is hard to define and measure. More importantly, to understand how to improve student learning requires that the assessment focus shift from how well students do on exams to *how students are thinking* and, subsequently, what educators can do to help students improve. Few assessment efforts, in 1940 or now, reflect a grasp of the critical nuances essential for understanding the way the structure of content in a discipline contributes to learning logjams, let alone how to improve instructional effectiveness. Unlike the outcomes revival, however, the Internet is still relatively new. Nonetheless, it is already changing educational practice dramatically. From synchronous (chats) and asynchronous (threaded discussions, blogs, wikis) communication to the integration of images, animations, and links to the new availability of resources from anywhere in the world, the portent for education is profoundly disruptive.

Technology projects funded by FIPSE have established invaluable models for exploring ways to preserve and extend the deeper values of education in times of disruptive change. The projects were funded to help innovators pursue ideas for improving student learning and for improving our understanding of the ways students learn in new technologically mediated environments.

For instance, the WebCLS (Web-based Education in Clinical Laboratory Sciences) project, developed in 2002 by a partnership of nine institutions, is a web-based strategy for engaging online in interactive course laboratories using video and animation, interactive discussions, as well as online testing and a virtual practice laboratory. In addition to providing access to under-served areas, the project targeted learning strategies that, more than simply identifying students' scores on exams, give insight into the ways students approached the material. The instructional strategy that guides the project complements the traditional exam with multimedia learning materials, opportunities to discuss or chat online, and share work in written form. The multi-pronged effort capitalizes on technologies and moves away from traditional notions of instruction in which "one size fits all." Every individual learns differently and, ultimately, for different purposes, so it behooves educators to use multiple strategies.

The WebCLS quizzing software, for instance, provides students with immediate feedback, an essential ingredient for effective instruction.

Equally important, the quizzing software allows instructors to monitor the kinds of choices students are making, helping them learn more about their students' learning. The online exams are available to learners anywhere and at all hours. This kind of extensibility, with the addition of video and audio, helps students and provides faculty with a stepping stone for envisioning and implementing the potential wealth of new strategies the Internet provides. The integration of chats and online asynchronous discussion environments available in WebCLS, when facilitated effectively, further deepens the learners' experience. Feedback from students who have used WebCLS has been quite positive, reminding us, further, that even students often need small steps for coming to understand online opportunities in distributed environments.

Finally, the WebCLS project marks an important step in moving toward a learning-centered strategy that focuses on learning rather than seat (or, in this case, lab) time. The online quizzes, although they branch in WebCLS only to one level (Skinnerian), nonetheless mark a subtle but profound shift that puts the quiz more directly to the purpose of learning rather than isolating testing for purposes of grading, and it does so in a way that advances toward realizing the potential of outcomes-based design by focusing on guiding students to competency or mastery of the material even as it helps them do so.

Instructional effectiveness is embedded in an overall strategy that helps students and faculty gain insight into not just what is learned, but how they learn. It is a shift that is essential if educators are to effectively close the gap between what is taught and what is learned, and close the loop by repurposing assessment from policing and sorting toward helping learners improve.

Unpacking Technology Assumptions

A new tenet in educational technology has not fully informed the larger educational community, but is the backdrop for all research on learning with technology: *Instructors with no knowledge of programming or a particular technology whatsoever can nonetheless reprogram that technology mediated environment without a single keystroke.* All they have to do is allocate more or less credit to an assignment. That students will generally study more and therefore get more out of studying a text, for instance, when the assignment is worth 20% of their grade than they will from the same assignment when it is worth 2% of their grade, is a phenomena that mysteriously eludes many educators when talk turns to technology. Distance education is the source of much controversy in the popular press and this simple tenet obfuscates the debate that would otherwise further our understanding of how best to teach with (or without) technology. From the broadly distributed and popularized diatribe, "What's the Difference?" by Phipps and Merisotis (1999) that lamented how little we know about online learning, to the more recent, but equally infuriating, "Thwarted Innovation" critique by luminaries like Zemsky and Massy (Zemsky and Massy 2004), the implicit assertion and profound misperception that *technology* teaches, at the heart of both articles, remains central to the debate about instructional effectiveness.

This heightened awareness in the media can be frustrating because inevitably only part of "the story" is told, but in this case distance education can use it to remember and refocus on the needs of learners. The potential of every technology project, now and in the future, is contingent upon the implementation and recognition of educators to situate technology in ways that complement the design of the technology and the proclivities, including motivation, of the learners. To that end, a particular FIPSE-sponsored project from JesuitNET is both illuminating and vital.

The Role of Design

The implementation imperative has been addressed with the deepest congruence of new knowledge about learning in the JesuitNET project. That project, initiated in 2000 out of the Center for New Designs in Learning and Scholarship at Georgetown University, presented and implemented a model of faculty development well suited for technology integration in the context of outcomes. The project leaders focused on competency and understanding rather than the accumulation of facts. To these ends, the strategy the project deployed was based on a process of reverse engineering of the design of the course. Beginning with the end—that is, with outcomes—helps faculty first identify, then clarify, elevate, communicate, and, finally, evaluate their efforts. The JesuitNET project, which worked with six graduate courses in the first phase, focused on alignment of content and student learning activities in order to create the appropriate context within which to situate any technology—from pen, pencil, and chalkboard to more online technologies and simulations.

In studies of a comparable outcomes-based design process, Brown, Myers, and Roy (2003) found that students in these online courses were significantly more engaged in several aspects associated with best practice than in parallel courses developed by faculty in isolation. Students in competency-designed courses spent more time on task, engaged in more student-to-student interaction, more faculty-to-student interaction, and were more likely to report increased development of their own learning by improving their learning in ways that do not come easily to them.

In a related study, Henderson and Brown (1999) found that courses that were developed in a formal design process comparable to the JesuitNET model were more cost effective. In this kind of course design, faculty time, usually the most expensive resource, is more fully focused on the design of the course, which in turn saves time developing (and invariably redeveloping) materials. Design time is inversely proportional to costs, or, in other words, an ounce of design saves a pound of development, which tends to be more expensive. Perhaps even more importantly, the design process helps faculty more fully articulate and communicate their goals, or what the JesuitNET project identifies as competencies, which in turn is more likely to help students attain those goals or achieve targeted outcomes.

Students in the JesuitNET project were not the only ones who benefitted. In order to more fully articulate goals and competencies, the project included the participation of graduate students and experts in the field to review content, skills, and the activities that engage students in the content and practice of those skills. The expanded collaboration is itself an innovation that merits consideration.

Perhaps the most difficult and yet profound aspect of the design process, however, is the focus on moving from teacher and content-centered to learning-centered instruction. Effective design focuses first on goals, and then the activities that students will engage in to meet those goals. When goals and activities have been identified, the content that is required to reach competency is identified as a resource, either provided by the instructor or, increasingly as the focus shifts to developing the critical skills of the learner, to activities that guide students in the search and evaluation of content increasingly available online. In other words, an effective design process promotes a vision of teaching and learning in which the content is not central, that is, in which a course is considerably richer than the material that needs to be "covered," a term that Wiggens (1993) identifies as synonymous with "hidden."

Content is a resource for learning. That simple conceptual shift challenges the way faculty think of themselves. Faculty are no longer math or physics or writing teachers. They become, rather, scholars *who teach students* about math, physics, or writing. This manifestation of moving from the "sage on the stage" to the "guide on the side," and a guide who is increasingly distributed and asynchronous from learners, is neither a subtle nor easy shift. Yet it represents the newly recognized core of what it means to be an effective educator in new learning environments in which there is collaboration with peers, graduate students, technology professionals, experts, or professionals in the field, and, ultimately the larger community of those who hold a stake in education.

SITUATED LEARNING AND RELEVANCE

When the larger community is engaged, another important aspect of instructional effectiveness comes more fully into relief, situating what is to be learned in the broadest most relevant context. In a recent study comparing two software applications designed to teach introductory statistics (Alldredge and Brown, 2006), it was found that one commercial application had significant gains compared to the other. Both packages were used in lab sections of the same course, and facilitators of the lab sections each taught with both programs in order to control for instruction and implementation variables, including points and test weight. Both packages were ostensibly the same—content, graphics, graphs, and tables and animations; however, the instructional approaches were very different. One program approached basic statistics in the traditional way, beginning with measures of central tendency and proceeding through t-tests, chi square, ANOVAs, regression. The program that evinced superior test results, however, had one perhaps subtle but important distinction. In the first program, the statistical concepts and operations were presented in sequence, moving from least to more difficult, but the operations were presented as ends in themselves. The implicit point of learning the statistical function, in other words, was to understand the statistical operation and the mathematical underpinnings. The program that had significantly better results, however, used a problem-based approach in which problems were presented to be solved, and the statistical procedures were presented as tools for helping students understand the problem.

The FIPSE-sponsored Earth Math program embraces and has extended this principle and reveals an imperative for design that integrates technologies to address subject matter that has been broadly recognized as the most persistently difficult to teach. The project was developed by educators at Kennesaw State and assessed between 1993 and 1996. Additional phases of the Earth Math and Earth Algebra effort were developed between 1997 and 2000 (phase three). The authors of the project designed it to focus on a guided inquiry format using web-based interactive materials and to apply mathematical concepts using real data.

Two aspects of this project merit particular notice. First, the project leaders emphasized the need for the web-based materials to be flexible for implementation in multiple learning environments, from the classroom to distributed environments. The flexibility of the materials demonstrated that it is possible to provide an adaptable framework for multiple contexts that supports student gains in learning within various instructional contexts. The extensibility of the effort was demonstrated in the successful use of the program in precalculus, teacher education, and in algebra.

The salient aspect of the success of the program appears to be two-fold. First is the focus on presenting and explaining the material in relevant situations. The materials were designed to be applied to "environmental problems or issues that confront us daily—in our neighborhoods, our cities and towns, and in the countryside and wilderness areas." Further, the authors state the "issues addressed include population growth, oil and coal consumption, air pollution, water availability, food supply, urban and rural development, and others." In other words, the Earth Math focus was to situate the content in "a meaningful real-life" context. Situating the learning within a broader context, as Bransford et al. (1990) and others maintained early at the outset of the technology revolution, yielded better student performance.

The project and its extensions again illustrate the primacy of the implementation of the technology within designed contexts—both worldly and educational. Students in the project evaluation (Anonymous 2002), report gains in algebra knowledge, data analysis skills, math modeling comprehension, and improved attitudes about math. The gains in one study reported success rate gains from 55.6% to 82.9% and subsequent course success improved 44% without the Earth Math algebra approach as opposed to 60% with it. At Navajo Community College the gains were similarly striking, going from 48% success rates in college algebra to 70%. In addition, the project leaders concluded the Earth Algebra project has provided a set of tools and a model that might "supplant" the curriculum of entry-level college algebra courses, an achievement that might, if more fully disseminated, help stem the decline of math and science performance in this country. The association of the gains to the strategy of situating math in authentic situations is captured by the instructors involved in the project who came to recognize that most of their students never understood how math could be useful in their lives until participating in the Earth Math program.

Second, however, and perhaps equally or more important, are the reported gains in attitudes and corresponding abilities to solve math-related problems, especially among the future teachers the program has already influenced. Not only might the relationship be attributed to the relevance of the strategy, it is also important to note that the attitudinal and even the learning gains might be reasonably attributed to the fact that students reported they were more likely to work together in small groups in class and on projects.

Another well publicized study in statistics education suggests a similar confound. When Schutte (1997) tried to compare learning in his conventional campus-based class with his online offering by randomly dividing up his own class, he was surprised to discover that the students he required to complete assignments online out-performed the group he taught in his traditional manner. Not controlled in the study was that the online students decided to meet and work through the material together. What was broadly trumpeted as a triumph for online technology-based learning was more likely yet another instantiation of the gains that can be attributed to collaborative learning.

INTEGRATING TECHNOLOGY IN UNIQUE USE AND ILL-STRUCTURED DOMAINS

These projects and their implementation have illustrated the goal of helping learners develop and grasp relatively stable or fundamental information —basic science, math, and algebra skills—and to attain outcomes that target what Ehrmann (1999) identifies as uniform impact approaches to instruction. Recognizing that even though the application of those skills needs to be flexible, the recognition of those competencies can be uniformly applied and objectively measured.

Competency is not always so easily determined. People have unique uses and purposes for learning, and effective instruction needs to recognize not just the individuality of learners, but the individual or unique purposes they have and will continue to have for their learning. Designing and implementing instruction accordingly and measuring those efforts all pose interesting challenges.

The Diagnostic Pathfinder, a FIPSE-sponsored project developed at Iowa State University, modeled one approach for helping students develop their diagnostic reasoning skills, essential for navigating the ill-structured domain that professionals encounter in clinical practice. The medical profession exemplifies the meaning of lifelong learning in that the reality of diagnosing various pathologies presents the consummate learning challenge because diseases *literally* mutate. Professionals in the field must confront a constantly moving target. Without diminishing the importance of mastering critical facts and key concepts, the medical challenge underscores the need to help students learn how to reason as well as what it is they need to know. That distinction, further, distinguishes instructional effectiveness from training.

Developed in 2002–2005, the Diagnostic Pathfinder was used in three schools and has gained additional dissemination. The software is a case-based strategy for guiding learners through the process of clinical diagnosis. The program includes predetermined gates that require students to complete aspects of the diagnostic before they are ushered into the next phase and, finally, competency. In addition to the learning gains the effort has evinced, the project team has also been developing an "analyzer tool" that provides instructors as well as students with additional feedback relative to individual cases. The Diagnostic Pathfinder is a wonderful example of technology-mediated instruction that helps learners learn and helps researchers learn more about learning. Like the Earth Math model the project challenges persistent, nominalist or chronological myths about learning that hold that the learning of basic facts must precede students' abilities to think or reason effectively about those facts. The Diagnostic Pathfinder is designed instead with a vision that helps learners navigate a context, like real life, where the facts sometimes change.

The flexibility of the Diagnostic Pathfinder moves in multiple directions. It has proven to be applicable in different institutions, extensible to specialties other than clinical pathology, and, more salient to our growing understanding of instructional effectiveness, it has extended the way we think about what can be effectively taught, online and otherwise, by moving clearly away from *what* students need to know, to *how* they might improve their thinking and subsequently deepen their learning. Hallmark transmission models of teaching that provide answers to questions students haven't yet asked and don't fully own produce superficial, short-term learning.

Models like the Diagnostic Pathfinder that promote inquiry and guide process help students understand and own the questions and subsequently construct understanding that is more substantial, enduring, and more readily adapted to meet the kinds of challenges that those who graduate from our institutions will undoubtedly face in their professional, civic, and personal lives. Finally, it is important to note, all of the projects reviewed in this chapter have effectively individualized learning by leveraging technology in terms of time, space, or style. Approaches such as these help us envision the distinctive features of innovative uses of technology to extend teaching and learning.

Now and Next: Technology and New Communities of Practice

As e-portfolios, blogging, wikis, and wik-a-longs emerge, the educational implications of these tools will, like the projects reviewed in this chapter, continue to subordinate the pre-eminence of traditional synchronous proximity to the needs of individual learners. Real time and space education is rapidly becoming, ironically, yet another option rather than a requirement, another of many means to instruction in increasingly diverse contexts. As we already are witnessing the demise of seat time and the traditional classroom-based community, we can anticipate individual learners, communities of learners, and professionals more and more often interacting with individuals and communities beyond the old boundaries of space, time, and status. The development and implementation of the projects reviewed here have assembled faculty, students, professionals (in and out of the "class"), instructional designers, assessment professionals, and even accreditors.

Staffing patterns at educational institutions will mirror and extend this trend. Some designs have already demonstrated the power of nontraditional groupings, including strategies where student teams do authentic projects for community partners, adding a new twist to the presumptions of face-to-face by demonstrating that even distributed learners can engage face-to-face with partners in their own communities, with distributed faculty and peers or classmates supporting their endeavors. Education, in this way, will reach out more and more directly into the community. These models anticipate science labs that communicate with others and share research and methodologies, bringing in expertise, when appropriate, from around the globe. Facilitating such learning environments is already changing the role of instructors even as they move, often begrudgingly, from sage on the stage to guide on the side. Now and next they will move their expertise online, well beyond the class and lab.

Any discussion of instructional effectiveness is incomplete if it neglects the role of the instructor, especially as we ponder the implications of online asynchronous models and emerging hybrid models. The latter models have been prompted, in part, by increasing enrollments in distributed courses by students who are on campus and choose technology enhanced courses. Convenience is certainly one reason for this choice, but more students are both comfortable with, even prefer, the type of community that online courses can provide. Students are increasingly comfortable communicating, gaming, multi-tasking, and experiencing the world from the vantage of the mobile and co-located. Think of a car of teens, each speaking into a cell phone as they wind through traffic. Community morphs. The Schutte study, discussed earlier, is a precursor of what is coming, where the implementation of online strategies increased the collaboration of students in the group and subsequently improved performance by 20% compared to students in the traditional lecture classroom. This group *self-facilitated,* instigated by a sense of shared task. Mindfully and expertly facilitated distributed communities of learners hold even greater promise.

A particularly rich example is the online Operations Management course at Washington State University. Students distributed geographically were assigned to work in virtual groups in order to apply the principles of operations management at a real site in their communities. Students in each group selected one project and collaborated to use what they were learning about operations management. No particularly sophisticated software applications were used in the course, although, anecdotally, students gained more knowledge of spreadsheets in the project-based course than the campus-based course did when a particular focus was placed on the importance of learning to use a spreadsheet. The course had three parts. Students read the text and did homework. They discussed what they were learning. They worked in groups on very real projects. The instructor, consistent with the discipline, strategically optimized his time. The text, he argued, was in its seventh printing and therefore it would be inappropriate for him to spend his time putting his own knowledge into text online. The homework was important to do, but the proof of the learning would emerge in the projects, so he minimized his attention to homework, noting only completion, not quality. He monitored the discussion, but observed that students were good at self-facilitating as long as he was available to guide, address egregious misperceptions, and answer particularly difficult questions. His time, he learned, was most effectively deployed mediating the group work that focused on the real projects and that most urgently called for his expertise.

The outcomes of those projects were phenomenal. One group negotiated for $95,000 to do a project that effectively reduced costs for a national bank. Another group saved more than $1,000,000 for a regional dairy plant, saving the plant and the jobs of the employees in that plant. Campus-based undergrads in the online course landed internships and jobs for their work. The list goes on, and in most cases the various recipients of the student insights in turn enrolled more of their employees in the program.

However, as pleased as administration has been with this model, they have nonetheless asked, ironically, for evidence demonstrating student learning that the course has generated. Identifying and communicating meaningful outcomes, it appears, is at least as urgent for educators as it is for our students and our constituencies.

CONCLUSION

To disseminate the messages and meet the challenges discussed in this chapter, staffing issues require a new vision of collaboration among educators and community. The projects here reflect successful collaborations between faculty content experts, instructional designers, technology professionals, and educational researchers and assessment experts. Even that is not enough. The collaboration now and next will require greater public participation. The Operations Management model increasingly involves leadership at the organizations where the projects were conducted. Accreditors need to work with educators and public stakeholders to help translate success in ways that are meaningful and useful for all.

Investments in technology in cost and labor are ubiquitous and growing. Employers and new generations of students increasingly expect quality experiences and outcomes. And the shortcomings of current models, particularly in math and science, are well known. Even today there continue to be news reports of the diminished and shrinking status of U.S. students' performance compared to global peers. Meanwhile, demand abroad and here for learning opportunities is increasingly expensive and the situation will not improve in the near term. *Subsequently, it is incumbent upon educators to mobilize technologies to meet these needs.* Finally, questions of the effectiveness and return on investment now press upon all sectors of the education community. How do we demonstrate to an increasingly curious and perhaps skeptical public that the investments in education pay off? The projects reported in this chapter have suggested a few ways that communicate to stakeholders and, perhaps more urgently, have helped sharpen the questions that we all need to ask.

Chapter Five

PROMISING PRACTICES:
USING WEB-BASED DISTANCE LEARNING
TO INCREASE ACCESS AND COMPLETION

by Julie Porosky Hamlin

OVERVIEW

This chapter focuses on the student support infrastructure that is an essential component of effective online learning. The chapter highlights progress higher education institutions have made in providing a comprehensive set of services and identifies continuing needs and challenges.

To characterize the state of the art in online student support services at this mid-point in the decade, the chapter considers such dimensions as what services best support retention of distance learners and eventual program completion; what strategies work best in online environments, and how campuses can integrate new services with their campus networks and data systems; how services can be provided cost-effectively; ways to promote efficiency, by, for example, collaboration among institutions or by brokering services from outside providers; services needed to support special populations of learners, such as students with physical disabilities and students learning in a second language; and increasing demand for online services from residential or campus-based students (i.e., not distance learners), and how important it is to meet this demand.

In addressing these questions, the chapter draws on the knowledge gained from FIPSE-funded projects designed to provide various online student services and on scholarship in the field of online student support services.

THE NEED FOR ONLINE SUPPORT SERVICES

Fully online postsecondary courses and degree programs began to appear in the late 1990s. By 1999, a handful of institutions had well-developed inventories of courses or complete programs being delivered wholly via electronic media. The target constituency for most online programs was adult students, who were thought to be in particular need of flexible learning options. Adults were also considered to be at an appropriate life stage to be able to benefit from an instructional format that, though not offering face-to-face contact with an instructor and fellow students, had many features that enriched learning.

FIPSE played a pivotal role in extending asynchronous, technology-mediated postsecondary education through its Learning Anytime Anywhere Partnerships (LAAP) program. This new program, authorized by the Higher Education Act of 1998, provided for the award of 10 million dollars in 1999 in single- or multi-year grants to support partnerships in innovative, collaborative projects that would broaden access to asynchronous, distance learning and ensure quality in technology-based programs. Focusing the attention of the postsecondary education community on the potential of distance learning to meet new challenges and provide new opportunities in lifelong learning, the LAAP program had a nationwide impact that is yet to be fully documented.

Another galvanizing development in the early years of online learning was the 2000 launch of a Department of Army initiative, called eArmyU, which invited institutions throughout the country to offer online courses to a ready-made clientele of service members within a consortial framework. The eArmyU initiative triggered the start-up of responsive online programs by institutions throughout the country. To a great extent the LAAP program, and to a lesser extent eArmyU, furthered higher education's internalization of online learning in the United States on a significant scale.

By 2005 online learning, often termed "e-learning," was almost wholly internalized in higher education. Few institutions are ignoring online learning. Even institutions that do not offer courses and programs in distance formats use Web applications and resources in classrooms. Today, e-learning is also thought to be appropriate for younger college students and high school students. E-learning has come a long way in a short time.

As e-learning has evolved, so has our understanding of what constitutes a fully-equipped and well-integrated online learning environment. The e-learning venture begins with an institution's decision that its student constituency can benefit from online learning. It proceeds with the design or adoption of an online learning management system, which necessitates the assembling and preparing of a host of staff with various specialties to produce and deliver instruction. At an earlier point in the short history of online learning, much of the higher education community assumed that getting the instructional production and delivery processes in place meant the e-learning enterprise was complete.

Soon, however, we discovered that digital instruction was only one piece of what should be a comprehensive infrastructure for online learning. A look at student persistence and success in online learning confirmed that sending instruction through the air did not ensure that it would be effectively received nor that it would produce intended learning outcomes. Not only must the classroom part of the campus experience become electronically accessible to those studying at a distance, but so also must the myriad of processes entailed in getting the student into the classroom and the array of academic and administrative processes required to facilitate the student's comfort with the instructional technology and his or her success in a course of study.

The LAAP program issued well-thought-out guidelines addressing areas of emphasis and concern in anytime, anywhere learning, and its guidelines on "improving support services" placed high priority on the quality of services that must go hand-in-hand with the instructional component. The guidelines noted that few comprehensive frameworks for the delivery of support services existed at the time the LAAP program began, and that for many institutions a reculturing likely would be needed in order to align the delivery of student services with the emerging anytime, anywhere forms of instruction. The guidelines envisioned to achieve this alignment would entail not only the integration of data systems, but also innovations that enabled learners at a distance to have routine, anytime, anywhere access to expert staff resources.

What are the core support services taken for granted on campus that must be available on the student's desktop or laptop to support digital instruction? A first category includes the most basic services: admission, registration, financial aid, tuition and fee payment, and book ordering. A second category of support services goes beyond what one FIPSE project featured in this chapter termed "the administrative core" (Western Cooperative for Educational Telecommunications 2003, 1). These other services essential to the online learner include library resources, assessment, tutoring, academic advising, mentoring, and personal and career counseling—all, ideally, available online. Online special-interest clubs and online moderated learning communities might also be included in this category.

There is a third set of support services, never a part of the physical campus inventory, which is unique to online learning. This set includes a student orientation to online learning and training on the learning management system, training in information literacy, around-the-clock technical helpdesk, and institution-hosted online learning resource centers on the Web. As noted by the Southern Regional Education Board, "because the distance learning environment places greater responsibility on the individual, students may require specialized services to support the learning process" (Chaloux and Mingle 2002, para. 2).

EVOLVING PRACTICE

Once e-learning institutions had surmounted the hurdle of creating and beginning to deliver online courses, most began to turn their attention to the matter of student success in the new modality. Integral to student success, most institutions began to realize, was a set of essential instructional and administrative support services that would be accessible in a format that worked for online learners, including learners with physical disabilities or other special needs. Institutions varied in whether they approached the design and deployment of support services in a piecemeal or a holistic way. In some cases, scarcity of resources meant that only the most basic functions could be offered electronically. In other cases, it took time for institutions to realize the extent of services needed, and the networks for sharing best practices in e-learning are only beginning to develop.

Nevertheless, progress in the development of services to support online learners was relatively swift. Over the past five years, innovative initiatives have begun to appear, and a momentum has begun to build as word of best practices spreads in professional forums. FIPSE, in its important capacity of stimulating and supporting innovation—and in extending the impact of innovation—funded a number of projects that directly addressed the all-important suite of student services on which e-learning must rest.

In the main, the FIPSE-supported projects that were related to student services addressed access and retention, or both. In keeping with FIPSE expectations, collaboration among institutions was a feature of the projects, with many collaborations involving non-institutional partners. The complexity and resource-intensiveness of e-learning often necessitates the involvement of commercial suppliers as well as of the institutions that are the educational deliverers.

Access and Retention for Distance Bilingual Learners

A FIPSE-funded collaboration was the "Forging Partnerships and Networking Learners with the HETS Virtual Learning and Support Plaza" project, managed by the Hispanic Educational Telecommunications System (HETS). HETS is a distance learning consortium hosted at the Inter-American University of Puerto Rico and made up of 17 colleges and universities from various states in the United States, Puerto Rico, and Latin America. The project sought to build a "virtual" (meaning non-physical) community for learning, collaboration, and support by networking students, faculty, and professionals through the Internet. The project used a bilingual portal, the Virtual Learning and Support Plaza, created and launched in 2001.

The components of the project were serving special populations—Hispanic learners—through the Virtual Plaza portal, increasing distance learning options through inter-institutional collaboration, providing online support to learners through mentoring and career exploration services, and providing support to instructors with Web-based training to teach online, a discussion forum, and online resources for distance learning and instructional design. External companies and associations also have played roles in this project.

The HETS project encompassed both access and retention goals. The virtual plaza enables students and prospective students to browse through an online catalog of credit and non-credit courses offered by all of the project partner institutions, receive mentoring, explore careers, and socialize. The project's mentoring program focuses on providing support to Hispanic students by linking them with Hispanic professionals who can provide the students with an orientation to their profession.

The HETS project's goals for increasing distance learning options were ambitious and reflected some of the reasons why institutions throughout the world have entered into online learning collaborations. As summarized in a study by Twigg (2003), these reasons include reaching educationally underserved communities, serving non-traditional students, providing for transfer of credit among institutions, and creating a mechanism to offer programs not offered by existing institutions.

The HETS project's original intentions for increasing access entailed using grant funds to support the development of individual online courses at HETS member institutions, but in the course of the project these plans changed in order to make more efficient use of funds. The objective was refocused toward the creation of joint degrees, continuing education certificates, and training and professional programs among small groups of member institutions. Some of these programs are bilingual online programs, and one features instruction in Spanish.

The HETS experience underscores the difficulty of managing and containing costs in inter-institutional collaboration. The project's mid-course correction shows the far-sightedness of the project participants and their willingness to explore a new approach to meaningful, sustainable collaboration.

Overcoming Disabilities through Web Access

Access to online student services must not ignore the need for special structures and features to reach students with varying capacities for working with Web resources. The FIPSE-funded "Accessibility to Learning Environments: Learning Anytime, Anywhere, for Anyone" WebAIM project focused on helping postsecondary institutions create a Web-based architecture that would be accessible to all individuals, including those with disabilities. WebAIM sought not to *serve* special populations but rather to help institutions make the commitment to do so and to provide these institutions with the necessary skills, tools, and administrative structures.

Compliance with anti-discrimination legislation and education-for-all sensibilities was a framework for the project, and five factors established the need for the project: (1) a growing population of Americans with disabilities over the age of 16, (2) the potential of Web-based distance learning to serve lifelong learners, (3) lack of accessibility by disabled people to three out of four web pages in postsecondary education, (4) workplace expectations for conversance with Internet tools and the fact that such skills are typically taught in secondary and postsecondary institutions requiring, in turn, Web access by these institutions, and (5) a 45% rate of unemployment or under-employment by adults with disabilities.

The WebAIM project partners, three of which included individuals with disabilities in their work groups, were Utah State University (USU), George Mason University (GMU), the Teaching, Learning, and Technology Group (TLT), and Blackboard. The project focused on four areas: serving special populations, administrative policy changes, system/resource design, and providing instruction within specific content areas. Each project partner had specific responsibilities aligned with the four main goals of the project. TLT and USU had primary responsibility to disseminate information to postsecondary institutions. USU was responsible for conducting training and providing technical assistance. Blackboard was assigned to create and disseminate an accessible course management system, and GMU and USU had primary responsibility for producing and testing a model for institutional coordination and reform. Partner activities were coordinated via feedback loops.

By the third year of the project, WebAIM had made significant progress in delineating and sharing the skills, tools, and structures integral to Web-based education that is accessible to all. Dissemination activities raised the awareness of an estimated 900,000 or more individuals. Blackboard, a national leader in Web teaching-learning platforms, released the first-ever course management system that implemented federal regulations for accessible electronic information technology. WebAIM partners reached more than 65,000 individuals with Web- or site-based training and technical assistance on accessible Web design. GMU has created and tested a model, also being widely disseminated, of accessibility system reform for postsecondary institutions.

In addressing its goal of providing instruction within specific content areas, the project sought to produce and disseminate high-quality instructional materials on accessible Web designs, and regularly placed new materials on the WebAIM.org site. These materials responded to specific needs encountered by project partners. The needs included faculty's need to create and post learning-disabled-accessible materials in a variety of electronic formats, such as PDF, PowerPoint, and multimedia, and Web designers' need to learn features such as Flash MX and learning-disabled-accessible chats, JAVA, or streamed video.

WebAIM conducted Web-based training, which was then converted to resources, in five learning modules: the user perspective, making the accessibility choice, HTML techniques and strategies, creating accessible media, and institutional coordination and reform. The modules were presented one per week for five weeks, and each module contained multimedia elements, text content, links to relevant sites, learner activities, and various interaction features such as live text chats and discussion forums. To the amazement of the planners, more than 3,000 people pre-registered for the five-week event, whereas only a few hundred had been expected.

The WebAIM project illustrates the power of collaboration between educational deliverers and a commercial provider. When a project's scope includes alteration of system features in order for the project's impact and dissemination goals to be realized, an industry leader in course management systems plays an important role.

Writing Support Online

A core support service required by students both online and on ground is assistance with writing. Extending help to students with writing promotes access and enhances student persistence. In an effort to provide online support services that parallel campus-based resources, Rogue Community College in Oregon in cooperation with seven partner community colleges launched a FIPSE-funded, three-year Online Writing Lab (OWL) project, "The Write Stuff at the Right Time," to provide interactive writing help to distance, non-traditional, and underserved students.

The OWL design focuses on discipline-specific modules around which other elements of OWL revolve. The OWL site includes discipline-based online tutoring assistance, multiple interaction features, assistance with college entrance and scholarship essay writing, instructions on Internet usage, faculty resources, help with documentation and citation, and English-as-a-Second-Language (ESL) resources.

The project had several objectives: building a flexible online writing laboratory that meets both transfer and professional/technical students' needs; creating a how-to manual and training CD-ROM for implementing OWL at other community colleges; establishing and field-testing a mechanism that would register and track OWL users from multiple campuses; assuring compliance with FTE audit guidelines in a virtual lab environment; preparing faculty and staff to develop, manage, and evaluate online instruction, tutoring, and student services; evaluating OWL's effectiveness, with particular attention to traditionally underserved populations; and disseminating the project findings and lending technical assistance to other schools wishing to replicate the project.

In the process of achieving its goals, the OWL project identified promising practices and strategies through feedback from users. For example, administrators, faculty, and students appreciated the simplicity of operations in OWL. No special software is required for OWL, and it runs on multiple platforms. The project designers kept in mind that the students OWL serves do not all have high-grade equipment and that certain graphics and high RAM usage would put the service out of reach for the target population.

A number of institutions beyond the project partners have responded with great interest in adopting OWL, and the scope of the project's intended national pilot has therefore increased significantly. Licensing arrangements, server capacity, remote access, and inter-institutional tracking have become new challenges for the project. The original plan to transfer OWL to individual institutions' servers was revised to a plan to move the site to an outside server and assist piloting institutions in building appropriate Web interfaces.

The popularity of the OWL approach to delivering writing assistance to students at a distance suggests that educators prefer a writing service that is incorporated in individual institutions, involves the campus community, is holistic, provides continuity, and tracks results. This approach is in contrast to the stripped-down, "quick fix" approach to tutoring that is offered by commercial providers.

Consortial Leveraging to Support Online Learners

Student advising, assessment, career counseling, technology literacy, and academic tutoring all are key services associated with student retention. The Connecticut Distance Learning Consortium (CTDLC) in its FIPSE-funded project "Supporting Online Learners: A Statewide Approach to Quality Academic Support Services" addressed all of these services within a framework designed to optimize inter-institutional collaboration and achieve cost-efficiency.

The 11 institutional partners of the CTDLC worked together to create a set of services that were shared, co-owned, and met the needs of all partners. The three project components were (1) designing and implementing an e-portfolio for advising, assessment, and career counseling; (2) identifying the levels of technology required for success in online courses, designing an assessment tool, and identifying appropriate training; and, (3) enhancing an online collaborative tutoring project.

The electronic portfolio component involves a shared platform that is branded for each CTDLC institution. Two pilots of the portfolio yielded revisions and enhancements that have been included in version three. The second pilot included career planning, first-year seminars, advising, selected classes, and programs. Version three was enhanced to include communication tools, career planning sections, and the capacity for students to customize e-portfolios for different uses.

Several strategies were used to help institutions and individuals implement the e-portfolios. Faculty members were commissioned to write handbooks on using e-portfolios for assessment, career counseling, and advising/first-year seminars. A listserv was launched to enable faculty and staff using the portfolios to consult with one another about strategies and problems. Finally, a faculty institute was held to focus on issues of e-portfolio implementation. In addition to the 11 CTDLC partners, six other Connecticut institutions participated in the institute. Among the purposes for which e-portfolios are being used by participating institutions are articulation, general education assessment, capstone projects, assessment within courses, first-year seminar courses, and assessment of program objectives.

The technical literacy component of the project began with a survey involving faculty and staff at participating institutions, the results of which led to the definition of three levels of skills. Level one included skills students were expected to have on entry to the institution; level two comprised skills needed for online learning, specific classes, and advanced office applications; and level three included skills required for specialized courses.

The project partners looked for existing instruments that might be adapted for measuring student technology skills but in the end designed their own tool in order to contain costs for repeated use of the instrument. Both the project-designed tool and commercial tools were piloted for comparison of results. The results of the initial pilot of the project-owned technology-literacy assessment tool showed that more students than anticipated lacked proficiency at level one. An online, self-paced remedial module was created for students needing help at level one.

The collaborative tutoring component, begun under another grant and grown with FIPSE support, was unique in involving both public and private, associate- and baccalaureate-granting institutions in tutoring solutions for online students. Using a single Web-based platform, the institutional partners each contribute a small number of tutoring hours. The hours are then combined so as to afford students from all institutions access to tutoring in several subjects, seven days a week, morning through evening.

By spring of last year, students had access to 142 hours of tutoring in five subjects each week. A measure of the success of the tutoring program is that an increasing number of faculty require students to use tutoring before submitting assignments. Another measure of success is that institutional partners have committed funds to continue participation in the tutoring project after grant funding ends.

The Connecticut Distance Learning Consortium notes a major change since it submitted its grant proposal to FIPSE. It involves the convergence of online and traditional learning: When we wrote the grant we envisioned that the projects would impact distance education programs and online learners (hence the title of our project) at each of the participating institutions. However, it has become clear that the impact is not only on online students, courses, and programs, but on the institution as a whole. The tutoring program in all institutions is marketed and used by all students. The technology-assessment instrument, in most institutions, is being given to all students (Connecticut Distance Learning Consortium 2004, 8).

This trend toward convergence is considered in the next sections of this chapter.

Student Services Beyond the Administrative Core

"Beyond the Administrative Core: Creating Web-based Student Services for Online Learners," a Learning Anytime Anywhere Partnerships project funded by FIPSE, examined the full spectrum of online services to support online learners and drew a distinction between commonly offered administrative services and a host of other services that also are needed. The three-year project was led by the Western Cooperative for Educational Telecommunications (WCET) and included three institutional partners—Kansas State University (KSU), Kapi'olani Community College (KCC), and Regis University—and one corporate partner, SCT.

The project's premise was that one of the biggest gaps in online education is the inability of institutions to provide anytime, anyplace access to a full array of student support services. Commonly offered online services considered to be within the administrative core were admissions, financial aid, registration, among others. Support services considered beyond the administrative core, often neglected, included some of those targeted in other grant projects described in this chapter—tutoring, academic advising, personal counseling, career counseling, and library services.

Goals of the project were to (1) recognize online learners' needs for student support services; (2) use the knowledge of needs to guide the development of commercial and home-grown Web-based products adaptable to online learners' needs in a variety of contexts; (3) develop customizable service modules based on individual student profiles, including the usually neglected services; (4) develop guidelines and Web templates for institutions that wished to create a comprehensive Web-based array of student services for online learners; (5) track the processes involved in creating online student services at the partner institutions; (6) produce case studies of these processes; and (7) disseminate widely the lessons and products of the project, including the software package, student services guidelines, and case studies.

Each institutional partner in the project developed a Web-based student service to meet campus needs and also tracked the institutional change process required to move the service to the online environment. KSU devised an academic advising model; KCC, a learning support model; Regis, an orientation to academic advising; and SCT, the e-education infrastructure together with additional functions in its existing products and new non-proprietary products. Other objectives of the project were implementing changes in staff roles at partner institutions resulting from the new approach, designing and initiating a process for exchanging information and ideas, and disseminating project results both during and after the project.

The deliverables of the "Beyond the Administrative Core" project were the student services models developed by the partner institutions, a set of guidelines for institutions desiring to build Web-based services, a commercial solution that expanded access to personalized student services, and the detailed case studies of change processes referred to above. The guidelines deliverable took the form of a set of "Guiding Principles" that will live on as a rubric for other institutions desiring to take their Web-based student services beyond the administrative core.

Resources for Promising Practices in Online Support Services

The projects cameoed in this section illustrate a growing awareness of the integrality of student services in the e-learning enterprise. Promising practices in student services are appearing in e-learning institutions throughout the country, and they receive regional or national exposure through the efforts of a handful of non-profit organizations concerned with e-learning policy and practice and which, as a service to members, conscientiously track and share best practices almost minute-by-minute, often through listservs.

A leading organization in this tracking and sharing effort is the Sloan-C Consortium for asynchronous learning networks, which is national in scope. The Sloan-C website features a section for showcasing "Effective Practices for Student Satisfaction," and the best practices by various institutions linked at the site include, among others, administering extensive satisfaction surveys to online students; using "course wizards" to help students ask for online assistance; customer service through a helpdesk; comprehensive online library services; telephone calls to students on their first day of class; online help with student writing; e-portfolios to help students evaluate their learning experiences; online prep courses and orientation; help with scheduling the student workload; and community building through sharing student photos and work (Sloan-C Consortium 2004).

Two regionally-focused organizations that provide leadership in e-learning policy and which also showcase and share best practices by member institutions are the Electronic Campus of the Southern Regional Education Board (SREB) and the Western Cooperative for Educational Telecommunications (WCET), whose project is featured in this chapter. WCET facilitates an Online Community with discussion threads subdivided by topic. In the sub-community called "Online Student Services," one finds a wealth of information about innovative practice as well as something of a live transcript of the evolving state of the art in student services to support e-learning.

For example, a college in the early stages of planning for electronic delivery has posted to ask for help from WCET members in narrowing down the long list of electronic student services it has compiled, and not all of which it can afford to deliver right away. The college asks, what process other colleges used to prioritize student services initiatives. A state university responds by listing advising, re-design of library services, and technical support, among other priorities. The importance of training financial aid staff to work with distance learners is also mentioned.

To the same question a SREB representative replies with the results of a SREB survey of online support services most in demand. In order of importance they were registration, admission, tuition and fee payment, library services, and technical support. A second set of services identified in the survey were tutoring, advising, financial aid, and bookstore. These interactions demonstrate collaboration and information sharing among the different online learning "think tank" and support organizations.

It is appropriate to sample best practices in online student support services within the context of the media through which those practices are being disseminated and discussed, because across the country a good deal of copycatting, in the best sense of the word, and collaborating is occurring in the sub-specialty of e-learning support services. In other senses, perhaps not enough sharing and collaborating is occurring, as is mentioned in the next section.

LESSONS LEARNED

Lessons learned in the course of the FIPSE-funded projects highlighted in this chapter provide traction for future forward movement toward the implementation of comprehensive and responsive student support services to promote e-learning access and retention throughout higher education. The lessons that stand out are summarized below.

Institutions Should Be Sure Students Are Technology-Literate

Planning for online student services should realistically assess the preparedness of student consumers. Increasingly, students entering college are "cyber natives," as contrasted with the "cyber immigrant" status of adults (including many faculty) who form the transitional generation of the Information Age. It would be easy, therefore, to assume that students arrive in virtual classrooms prepared to operate the basic technology of online learning. In the technology literacy assessment component of its project, The Connecticut Distance Learning Consortium (CTDLC) discovered that a much larger percentage of students than anticipated lacked the basic computer skills identified as essential for learning success. Other institutions have made the same discovery, and many have incorporated mandatory orientations to online learning or information literacy short courses, sometimes including self-assessments. eArmyU, which works with more than 30 institutional partners, requires that all member institutions offer such orientations.

Results Must Be Measured in Order to Be Meaningful

FIPSE requires that the impact of innovative practices be measured, and all projects have included provisions for assessing the success of their projects. It is also important to build in provisions for ongoing measurement, as the Online Writing Lab (OWL) project did with its objective of creating and field-testing a mechanism for tracking OWL users in a multi-school environment. Testing and measuring also played a prominent role in the WebAIM project's deployment of an eight-point model of institutional coordination and reform.

Collaborations Create Cost Efficiencies ... and Complications

All of the projects highlighted in this chapter included collaborations among institutions and associated entities, and throughout the country e-learning cooperations literally abound. In the simplest terms, collaboration pools resources and guards against a costly reinvention of the wheel. The CTDLC found the cost savings of providing a collaborative solution to online tutoring to be enormous. The platform, coordinator, and instructor costs that are shared by participating institutions would have had to be borne separately by each institution without the consortial framework. The WebAIM project realized economies of scale in dissemination, training and technical assistance, tool development, and institutional reform.

Working with partners also can cause complications and delays. The WebAIM project partner cohort fluctuated for two years before it stabilized. Sometimes partners, with the best of intentions, encounter resource deficits and cannot continue. Too, some collaborations are formed without a full understanding of what each partner is prepared to bring to the table. As phrased by WCET (2003) in the lessons learned from its Beyond the Administrative Core project, "there has to be a reason to collaborate."

Institutions sometimes do undertake online student services innovations in vacuo, without an awareness of identical services already well-established at other institutions. In so doing, they incur costs that might have been avoided. Because online student services are usually technology-intensive and therefore costly, e-learning institutions should develop a reflex of looking afield before plunging forward. The best practices networks mentioned earlier are an excellent source of information on innovations other institutions have mounted. An increasingly popular form of collaboration is the licensing of online products among institutions, student services products as well as online courseware. The OWL project pursued this option.

Partnerships between Business and Education Are a Plus, Sometimes a Necessity

Blackboard played an essential role in the goals of the WebAIM project; the project required the company's commitment to enhancing the accessibility of its products to the project's target population. The Hispanic Educational Telecommunications System (HETS) project likewise benefitted from partnerships with commercial entities. Ideally, such partnerships will be win–win rather than relying on companies to donate services for a "good cause." IBM viewed its support of HETS's e-mentoring program as an opportunity for IBM employees to serve as role models for students and to recruit future employees, as did Banco Popular of Puerto Rico, another commercial partner that participated in the e-mentoring program.

SCT, the commercial partner in the WCET project, was able to bring new products to market through its participation in the project. "The idea of weaving all kinds of technologically unique, personalized, and customizable online student services modules working seamlessly beneath one student information system is what SCT has been working on since taking part in this project" (Shea 2002, para. 20). More important, "the ... legacy of this project may be in helping to broaden this corporation's vision to embrace a comprehensive and integrated view of student services" (WCET 2003).

Staffing Projections Must Be Realistic

To the dismay of presidents and chief financial officers throughout academia, educational technology does not replace people nor reduce the size of the workforce. If anything, human labor-intensiveness increases with the customizability that technology brings to the student services sphere. Both the OWL and HETS projects experienced realizations about the extent of staffing required and made mid-course corrections. The WCET (2003) project commented on this fact, as well: "It's about people, not technology. Moving student services to the online environment is primarily a challenge of leading people in a new direction. Dealing with politics, policies, practices, and culture are human, not technical, issues."

Tutoring Might Be More Broadly Conceptualized as "Learning Support"

Tutoring, as represented in the successful CTDLC and OWL projects, is a direct intervention to promote persistence in online learners. The WCET project, along the way, reconceptualized tutoring in a way that points toward the future. "Kapi'olani [a project partner institution] started out by focusing on tutoring but figured out that they needed to more widely define tutoring, so they are calling it learning support services" (Shea 2002, para. 13). The Kapi'olani-managed segment of the Beyond the Administrative Core project anticipates providing a wider, long-lasting spectrum of web-based services to online learners.

Planning for Sustainability Is Important

Online student services that begin as innovations with external funding are at risk of running out of gas if their future is not anticipated from the outset of the implementation. Sustainability of the WebAIM project was a priority from the beginning, with the project partners realizing that sustainability could be limited unless partners leave the period of grant funding with revenue-generating products that can position the grant initiatives for continuation.

The CTDLC project has addressed sustainability by creating a package of marketable tools, including e-tutoring, an e-portfolio, and a technology-literacy assessment. The OWL project is addressing sustainability in part through licensing the OWL product.

It Is Desirable to Strive for a Holistic Approach to Online Student Services

Online and traditional learning are converging. Students in dormitories want and deserve the same Web-based student support features that are available to distance learners. As noted in an earlier section, the CTDLC project adjusted its plans and scope upon the realization that the clientele for the services it was developing was not limited to online learners. Early adopter e-learning institutions may already have developed a parallel set of student services for online learners and now must backtrack to integrate land-based with online-only services. Institutions just beginning to offer e-learning can benefit from what has been learned and avoid the trap of creating a separate set of services for "distance" students, who increasingly look like *all* students.

Approaching the development and delivery of student services in a holistic way that equally serves online and campus-based learners entails adhering to principles that were captured in four of the Beyond the Administrative Core project's "lessons learned":

- IT'S TIME TO END THE SILOS. Student services have developed over time as the need for them arose on campus. Many have separate policies, practices, and technical infrastructures. New technologies make it possible to integrate services into a cohesive system of student support. This requires re-engineering student services—designing new policies and practices—and takes a cross-functional campus team to make it happen.

- INTERNAL CONSISTENCY AND INTEGRITY ARE VITAL. The extent to which an institution puts its student services online should be consistent with its mission, culture, and priorities. If an institution is enrolling distance students in online courses, it must provide those students with accessible services of equal quality to those for campus-based students. Otherwise, these students cannot be expected to succeed at the same rate and it calls into question the institution's commitment to learning for all of its students—not just those privileged to come to campus.

- TECHNOLOGY SHOULD ENABLE NEW SERVICES, NOT DEFINE THEM. At a rapid pace, new technologies are coming onto the market. New versions of existing software are common. In envisioning new services, the focus should not be limited by what is possible today. By defining the ideal and then phasing in the solutions as the technology becomes available, the best service will result.

- A CROSS-FUNCTIONAL TEAM IS KEY. To integrate student services and create a new way of serving students, institutions need broad representation from admissions, registrar's office, student services, disabilities services, marketing, faculty, IT, and students (WCET 2003).

The OWL project, in catching faculty unprepared to use the features of the online writing lab, experienced the disconnect that can occur when the whole campus community is not operating cross-functionally.

FUTURE DIRECTIONS

Institutions and organizations concerned with the quality of online programs are on the way to a consensus about best practices in online student support services; yet, while agreeing on models, institutions face challenges in implementation and integration. At the same time, something new is happening. Just as we are becoming more knowledgeable about the total environment required to support learners at a distance and are wrestling with the logistics of creating that environment, the framework for our efforts has morphed. As indicated in the term "distributed learning," the community described as "online learners" or "e-learners" has broadened to include students in physical classrooms as well as those on computers across the campus or across the country. With information-age gradualness—meaning over a period of about three years—what some call "bricks and clicks" have begun to converge, as the Connecticut project discovered.

No longer does e-learning serve only students engaged in study at a distance. Online learning is becoming a standard component of the physical campus through hybrid formats that combine face-to-face class meetings with online elements in a single course and, increasingly, through Web-enhanced instruction in face-to-face classes. Suddenly the constituency for online support services has expanded to include nearly all postsecondary learners worldwide.

A nuance is in play regarding the "need" for online student services. Learners studying wholly at a distance, sometimes a continent away, require services online because they cannot or should not be expected to go to campus; or, in the case of online-only universities, because a physical campus does not exist. Learners on physical campuses, however, are coming to *expect* academic and administrative support services online, just as they expect faster computers, because the services are more convenient via desktop or laptop than through standing in line at the campus administration building. The provision of support services online is likely to be a factor in on-campus student retention just as it is a factor in the success of learners at a distance.

For all institutions, the implications of the convergence of online and traditional learning are enormous. Clearly, institutions with a distance-learning mission or component must provide the complete online support infrastructure to undergird online instruction. Moreover, even institutions that do not emphasize online delivery, because of the importuning effect of student expectations, must consider putting all of their student support services online in order to stay competitive. The comprehensiveness and effectiveness of online support services, therefore, become important topics for all of higher education.

The higher education e-learning community, greatly broadened in the past five years to include a majority of institutions, is approaching consensus on best practices in online student services to serve the goals of access and retention. At this point, progress depends significantly on getting the word out, which in turn is dependent on keeping the networks of dissemination and discussion robust, visible, and accessible. A long road lies ahead before institutions will uniformly offer a comprehensive suite of services for online learners.

One of the most exhaustive lists of best practices in the use of technology to deliver instructional support services was compiled by Steven Sachs of Northern Virginia Community College (Sachs 2003). Drawn from best practices identified through work undertaken by some of the organizations mentioned earlier in this chapter, the list contains more than 230 best practices (some overlapping) organized by the categories of Orientation Services, Tutorial and Mentoring Services, Learning and Information Resources Services, Enrollment and Student Records Services, Financial Aid Services, Advising Services, Help Desk Services, Bookstore Services, and Coordination of all of the above-listed services. Within each category, the services are subdivided by basic, intermediate, and advanced level. A scan of the list, which includes such items as "students can electronically access staff who speak foreign languages" and "students have access to a math tutoring center or on-call math tutors from off-campus," reinforces the enormity of the challenge of reaching the ideals envisioned by e-learning leaders and by the FIPSE Learning Anytime Anywhere Partnerships program.

Future directions for student services to support e-learners can be gleaned from the experience of the participants in FIPSE-sponsored projects and from watching trends. Our predictions suggest the following directions.

Online Student Services of the Future Will Not All Be Home-Grown

Commercial products will become more varied, sophisticated, and, likely, affordable. Thus, institutions that have difficulty now deciding whether to buy or build their online student services may find their decisions even more difficult in the future. The Connecticut project recognized the challenge to its e-portfolio from commercial products released after the grant had begun. The partners also are now under pressure to integrate the portfolio platform with course management systems and student information systems, a costly process.

The question becomes: Is this process a job best done in-house, or must it be outsourced? Could the OWL project be accomplished more efficiently by a commercial supplier like SmarThinking? As shown by Blackboard in the WebAIM project, and by SCT in the Beyond the Administrative Core project, with appropriate incentives companies can customize their products to meet campus clients' needs and can even be good neighbors.

Students Will Expect Progressively More Personalized Online Student Services

The extent to which institutions can provide customizable and "right now" services will be a factor in the institutions' competitiveness. "The user is king" is a lesson mentioned in the Beyond the Administrative Core project report:

> Web-based services should be designed from the users' perspective. Students are primarily task-oriented—they want to pay a bill, run a degree audit, schedule an appointment—and they don't want to think about which department provides what service. They prefer a single sign-on to integrated, personalized, and customized services and the options of self-service, general help, and personalized assistance. The full range of optimized services includes online and real-person/real-time resources. (WCET 2003)

Another lesson learned notes that "student information systems (SISs) and portals play critical roles in the provision of personalized and customized student services" (WCET 2003).

Bilingual Online Student Services

This will occur as the Latino population grows and makes its expectations heard and felt in higher education. Initiatives like those modeled in the HETS project will begin to appear throughout the country. A need exists for all institutions to address a bilingual population, since bilingual learners at a distance have access to all online programs.

Online Student Support to Emphasize Learning Outcomes

A new category of increasingly integral online student support services is likely to develop around the accrediting community's emphasis on the assessment of learning outcomes. Beyond tutoring, beyond "learner support services," students will require technology-based mechanisms for self-testing mastery of course content and even of whole-program learning objectives. The self-tests will require links back to reinforcing course content.

CONCLUSION: SETTING PRIORITIES

The old joke goes, "Q: How do you eat an elephant? A: One bite at a time." In keeping with that sensible approach, it is useful to return to the principle underlying another lesson reported in the Beyond the Administrative Core project: "First things first":

> It is ideal to put the administrative core services—admissions, registration, financial aid, student accounts—online first so that you can build upon them. These centralized services have many established rules, regulations, and operating procedures so it is easier to achieve consensus about what the new services should be like. Then you can move on to the decentralized ones where each department may have its unique needs. (WCET 2003)

This advice is echoed in one university's response to the "what do we put online first?" question posed by the college just beginning electronic delivery of student services. The university first identified the must-have services required for a student to take a class without having to physically come to the campus. These included application, registration, financial aid, payment, technical support/help desk, and library services. The next tier included degree advising. Next came services that directly support degree programs: tutoring, placement, and tools that enhance students' success in courses that rely heavily on process, such as math, computer science, and information systems (WCET 2005). This first-things-first wisdom is helpful in contemplating one successful way to engage in innovative technologies and begin institutional transformation.

Chapter Six

INCREASING EQUITY:
SEEKING MAINSTREAM ADVANTAGES
FOR ALL

by Chère Campbell Gibson

OVERVIEW

The title of the 2005 annual conference of the American Council on Education, *"Educating All of One Nation: Realizing America's Promise: Embracing Diversity, Discovery, and Change,"* is telling. It suggests that equity of access to and success in education for all is not yet a reality and remains a topic for serious consideration. Moreover, many would suggest that this is particularly true of those described as "special populations"—persons of color, those whose first language is not English (often referred to as language minorities), those who are differently-abled, as well as those who are denied access to traditional higher education due to geographic location or life's work. While the introduction of a variety of distance technologies has begun to overcome some of the barriers to access to education, additional barriers emerge when addressing the equity needs of these special populations.

NEEDS

How critical is the need that distance technology stands to address? "Special" populations are at greater risk of being left out of postsecondary education. For example, students from historically disadvantaged minority groups (American Indian, Hispanic, and Black) have little more than a 50–50 chance of finishing high school with a diploma. By comparison, graduation rates for Whites and Asians are 75% and 77% nationally (Swanson 2004). However, race–ethnicity is only one of a number of closely linked factors that mediate the dropout decision. Socioeconomic status, the ability to communicate in English, and geographic region of residence are all highly correlated (National Center for Educational Statistics 1995). Sadly, but not surprisingly, while the number of persons earning a bachelor's degree has increased during the last 30 years, the Black and Hispanic gaps with Whites widened slightly (NCES 2002). Further, while 6% of all undergraduate students reported a disability, postsecondary students with disabilities were less likely than those without disabilities to have attained bachelor's or associate's degrees (NCES 2000).

In 1992, a report from the National Center for Research on Cultural Diversity and Second Language Learning noted that while "the number of students from linguistic and ethnic minority backgrounds is expected to increase," there also exists an expectation that the number of jobs requiring at least a baccalaureate degree will increase, coupled with the realization that students from these backgrounds are neither performing well in high school nor enrolling in college in sufficient numbers to qualify for these new jobs (Mehan et al. 1992). So, although the last 10 years have seen improvements, we still have a long way to go.

One solution to the issue of access to education is to provide access to technology to overcome barriers of time, place, pace, and disability; but special populations can present special challenges when confronted with technological solutions. How do we ensure equity of access to technology? Even more so than for other distance learners, special consideration needs to be given to designing for and ensuring that learners have appropriate technology skills, academic preparation, learning skills, language skills, and self-management skills. Further, how do we design educational experiences that are relevant to the distinct aspects of these students' culture, life situation, and language abilities? Finally, how do we support these same learners regarding success and retention in learning? These are not new challenges, but addressing them with particular attention to those less well served by education and training—those who are ethnically diverse or disabled—is a unique LAAP contribution.

EVOLVING PRACTICE:
PROGRAMS EMERGE TO ADDRESS CRITICAL NEEDS

Compared to the general population, these learners' needs include even more acute awareness in the areas of access to education, access to technology, inclusion in education through technology, and designing for success in technology-based education. These themes echo many of the issues that have confronted education and distance education in the past, but the solutions are modern and evolving. And we are beginning to recognize the additional challenges and benefits these solutions present to special populations.

Access to Education

Flexible access to education is essential for working adults and nowhere is that flexibility more critical than in the health care field, with its 24/7/365 schedule. While rural working adults, including many from reservations, were served by the Montana Consortium and needed flexibility in their access to instructional technology baccalaureate degree, health care workers in long-term care facilities in Iowa needed maximum flexibility to accommodate their ever-changing work shifts. Others needed educational access that afforded flexibility in place of learning.

Nowhere was this more challenging than in working with migrant families. The University of Wisconsin System Administration's Alcanza grant recognized the need to serve individuals whose very vocation moved them and their families between and within states throughout the year (Carranza 2004). Providing training to those differently-abled and homebound provided yet another challenge. The pace of learning is also a challenge for many students due to limited language skills, physical disabilities, learning disabilities, and limited personal learning skills and abilities, including computer skills. Based on our knowledge of distance education today, a solution is the use of technology for teaching and learning with a heavy dependence on computer-based education and training, but another issue emerges—access to the technology needed in order to provide access to education.

Access to Technology

These projects revealed that many of the access issues experienced by special populations are parallel to, but greater in comparison to, other distance learners. For Project Alcanza, the answer to the question, "How do we ensure access to the necessary technology?" was to provide computers both at the migrant labor camps for youth and adult access as well as at the food processing plants, job centers, and other migrant serving agencies. However, a new realization emerged—the computers, especially at the plants, remained unused. Providing access to the necessary technology was not enough for this particular special population.

For others, access to technology was not the issue, but rather the nature of the technology and its network capabilities presented the challenge. As the Montana Consortium discovered, older computers and dial-up access limited accessibility and had design implications for slow downloads or incompatible files for their largely rural and Native American population. These issues arose more often for marginalized groups who do not have the income or do not receive funding for the latest equipment.

Technology selection was also a consideration. Computers alone may not always be the answer for either conveying content or communicating with the learners. Designing call center training for homebound adults with disabilities, the National Telecommuting Institute discovered that a mix of technologies, for both synchronous and asynchronous communications, enhanced teaching and learning.

However, physical access was not a sufficient condition to provide access to education. Computer competence was another critical issue. The University of Iowa's certified nursing assistant program and the Montana Consortium's access to baccalaureate degree programs discovered the importance of determining learners' access to technology and its capabilities as well as the capabilities of the learner or user. The value of orientations to technology-based learning, including navigational skills, emerged as well as perhaps more prominent issues than had been expected.

English proficiency is also critical. One solution to address multiple challenges was to teach basic computer skills as subject matter while teaching English simultaneously. This was the strategy employed by Project CONNECT, a web-based English as a second language project. Others, such as Alcanza, provided training to adult migrant workers in both Spanish and English, both via computer and face-to-face.

These examples illustrate the need to reach deeper into issues of access to education and technology for special populations. Additionally, particularly for ethnically diverse and differently-abled learners, they need to feel included.

Inclusion in Education

Several projects, especially Alcanza, Project CONNECT, and the University of Iowa nursing education program, dealt with potential exclusion from education and training by addressing the challenge of language. Multiple language teaching or imbedded glossaries were perhaps the most obvious strategies to ensure inclusion. The Hispanic Educational Telecommunications

System's Virtual Plaza provided a system allowing students to access the news in both Spanish and English.

What about cultural inclusion for an ethnically diverse learner population? Learners of color and those who are differently-abled often do not "see" themselves represented in their coursework, nor are courses designed with cultural diversity in mind (Gunawardena, Wilson, and Nolla 2003). Their contexts for living and learning are not always represented in course materials or in interactive activities that involve their communities, their families and their world of current employment, or the jobs they aspire to hold.

One solution was to identify existing courses that were culturally appropriate within already existing partnerships. This was the strategy employed by the Hispanic Educational Telecommunications System (HETS). They sought out unique offerings that represented educational and professional development opportunities for Hispanic learners, represented Hispanic, multicultural or bicultural perspectives, and had the potential for overall development of Hispanic communities. In addition, their Virtual Plaza portal provides links to culturally relevant news, events, and other resources.

Others sought to develop culturally appropriate courses and experiences. Working with Native American communities and learners, the Montana Consortium of colleges, including tribal colleges, not only ensured that course materials were culturally appropriate, but linked actual course projects and other learning experiences to the communities in which the students resided. The particular content of the degree offered by this Montana Consortium was information technology, including Cisco Certification—content and credentials necessary in the rural communities where the learner lived and hoped to be employed.

Others designed portions of courses to reflect the context of practice, using a case-based approach to teaching and learning. The certified nursing assistant program incorporated stories that helped convey the necessary content tied to the context for application leading to an authentic interactive experience. The online Plant Safety and Consumer Education programs, designed for migrant workers and their families, respectively, highlighted the work and family contexts to convey the content and the context in which it is applied. Hispanic actors also were evident in this multi-media program. Teaching civics and the American system of education while teaching English to second language learners provided yet another example of inclusion in education with a focus on learners and the context in which they will apply the new learning.

As Alcanza sought to prepare young migrant high school juniors and seniors so they would be better qualified to enter college and motivated to do so, they brought them to college—to the context of their future. Advanced placement as well as remedial course work was held on college campuses. Students lived in dorms and ate with other college students, attended their own special classes, and "became" college students for a short period of time.

Success in Technology-Based Education

Access to education through the use of educational technology, even with culturally appropriate educational materials, activities, and locations, does not automatically lead to success. As Dhanarajan (1997, 7) notes, "Equality of opportunity is a matter of outcomes, not merely resource availability; in other words, providing access is merely a starting point and equality can only be achieved if the people provided with such opportunities are helped towards achieving their own goals."

Both the HETS project and Alcanza used mentors as a way of supporting their learners to enhance retention and learning. Moreover, these mentors spanned the age spectrum from business people to collegians. The Hispanic Educational Telecommunications System-based grant focused on the design and delivery of a Virtual Plaza to support both learning and networking. One of the key elements in this bilingual portal was online mentoring and career exploration. To do this, HETS recruited Hispanic business people to mentor learners whose career aspirations matched the mentor's current vocation. Developed to enhance retention and learner self-esteem, as well as technical literacy, these relationships also gave students a virtual look at the day-to-day life of professionals in their chosen careers.

In contrast to using adults as mentors, Alcanza focused on employing youth to mentor the migrant youth participating in the program. Young college students, Spanish-speaking and most often Hispanic, worked both in migrant camps and in the on-campus pre-college programs to accomplish similar goals to the HETS project. The focus was to broaden the migrant youths' aspirations and motivate them to remain in high school, take appropriate college preparation courses, and follow their role models' example.

Working with rural students, predominately Native American, the Montana Consortium mentored both on an individual and on a cohort basis. Each cohort entering the baccalaureate program in information technology was assigned a Personal Service Adviser (PSA). This PSA mentored each cohort member from recruitment to graduation. Similar to the mentors in the

HETS and Alcanza programs, these PSAs represented the ethnic makeup of the learner population and understood the economic, social, and cultural context of their learners.

POTENTIAL PITFALLS AND PROMISING PRACTICES: LESSONS LEARNED

Many lessons learned emerged from formative evaluation of the projects above. These insights led to project adjustments, enabling the projects to be more successful, and providing additional lessons learned. These included: the importance of the supporting infrastructure and technology support; the need for appropriate instructional design, including needs assessment and pilot testing; a provision for faculty support to enhance the design and delivery of education and training; and learner support. Partnerships played a vital role in each of the projects and much was learned from these evolving relationships.

The Importance of the Supporting Infrastructure and Technology Support

One of the first realizations by all who use technology to enhance access to education and training, regardless of the population served, is the importance of the technical infrastructure of the agency or organization providing the programs and, for the ultimate recipient of the education and training, the learner. However, in order to serve special populations, additional features are often incorporated into technological solutions, making the solution technically complex.

Nowhere was that more evident than in the innovative web-based educational programs for health care workers in long-term health care facilities, where technical implementation problems emerged. The bottom line—sophisticated web-based templates with their imbedded glossaries that emerged from the collaboration of a computer programming or design vendor and the subject matter design team, needed an infrastructure that exceeded the capabilities of the University and many of the collaborating nursing homes. In addition, the templates needed to have an easy-to-use interface for content specialists to input course content. Technical service providers are most used to importing content into templates they design themselves, and thus fail to consider the technological infrastructure and expertise of their partners. Designing a simpler and easier set of templates solved exportability and usability challenges. This redesign served both content specialists and learners alike. Further, once the extensive documentation was received, the University of Iowa and its collaborators were able to understand and work more effectively and efficiently with the interface.

As part of the Hispanic Educational Telecommunications System (HETS) managed project, the partnership developed a multi-language Virtual Plaza portal for learners, faculty, and other interested parties. Early in the project, the staff had neither direct access to update and upgrade sections of this web-based interface, nor did they have the necessary documentation. Once again, the development of the interface was delegated to an outside technical service provider and extensive documentation was not originally provided. With both access and documentation, the Virtual Portal is up-to-date and dynamic with the addition of many new features, including news headlines and animated promotions, added by internal staff. Another additional lesson learned seems noteworthy—the need for a mirror version of the portal's website as a "staging server" for updates and testing. This strategy heads off course downtime and provides a protected environment for instructional and design innovation.

While some projects experienced challenges with technical infrastructure early in the project, others found that technical infrastructure considerations could also solve some of their challenges. As it approached the conclusion of its funding and the question of sustainability, Project CONNECT considered achieving an economy of scale as part of their plans. By sharing an online platform, including the learner management system, with another online project for adult English as a Second Language teachers, cost savings accrued for both programs.

The Need for Learner Appropriate Instructional Design

The challenge of time has been a constant in instructional design, distance education, and funded projects that link them both. There is never enough time. As a result, many externally funded distance education projects abbreviate the instructional design process. The two facets most often ignored are the initial analysis phase, including the needs assessment and learner analysis, and the formative evaluation of instructional materials. These formative evaluations may take the form of a one-on-one evaluation, a small group evaluation, or an actual field-test in the learners' context (Dick, Carey, and Carey 2001). Several of the projects learned the hard way about the importance of this initial analysis and formative evaluation in instructional design.

For example, Project CONNECT discovered a substantial disconnect through its evaluation and field testing of their educational modules. The project discovered the learners' goals focused on learning to speak English, especially informal English. The modules designed, however, focused on enhancing learners' English *reading* abilities. In another example, formative evaluation of the University of Iowa's educational programs designed for the certified nurse assistant and the pre-certified nursing assistant indicated that the modules tested were user-friendly and easy to navigate; however, they discovered that learners had little or no technical experience, a considerable limitation in their technology learning skills.

All of these findings—disparate learners' goals, the overestimation of learners' entering experience with technology, and the capability of local technology—have major implications for the design of instruction. Determining these factors after several modules of instruction were developed and piloted required modifications that may not have been necessary had both needs assessment and learner analysis been conducted early in the design process.

In addition to the reaffirmation of the importance of early analysis and formative evaluation, we have learned a lot as projects designed and developed education and training materials for special populations and conducted formative evaluation. Some of the lessons learned are unique to special populations, particularly language minorities, while others are simply principles of good practice that benefit all learners.

Language is one area where a number of recommendations emerged. Multiple language delivery is suggested, if possible. While expensive, it does provide an opportunity for both accessibility of content and second language learning. An alternative is the use of simpler language for second language learners or those with limited educational backgrounds. Language level and culturally appropriate glossaries hyperlinked from textual material is also recommended as well as less text density per page, again especially with second language learners.

The use of multiple technologies to encourage the use of multiple learning channels also emerges as a lesson learned. Incorporating the use of audio, video, and graphics can enhance learning and provide variety beyond the text on a computer screen.

The challenges faced by special populations goes beyond simply language; they include limited educational experience and no experience learning independently on computers, so built-in scaffolding is important. The following instructional designs can build upon one another and lead to the respective learning outcomes:

- LADDERING: learning skills, independence

- COLLABORATIVE DESIGN: problem-solving, learning, and working together
- IMBEDDED HELP SCREENS: scaffolding learning

Creating a community of practice online or bringing students together to create a community of learners emerged as an important facet of design for special populations. Working together with a shared understanding of cultural and life experiences in the case of the differently-abled, language minorities, and race–ethnicity diverse students, is important. Thus, efforts should be made to design group activities for online and in-residence learning and assessment activities. In addition, giving learners choice within their educational materials in terms of pathways to learning develops self-directed learning skills.

One recommendation that always emerges for instructional designs with technology is to design for interactivity. This interactivity may be individual activities built into educational modules for the independent learner, or it may be activities designed for small group work. Using the learner's context as an arena for practice and the use of authentic story or case-based learning is also suggested. Activities that encourage the movement from theory to practice in the learner's own context ensures transferability of learning. Ensuring that the learner "sees" him- or herself represented in the cases or stories enables inclusivity. Both will promote learning.

Assessment recommendations include the use of self- and authentic online assessment, including why answers were wrong. The provision of feedback from both the instructor and fellow students can be particularly helpful.

One additional finding was the importance of a part time option for learners pursuing baccalaureate degree programs. As the Montana Consortium discovered, learners need more flexibility in their educational pursuits. Enrolling in the same number of credit hours as a traditional undergraduate student does not allow for the flexibility needed by an adult working in or out of the home.

Supplementing online teaching with face-to-face meetings emerged in several projects including the Call Center Training, the Montana Consortium degree program, and Alcanza. The Call Center Training project found that multiple media training (WebCT, video- and audio-based instruction) were particularly successful when coupled with intensive classroom-based small group work resulting in a hybrid offering. The learners pursuing their information technology degree through the Montana Consortium found meeting face-to-face was important for forging relationships and creating a foundation for support as the cohort progressed together through their studies. Lastly, the adult members of the migrant families seemed particularly reluctant to use the computers in the plant; however, the addition of a facilitator who both spoke their language and had computer skills greatly increased the computer usage and learning.

While these lessons learned are not necessarily unique, they do emerge from a careful analysis of education and training activities with culturally diverse and differently-abled populations. The voices of these individuals are often missing in the data that supported instructional design recommendations, thus these projects give further credence to past recommendations (Dick, Carey, and Carey 2001).

The Need to Support Learning with Technology

While educators may be proficient at assessing their learners' cultural background and previous educational experiences, they may too often assume to know about students' experiences using and learning with technology, let alone their access to it. Not only do these learner/technology characteristics have implications for instructional design—including instructions, navigational aides, page designs—they also have implications for learner support before *and* during the educational process.

Both Project CONNECT and Alcanza noted that clientele with limited language skills needed additional technological help. Alcanza discovered that, without dedicated personnel available in the food processing plants to help learners with computers, the computers were not used. Individual assistance was also a need in the pilot testing of the modules of Project CONNECT, again for those with limited language skills. The evaluators suggested that this finding needs further study, but intimated that, for this particular population, the learners should use the educational materials within the context of a lab or classroom where assistance is available. Alcanza's experience provides additional support for this suggestion. The considerable and successful computer use of one of their partners, the United Migrant Opportunity Services offices, where educators were available for motivation and assistance, stands in sharp contrast to the initial low plant use of computers in the absence of help.

Despite the fact that students were entering an information technology degree program, the Montana Consortium not only provided the Personal Service Advisor but also required learners to attend an orientation to asynchronous learning. This orientation to learning online, including use of the e-library, was provided in addition to the continual technical support and troubleshooting available throughout the semester. After evaluating the first two cohorts, it was discovered that the orientation and technical assistance were having a positive impact well into the students' first web-based class, which is a critical time in the retention of distance learners.

While not a requirement for all learners to pursue, the Virtual Plaza portal of the HETS consortium provided a link to a module entitled "Learning Effectively Online." This module, offered in both English and Spanish, focuses on the basic elements of learning online, the tools used for synchronous and asynchronous teaching and learning, as well as a self-assessment component.

Ongoing support for distance learners is essential if they are going to achieve success; this is particularly true for special populations who may also bring limited language skills, academic readiness, and technology experience to the online environment. The projects discussed here have not only recognized these needs, but in many cases successfully designed and delivered solutions that help ensure success for special populations among distance learners.

Provision of Faculty Support

In setting our sights on providing and improving access to technology for special populations, however, it may be all too easy to neglect the other important part of the equation—faculty. Faculty development and support presents another ongoing challenge to those delivering technology-based education and training. While little was said about the need for faculty development relevant to culturally appropriate instructional design, teaching diverse audiences, and making technology-based education accessible for those differently-abled, two projects did address the critical faculty component.

The HETS Virtual Plaza, for example, provides on-desk, on-demand faculty support. The Plaza provides a variety of resources, including instructional design support pages and links to many online resources to enhance course design. An online faculty forum provides peer support and discussion. Weekly communiqués of interest to those teaching online are also sent to facilitate communication among and between faculty members in partner institutions. Lastly, HETS offers face-to-face workshops on teaching online, in both Spanish and English.

The evaluator of the Montana Consortium informational technology degree made specific recommendations related to faculty support. Students generally found faculty to be helpful and flexible, perhaps due to the early addition of a full-time distance education coordinator to make the transition from face-to-face to technology-based instruction smoother. Even with this support, the evaluator suggested additional faculty development. Specifically, faculty needed to better understand adult development and learning, and they need access to a part-time adult educator or curriculum development specialist to enhance course design.

Consortia Arrangements to Expand the Possibility, Reach, and Resources

"It takes a village to raise a child" is a wonderful African proverb that says it all. In all cases, pooled resources created a greater impact than one organization alone could accomplish. Three key facets of the successful partnership emerge—the need for a dynamic definition of the partners and consortium, partnerships based on a shared mission or shared audience of emphasis, and early and frequent communication among and between partners.

DYNAMIC PARTNERSHIPS

Alcanza, with its focus on the education of migrant families, serves as an example of growing dynamic partnership. Initially, the University of Wisconsin System project had two key partners—the Midwest Food Processing Association (MWFPA) that employs many migrant laborers and the United Migrant Opportunity Services, in addition to four of its 27 institutions. Soon, a job center located close to a major hub of migrant laborer activities joined the project based on a shared interest in serving migrant families. A small literacy council serving a diverse population, including families employed by one of the MWFPA plants, became aware of Alcanza's work with migrant families. As both organizations served similar populations and had the shared goal of education for personal and professional growth, the literacy council became a partner. The Department of Public Instruction joined as an informal partner with its interest in and mandate to serve the children of migrant workers. School districts with a growing number of Spanish speaking students and migrant families became aware of the computer-based educational tools and piggybacked on the use of these tools, expanding Alcanza's reach.

The Montana Consortium is an example of building partnerships based on past partnering relationships. Rocky Mountain College, Little Big Horn College, and Fort Peck Community College had worked together on past inter-institutional arrangements. However, as they soon discovered, developing interest in other schools and colleges was reasonably easy given a shared desire to ensure access to baccalaureate degrees to those who did not have ready access. Stone Child College, Chief Dull Knife College, and Miles Community College soon joined the consortium. Other regional schools and colleges also expressed interest, but changes in administration within one of the key partners has led to less enthusiasm for collaborative programs and, thus, lost opportunities.

Partners were lost. Change in one or more partners is one of the many challenges. In the case of Alcanza, several food-processing plants were sold, requiring the project director to build relationships once again towards the redevelopment of a partner relationship.

POOLING RESOURCES FOR MAXIMUM MISSION IMPACT

Resources come in many forms and at many times during the life of a program or project. Some partners are active in the initial phases of a project, pooling assets to accomplish a mission. The HETS consortium provides a vivid example. The consortium made the decision to place a major emphasis on the development of online programs through inter-institutional collaboration and based on existing unique online educational offerings. Unique offerings were those that "... represented professional and educational opportunities for Hispanic learners leading to the development of Hispanic communities and with the potential to bring about a Hispanic, multicultural, or bilingual focus" (Hernandez 2003, 7). Based on the analysis of existing offerings by the partners, cluster subgroupings of partners were established for potential inter-institutional collaboration and to help each collaborator meet their mission of serving Hispanic learners by providing greater access to education through technology.

Three different interests came together in the University of Iowa partnership with its focus on providing training for certified nursing assistants (CNA). One set of partners, community colleges, brought education and training resources and a mission to provide the 75-hour nursing assistant certification program. Long-term care facilities, while active in the initial phases of the project in terms of service on instructional design teams, played a unique role in the latter phases of the project, providing sites for aspiring CNA candidates to learn and practice application of their new knowledge. Regulatory and advocacy organizations brought energy, expertise, and political savvy throughout.

Legislative mandates also create partnerships. The Javits–Wagner––O'Day (JWOD) Program creates jobs and training opportunities for people who are blind or who have other severe disabilities, empowering them to lead more productive and independent lives. Its primary means of doing so is by requiring government agencies to purchase selected products and services from nonprofit organizations employing such individuals. The Call Center Training program of the National Telecommuting Institute, Inc. project began with three key partners: Task Force on Employment of Adults with Disabilities, the New York State Vocational Rehabilitation Agency, and Willow CNS, a provider of virtual contact center services and solutions. Two key groups interested in the full implementation of the JWOD program have since joined the partnership based on shared missions—NIB (National Industries for the Blind) and NISH (Creating Employment Opportunities for People with Severe Disabilities).

COMMUNICATION IS VITAL

Like so many distance education projects, one discovery by these projects was the importance of communication. Many used technology to maintain this communication link. Alcanza used both face-to-face and e-mail for communications among the many partners. Geographic proximity made face-to-face contact possible for this and several other projects. Project CONNECT increased their partner communication through the life of the project to gain consensus, maintain focus, sustain progress through ongoing email, two conference calls per month and four meetings face-to-face per year. The HETS consortium recognized the need for communications and a portion of the Virtual Plaza was dedicated to academic collaboration in order to foster inter-institutional communications. Requests for proposals and other information of importance were posted in this area encouraging partners to maintain contact with this dedicated section of the portal.

As HETS points out in their report, partnerships take time and energy to establish and maintain. In recognition of the importance of partnerships and the demands of partner development, HETS assigned one individual to partner recruitment and development as well as fund raising for the partners' activities. Given the large number of partners and the reliance on these partners for both online courses and mentors for Hispanic students, the money and time seem well-invested.

Partnerships are dynamic and partners may play different roles and have different levels of activity depending on the phase of the project. Pooling resources to accomplish a variety of missions enables greater effectiveness and less duplication in times of limited resources for all. Throughout, communications must be maintained in order to sustain the partnerships, and time and effort is needed to advance and expand the partnerships over time. And strong partnerships with a past record of accomplishment can be successfully leveraged for additional funding as demonstrated by most projects reviewed.

FUTURE DIRECTIONS: ACTION STEPS FOR ACCESS AND SUCCESS

Both access and success need to be addressed as we consider ethnically diverse, language minorities, and differently-abled populations. These special populations need additional considerations but few, if any, major changes. Whatever changes seem indicated are changes that would benefit all learners.

The challenges we face in providing both access to and success in education and training are not new. Distance education, with its roots in correspondence education, has wrestled with these same challenges over its more than 150-year history in the United States. Technology has enabled us to respond in new ways to the old challenges.

Our reach is greater but, as there were individuals beyond the reach of the penny post and later telephones for audio conferencing, not everyone has access to computers with the necessary connectivity, especially those who are living in rural areas or are low income (Bell and Reddy 2004, Pew 2001). Access is still an issue for those differently-abled, for even with robust computers and connectivity, websites may be inaccessible for them. Language skills, or lack thereof, may add another layer of inaccessibility.

Success remains a challenge as well. The limited dollars for distance education programs most often find their way to the purchase of technologies and infrastructures. Sadly, learner support as part of that infrastructure is often given short shrift. This is especially true in adult programs where accessibility, computer, technology-based learning, and language skills are assumed.

The U.S. Department of Education's Learning Anytime Anyplace Program (LAAP) has given practitioners a ready checklist of areas to consider when providing education and training to ethnically diverse and differently-abled populations. These include the importance of the following:

- Support for the technological infrastructure;

- Inclusive instructional designs that are not only culturally appropriate, but also accessible for differently-abled or those for whom English is not their first language;

- Learner support including preparatory educational experiences to help learners learn at a distance, learn with technology, and learn in adulthood;

- Technology support to ensure both faculty and learners are able to function in the environment and have ready help when needed;

- Faculty support for teaching with technology and the design of instruction.

We need more research to further document the need for supporting technology, faculty, and learners, and more critically, research towards the end of determining which support "solutions" prove most effective for which audience and under what circumstances.

Teaching and learning with technology is expensive and there is an economy of scale that can be achieved through partnerships (Gibson 1998). Partnerships take time, energy, communications, a willingness to work across boundaries, and the ability to discard past territorialism towards providing access to and success in education for all. While not easy, there are models that have proven successful and a body of research that needs to be re-examined in light of new times, new tools, and new contexts. These partnerships can be leveraged to enhance funding of these efforts, leading to a greater ability of all partners to meet their missions.

It has been said that, "Educational attainment is a critical determinant of employment and future economic well-being [and that] ... The racial and ethnic context of disparities in educational attainment will have to be addressed by education policy makers" (USDA 2003, para. 7). Policy makers must understand the social, psychological, and economic impact of education—education that we can offer at a distance to local communities. Looming shortages of health care workers, the growing need for technologically savvy workers in rural America, and the importance of an educated citizenry able to compete in the global economy cannot be overstated. The LAAP technology-based projects have begun to address these and many other challenges facing geographic and professional communities of practice.

Warschauer would also encourage us to consider technology for social inclusion. Social inclusion and exclusion, concepts prominent in European discourse, refer to:

the extent that individuals, families, and communities are able to fully participate in society and control their own destinies, taking into account a variety of factors related to economic resources, employment, health, education, housing, recreation, culture, and civic engagement. (Warschauer 2002, para. 27)

He argues that what is truly important is not simply access to computer technology and a line to the Internet, but people's ability to "make use of the device and line to engage in *meaningful social practices*" [emphasis in original] (Warschauer 2002, para. 32). This position further illustrates the necessity to build upon the progress of these projects in creating viable distance education programs and support for special populations.

Chapter Seven

No Time to Spare: Technology Assisted Professional Development

by Darcy W. Hardy

OVERVIEW

In this chapter we examine the emergence of online professional development programs available to K–12 and college/university educators, as well as what makes these programs successful. Educators today spend a great deal of time collecting and analyzing data for reports that must be provided annually, monthly, and sometimes weekly. The amount of time available to attend all-day professional development workshops has diminished significantly, yet these workshops are critical for teachers and faculty to keep up with an ever-changing world.

In an effort to define what makes online professional development successful, this chapter will highlight several innovative LAAP-funded projects delivered as hybrid courses (a mix of face-to-face and online instruction) or fully online workshops and programs. Some have been designed for traditional, face-to-face instructors, while others target educators teaching online. All are well-planned, comprehensive projects containing creative techniques used to build communities of educators. While face-to-face workshops end after a day or two, online professional development programs provide an avenue for continuing discussion.

THE NEED FOR ONLINE PROFESSIONAL DEVELOPMENT

In *Goals 2000: Educate America Act,* the Department of Education stated that "professional development serves as the bridge between where prospective and experienced educators are now and where they will need to be to meet the new challenges of guiding all students in achieving higher standards of learning and development."

The explosion of the Internet and of Web-based courses has led to a rapid change in how professional development programs are delivered. Five years ago, most professional development was delivered entirely face-to-face. We were just starting to really understand the benefits of delivering courses and programs for academic credit. Today, all types of programs are appearing online. Why have these programs emerged?

As revealed in conversations with FIPSE/LAAP project directors, the primary reasons for developing online professional development programs relate to time and convenience. Most of these projects have been developed for educators who need professional development but find it difficult to be away from the classroom for full days at a time, particularly K–12 teachers. In some cases substitute teachers do not do their job well, which can cause more work for the teacher upon return to the classroom. Faculty at colleges and universities are commonly involved in committee work, research, and service. Making time for professional development during the week is not a high priority, and many do not wish to have their weekends disrupted by attending face-to-face workshops on campus. Providing professional development online (where educators can access content 24 hours a day, seven days a week) gives instructors control of their time. All of the project directors interviewed felt strongly that by placing their programs online, the overall attitude of participants improved significantly.

Another reason for placing professional development online is the need for consistency of message. When face-to-face workshops are delivered to multiple audiences, the experiences can vary depending upon who is facilitating the workshop and how the content is presented. In an online program, the basic content is created once. Although interactions will differ for each group of participants, administrators can be assured that the core content is consistent. A consistent message ensures that all participants are receiving the same information, therefore making it easier to provide evidence of compliance.

A number of project directors described a need for developing communities of practitioners who are geographically isolated, either in groups or alone. Research indicates that most workshop participants leave, go back to work, and simply pick up where they left off. Face-to-face workshops seem to have the advantage of bringing people together in one place, but they lack a way to help those people sustain relationships with other participants. Until fairly recently (within the past seven years), placing materials online would not necessarily help solve this problem. However, chat rooms and discussion forums are now a viable means to encourage the development of online communities where participants can continue their discussions and consult with each other as issues arise.

Limited resources present another reason for moving professional development programs online. All levels of education have dealt with extensive budget cuts, yet the need to keep teachers and faculty abreast of new techniques and changes in processes still exists. Online workshops eliminate the need for travel, as well as the need to provide a substitute teacher in the case of K–12 educators. Further, the idea of developing a workshop once then delivering it to many participants can save a school district thousands of dollars in workshop expenses, especially if the district is large and workshops must be presented several times in order to accommodate all staff.

Although each organization involved in providing professional development to staff can have unique needs for placing programs online, the reasons listed above—time, convenience, consistency, building communities, and limited resources—seem common among the FIPSE/LAAP projects discussed here, as well as within the research reviewed.

Evolving Practice: Successful Models

This section provides a summary of each project and a look at the innovative techniques utilized to design and deliver online PD.

Achieving Accountability: Standards-Based Teacher Professional Development, Fordham University

This project was based on an "enormous need for effective, high-quality professional development programs to prepare new and existing teachers to design and deliver standards-based instructional programs." Fordham University worked with both academic and corporate partners to develop "Anytime Anywhere Learning Professional Development School (AALPDS)," an online curriculum that helps teachers learn to design and develop instruction that will produce objective measurable gains in student achievement. Courses were developed in several areas at the K–2, grade 3–5, and grade 6–8 levels. As a result of this project, Fordham University decided to support and expand the university's Regional Educational Technology Center (RETC), which now oversees the AALPDS.

Virtual Instructional Designer (VID): An Internet-based Faculty Development Tool for Designing Online Instruction, Indiana State University

Indiana University, Vincennes University, and Ivy Tech State College created a partnership called DegreeLink in order to address the low rate of Indiana residents aged 22 and older who have earned associate or bachelor degrees. The partnership focused on developing and delivering anytime, anywhere online courses and programs that lead to the completion of a degree. Faculty required instruction on the effective design of online courses in order to successfully deliver these programs. The challenge for the partnership was to create a "just-in-time" tool rich in media and resources to help faculty transform traditional courses to asynchronous online courses. The VID includes a Faculty Needs and Skills Survey that generates a customized learning plan that makes it easy for a professor to jump into the site and get the information necessary to create an effective online course.

The Crossroads Online Institute, Georgetown University

The Crossroads Online Institute was created to guide national cohorts of faculty "through a process of reflection and redesign of their courses for technology-enhanced learning environments." The project addressed three challenges in effective online professional development: (1) a shortage of excellent faculty development models, (2) a lack of discussion in most curriculum resources about the transformation of teaching and learning, and (3) the misunderstandings about hybrid teaching and technology innovations. The core element of the Institute is a 10-week online workshop that addresses these challenges as faculty develop modules that utilize technology-enhanced pedagogies and student assessment techniques. A blog approach is used throughout the workshop so that participants can share their thoughts and ideas about each segment of the workshop. Although the workshop is delivered online to a national audience, faculty are encouraged to sign up in pairs so that face-to-face collaboration can take place as well. The culmination of the workshop is the development of an online "poster" where participants summarize their experience as it relates to the courses they teach.

CREOLE—Creating Optimum Learning Environments, Florida Community College at Jacksonville

The CREOLE project used online professional development as a way to facilitate faculty expertise in both the classroom and online. Four modules were developed: Applying Teaching/Learning Research, Applying Motivation Research, Revising Traditional Lecture-based Courses to Incorporate the Internet, and Developing Interactive Web-based Courses. Each module consists of several chapters written by a variety of authors. Although FCCJ coordinated the project and developed some of the content, CREOLE also involves authors from universities and consulting organizations. CREOLE Module Four, *Developing Interactive Web-based Courses,* has been offered for professional development at FCCJ and for postgraduate credit at the University of Utah. Because the goal of the project was to address an international audience, it was developed independently of any specific course management system. The content is largely text-based and can easily be embedded in the course management system of choice.

Competency Assessment in Distributed Education (CADE), Association of Jesuit Colleges and Universities

The goals of this project were to develop and evaluate a distance assessment model using evidence-based design to identify and represent student competencies, and to embed performance and assessment tasks in online courses. The project began as a face-to-face workshop and evolved into an online workshop in order to reach more faculty across several schools. CADE has since evolved further, using both online and hybrid approaches. The online workshops are delivered in eight weeks, while the hybrid workshops are four- to five-week efforts and institution-specific. Faculty leave the workshop with a full design portfolio which serves as the blueprint for a course that focuses on assessing students using parameters of expertise (e.g., novice, graduate, or expert) in a scoring rubric. CADE requires participants to complete an evidence assessment first and then to determine the learning objectives. The evidence analysis helps them determine what the various tasks should be, and then identify the appropriate technology. This "backward" approach, whereby competencies are identified first, followed by evidence that indicates mastery, required student behaviors, and the identification of necessary instructional tasks, helps faculty think strategically about course design.

University of Minnesota School Technology Leadership Initiative (STLI), University of Minnesota Twin Cities

This hybrid K–12 professional development project is "designed to help address the nationwide shortage of school administrators who can effectively facilitate the implementation of technology in schools and school districts."

Fifteen one-credit hour courses (eight online, six on campus, one independent study) were developed to address the International Society for Technology in Education (ISTE) National Educational Technology Standards for Administrators (NETS-A). Students may take all 15 courses and receive a School Technology Leadership graduate certificate from the University of Minnesota, or they may choose to take individual courses (on a space available basis) to meet their needs. Online courses include a customized Flash interface to facilitate online guest speakers. In addition, STLI has created lessons, teaching activities, reviews, decision-making guides, and comparison charts to help teachers and administrators deal with technology issues in schools. Through a partnership with Microsoft, they have developed self-contained electronic lesson plans. The project includes other corporate and educational partners, which makes STLI an outstanding resource for K–12 technology leadership.

Learning to Teach with Technology Studio (LTTS), Indiana University

The LTTS was developed to provide standards-based individualized professional development to in-service teachers, assisting them in the integration of technology in the classroom. With almost 60 online courses in science, mathematics, language arts, and social studies (17 are cross-discipline), LTTS has created a comprehensive catalogue of courses that take a guided problem-solving approach to teaching. All courses follow a common methodology that culminates in a lesson plan that is inquiry-based. The courses are self-paced, and participants may begin at any time. Participants begin with a curriculum problem, receive individual mentoring, and end with a classroom lesson plan. In addition to Indiana University, program partners include PBS TeacherLine, University of Colorado Denver, University of Georgia, Alliant International University, KyEducators, and Kentucky Virtual University.

Professional Development for New Faculty, Riverside Community College

The 4faculty.org project was developed by Riverside Community College as a way to improve the quality of first-time faculty teaching and also to involve adjunct faculty more fully into the campus community. RCC formed a collaborative partnership with eleven other California community colleges due to the dramatic increase in adjunct faculty across the California Community College System. Courses cover basic information from how to develop a syllabus to understanding copyright in a digital world. Although the modules were originally designed for adjunct faculty, today they target all community college faculty. The courses follow the D.R.E.A.M. system, created by Riverside for this project. Lessons include Discover, Read, Explore, Apply and Measure sections, which take the user from introduction through assessment. Because 4faculty.org runs on software independent of an outside course management system, other colleges can easily become partners by adding content that is specific to their colleges. This allows all partners to experience a level of ownership in the project. Feedback from participants has been highly positive and membership now includes 41 California community colleges.

LESSONS LEARNED

Overall, each of the projects described above saw positive outcomes as a result of moving their professional development programs online. Most indicated a greater level of access than they did with face-to-face workshops, and all agreed upon the need to make professional development convenient, particularly for educators. The latter appears to be a driving force for putting content online: convenience. In today's busy society, people have to make choices regarding their time. Making professional development more convenient is a step in the right direction. Convenience was the number one reason cited when project directors were asked why programs were put online.

Lessons about Participants

Faculty participants are a key component to consider when developing professional development programs online (Cooper and Boyd 1998, Cyrs 1997, Gaff 1975). Several project directors spoke about the need to research what will motivate teachers or faculty to participate—before the development of the program begins. Finding out after the fact that there are no incentives for participation can impact the overall success of the program in a critical way. It may be necessary to create incentives for participation if they do not already exist (Gandolfo 1998). In the case of the 4faculty.org project (Riverside Community College), the modules were designed to help adjunct faculty become better instructors. However, by requiring adjuncts to enroll in these modules, colleges can demonstrate compliance with accreditation standards and policies. In addition, according to an independent evaluator of 4faculty, "The majority of faculty (88.4%) said they plan to modify the way they teach their [face to face] course as a result of taking the online course" (personal communication).

Financial incentives also exist, although not all are related to providing stipends to participants. For example, if each faculty member in the 4faculty program retains just one student as a result of what they learned, the full time equivalent funding (at $3,500/FTE) cumulatively for the colleges involved is increased by approximately $532,000 if growth caps are not in place.

The CREOLE project has benefitted from a financial stipend program for participation in the Online Professor Certificate Program (of which CREOLE is a part). The program is optional, but faculty are provided with a $500 stipend as an incentive for completing the program, and a $500 award is provided to the academic department of full-time faculty completers. Full-time faculty are often in need of materials or other professional development opportunities that are not annually budgeted. Professional development providers should continue to explore this option; however, if the award is for the particular faculty member involved in the program, this must be clear to the department receiving the award. If not, the funds may fall into the "black hole" of budgets and the faculty members may never see any benefit. Plans are to deliver the entire CREOLE program on its own and provide three doctoral credits for completers. Community colleges that employ a large number of adjunct faculty can reap multiple benefits when this type of incentive is employed. All faculty will improve their online teaching capabilities and adjunct faculty can move closer toward completion of a terminal degree.

Participants in the programs reviewed are K–12 teachers, pre-service teachers, and higher education instructors and professors. Like most working adults, they all have very busy schedules and sometimes fall behind in an online course or program. Several projects reported that explicit prompts proved to be helpful as participants completed assignments or projects. The Crossroads Online Institute found that prompts assist participants in their understanding of the process of creating their online posters and in adhering to the provided timelines. Prompts or reminders can be delivered via email, threads in a discussion forum, or as announcements on a portal. Completion rates for assignments increased when prompts were included, and the Institute plans to implement prompts for other course assignments in the future.

Clearly, when working with teachers and professors, there will be generational differences with regard to technology. While some participants in their 50s and 60s (or older) have embraced technology, many have not. The same holds true for younger participants, although it is likely to be the reverse. Teachers and faculty will have varied levels of comfort using the Internet and other computer technologies. It is important to recognize these differences when considering online professional development (Baumgardner 2000). The AALPDS project recognized the generational differences of their audience in technological skills, learning styles, and in professional development expectations. In addition to the frequent review of formative assessment instruments, AALPDS provides toll-free technical assistance and online help, and facilitates communication among local teachers, technology coordinators, and focus groups. Partnering computer- and web-literate participants with those who are less comfortable with technology can also help to bridge the gap. Specific instructions on how to navigate the professional development site or the course are important and assumptions should never be made that instructions are not necessary. Links to free online tutorials that have been reviewed by the project organizers may also be helpful.

Lessons about Developing Content

The lesson of separating course development from course production is one that has been learned by many online educators. Authors or content experts should focus on the objectives of the course or module, the development of the content, the instructional strategies that will be used, the level of interaction, and the methods for assessment. They should not be asked to produce the course as well. Staff whose skill sets include HTML, graphics design, and multimedia are best positioned to take content that has been developed by the author and make it "come alive" in the online environment. Too often it is assumed that those who develop content will be able to produce the course as well. When that happens, modules and courses can become a series of PowerPoint slides or Word documents with very little interaction and traditional assessment measures which are inappropriate for the online environment. While this is primarily due to a lack of time on the author's part, often the author does not have the skill set required to produce the course alone. Keeping these functions separate will greatly improve the quality of the course.

The Anytime Anywhere Learning Professional Development School (AALPDS) developed through Fordham University provides an excellent example of this separation. Fordham and the North Carolina Partnership for Excellence were responsible for developing content for the AALPDS courses. The third partner in the project, Classroom Connect, employs a staff of instructional designers, graphic artists, and multimedia developers. Classroom Connect provided production support for the project, thus allowing the academic partners to focus on pedagogy and content accuracy.

The use of diverse instructional strategies to target various learning styles and to maintain interest is highly recommended, particularly for busy working adults. The Learning to Teach with Technology Studio Project (Indiana University) in using a guided problem-solving approach, has implemented Macromedia Flash animations in two of their courses that present the problem and engage the participant. This approach has proven to maintain participant interest and there are plans to include this element in all courses in the future. They have also experimented with a conversational electronic agent. The agent, Karen, gives an introduction to the course the first time a participant logs in, provides direct instruction and information, and can even provide encouragement.

The School Technology Leadership Initiative (University of Minnesota) implements a variety of instructional strategies. Although the Initiative is considered a leadership program, and not a technology skills training program, innovative uses of technology are regularly incorporated in the project. Participants use office software and online collaboration spaces, as well as course management systems. Online survey and assessment tools, corporate mind-mapping and e-learning software are also utilized. Participants create video-accompanied presentations and participate in online videoconferencing and guest speaker sessions. They also implement a database-driven teacher appraisal system. Efforts are made for participants to gain hands-on experience with district-level data warehouse systems, formative assessment management systems, and student response systems. Video-based case studies and electronic lesson plans are regularly incorporated into the instruction and program participants are exposed to cutting-edge tools such as the Gartner/CoSN Total Cost of Ownership Tool, the IBM Change Toolkit, and others. The Institute provides a technology-rich learning experience for school leaders, and one that can serve as an example for other projects in the future.

Interaction is a key component to keeping participants engaged in any online program. The use of web logs, or blogs, has proved to be a powerful interactive element for some of the projects. Blogs allow participants to write about their thoughts and ideas in an unstructured environment. For example, in the Crossroads Online Institute (Georgetown University) model, discussions and seminar materials are contained within a blog and documentation of new learning activities is captured in an online "poster."

The poster outlines a quick glimpse of the participant's activity plan and allows other participants to view the process. After the participants implement the new activities and document outcomes, they meet again in the blog for "Evidence Week" to reflect on the implementation. The blog discussions are facilitated by past participants and include student evidence gathered from the implementation, and reviews and comments by colleagues to help determine if changes are necessary. The poster and blogs also functioned as tools for a community of learners working in a similar environment. As one Crossroads participant noted, "By looking at previous work, we could see a connection to what we were doing. By reading the blogs and seeing the posters, I had a better sense of my own place in this [workshop]."

The Virtual Instructional Designer (VID) project, led by Indiana State University, took the approach of "just-in-time" training to keep participants involved. In the VID, every lesson allows the participants to apply their own teaching materials and styles to the designated outcomes. Participants can see immediate results as they build timed online quizzes, manage email, create their own learning communities, apply audio and video to their courses, build web pages with HTML, and transform documents to PDF files—all with pedagogical assistance. And because the VID itself is asynchronous, it is scalable and able to meet faculty demand. The success of an online program also brings the challenge of how to grow the program while sustaining quality. The VID has addressed these issues and effectively scaled the program. Faculty leave the program with enhancements to their existing online or face-to-face course or a complete course, whichever option meets their need.

Another project, the Jesuit Distance Education Network (JesuitNET) Model for Competency-Based Distance Assessment (CADE) provides participants with the opportunity to develop a design portfolio for their online course. The faculty receive instruction that helps them describe their design thoughts for the course while working with an instructional technology staff member to take those thoughts and develop multimedia elements. The CADE program involves a process that uses "evidence-centered design to identify and assess student competencies, and cognitive apprenticeship to promote mastery of higher-level thinking skills." Instructors are able to create scoring rubrics that are cognitive in nature and based on novice, graduate, or expert ratings. Leaving the workshop with a portfolio that will ultimately lead to an instructionally sound online course helps faculty stay focused throughout the process. As stated previously, this project also addresses the need to allow faculty to do what they do best—develop instructional content—while skilled staff develop the technological aspects of the course.

All of the projects that included discussion forums highly recommend the use of a qualified facilitator. The AALPDS uses only experienced online instructors who interact both individually and collectively with participants during each course. Several projects began without a facilitator in the discussion forums and found that participation was very low. A trained facilitator can prompt discussions, raise provocative issues, and keep the conversation flowing. The CREOLE project (Florida Community College) found that good facilitators ensured a high level of participation in the discussion forums, chat rooms, email, and other interactive course elements.

The first time the course, lesson or module is offered, it will likely be far from perfect. While accepting that fact is a lesson in itself, the bigger lesson is to design the program for easy content revision and additions. It is important to have an infrastructure that allows program developers to make corrections easily. When course management systems are used for professional development programs, content should not be so closely tied into the system that moving it elsewhere or making changes becomes difficult. In addition, the design of the content should be such that revisions or additions do not have to be made in more than one place. For example, if a topic of discussion in an early lesson is referenced again later in the course, linking back to the original content rather than repeating it again will ensure that revisions or additions have to be made once. The 4faculty project chose to build the program independent of any course management system and designed and wrote to Java 2 Enterprise Edition specifications. Because the project would allow for multiple colleges to add content, they needed software that would allow for dynamic content distribution and user-need adaptation or customization.

The Learning to Teach with Technology Studio (LTTS) project started as a group-based program. However, over time the LTTS has moved to individualized instruction and a more self-paced environment. The experience of the LTTS was that although the participants recognized the benefits of community interaction, their schedules kept them from being fully engaged. Moving to a self-paced model has allowed LTTS to add a one-on-one mentoring element for each teacher that, while different from community discussions, provided the necessary level of interaction for this audience. On the other hand, the Crossroad Online Institute (Georgetown University) has observed that participants enjoy being able to see each other's work and making comments to better build community. The project utilizes electronic "posters" as part of the course modules. Participants create posters and post them online, thus providing other participants the opportunity to share comments in the discussion forum about each one.

It's easy to include too much content in the online environment. Working with authors who are writing content for an online course is similar to working with authors who are writing a book. There may be so much information that the author wishes to convey that it's difficult to draw closure. A solid outline of required content elements (developed by the project team) can help guide the author. Participants in the CREOLE project found that some chapters were too long to complete in the timeframe provided and adjustments had to be made. When adjustments are not made, word travels fast among potential new participants. Again, due to the very busy schedules of teachers and faculty, providers of professional development must adhere to the timelines promised. While there will always be additional content that would be beneficial to the program, decisions about how much content to include must be made early in the process. If too much content is placed in the course, participants will become frustrated with being unable to complete the course in the time anticipated.

Sometimes professional development programs are built for community purposes. In other words, the program will be open to the public so that other organizations may use it and make changes that fit their own purposes. If a program is developed for this reason, developers of the Virtual Instructional Designer recommend that you consider designing for *Open Source*. This will allow other institutions to download your source code and customize it for their own institution. The basic idea behind the Open Source movement is very simple: When programmers can read, modify, and redistribute the source code for a piece of software or an online program, the software or program evolves. For the purposes of professional development, creating projects that adhere to the open source concept will extend the life of the program well beyond the original developer's audience. Of course, when programs are developed strictly for financial revenue, any plans to follow the open source standards must be agreed upon by all parties involved.

Professional development for educators should be research- based and/or standards-based as much as possible. The LTTS program includes specific language regarding the use of national, state, and local standards in all new courses. Their decision to include such language was "based on the emerging emphasis on aligning all teaching activities to curriculum standards." While opinions and observations from developers are appreciated, participants need to be certain that the content they are receiving is factual and based on valid research and theories. For K–12 teachers, standards are a driving force in their curriculum and instructional deliveries. Professional development programs that address those standards in a deliberate manner will be more highly attended than programs that do not.

Lessons about Delivery

Several of the programs described above found a hybrid approach (part on-line and part face-to-face) to be an excellent model for professional development. For one project, this allowed all of the teachers to work together on-line, and then subgroups of teachers from each participating campus could address campus-specific issues in a face-to-face setting. The professional development program can even be designed primarily for online use but provide suggested group projects for those who are participating as a cohort. Hybrid programs are also appropriate when a large number of participants are uncomfortable with technology and the Internet. For example, the AALPDS staff has encouraged school districts with concerns about fully online programs to use the AALPDS online courses to complement their face-to-face professional development. As a result of engaging several new partners and by earning contracts from the NYC Department of Education, the AALPDS project has now evolved to include both fully online and hybrid courses. Project staff see the hybrid model as a way to help sustain the AALPDS.

The CADE program began with face-to-face workshops—even though an online program was the final goal. It is not uncommon for course and program developers to feel that it is necessary to conduct a workshop face-to-face before building it online. However, the JesuitNET project director highly recommends against that process, citing wasted time and the forced redesign of the workshop that should have been designed for the online environment from the beginning. The lesson learned is not to be afraid to move the professional development program directly online if that is the final goal.

Although it is much easier to go online today than it was when some of these projects began in 1999, there are still access issues. Project directors recommend that when designing online professional development, be aware that many K–12 teachers will be accessing the program from a school computer. These computers may be older, with connection speeds as low as 28.8K, and the school may have blocked some plug-ins necessary for multimedia. If the professional development program is being designed for a specific school or school district, research should be conducted to determine if the planned delivery of the program will be possible.

Lessons about Support

Marketing materials as simple as posters or as complex as brochures can be used to alert participants of the benefits of a program. Several of the projects discussed above realized only after the online course or program was developed that they had no method for getting the word out to potential participants. The Learning to Teach with Technology Studio staff sees marketing as their biggest issue because they are not marketing people-based services. Marketing funds were not included in the LTTS project; however, staff are now seeking other sources to assist their efforts. They recommend that consultations with communication and marketing specialists take place prior to putting a program online. For-profit organizations generally apply large marketing budgets to their products, which means that non-profit programs are overshadowed by corporate exhibit booths and marketing materials. Although non-profits are not seeking revenue, they are usually seeking enough participation to keep the online program operational. Budgeting (at least) for exhibit booths at educational conferences should be considered.

There does not appear to be enough support and recognition for teachers participating in K–12 professional development. This is not to say that the professional development is unappreciated. However, several of the projects noted that administrators must be informed about the amount of time teachers will spend in the online professional development program. When the professional development program is conducted face-to-face, administrators can clearly see how much time is spent in a workshop. In an online program, the expected time for participation or completion should be included in all materials that administrators review.

Lessons about Maintaining and Sustaining Programs

The projects discussed suggest that plans and budgeting for maintenance and program update costs be developed ahead of time. Riverside Community College's 4faculty.org project may have to close the project if funding is not secured this year. Although member schools contribute to the project, it is not enough to sustain the operation. In addition, authors and production staff who will be responsible for updates to content should be identified, along with a timeframe for expected updates.

Most online programs calculate development costs, some of which are based on grants such as FIPSE or LAAP grants. Regardless of who provides initial funding for a program—internal or external—the providers must build a financial model for sustaining the project after the funding cycle is complete.

FUTURE DIRECTIONS

It is obvious that online courses are a convenient method of delivering professional development programs. Busy schedules, unpredictable life experiences, and family obligations all play a part in how and why individuals appreciate the flexibility of this format. All of the projects identified in this chapter (and many that were not) plan to continue and even expand their online offerings. It is important for developers and providers of online professional development programs to be aware of the benefits as well as the challenges they may face.

Thomas Duffy, with the Learning to Teach with Technology Studio project, predicts that online learning in general will lead increasingly to life-long learning. Working professionals will continue to need short courses and discussion around the content of those courses, while meeting the demands of busy schedules. He stated:

> Right now people are either focusing on community or on learning objects—but the need is to combine them so that we have community discussion center around the objects as they are relevant to individuals. Additionally, there could be expert commentary—discussion on current events relevant to the area and a variety of other community resources. (personal communication, April 14, 2005)

As discussions continue regarding the need to place professional development courses and programs online, those who are responsible for funding these initiatives should remember the many benefits of online delivery. According to the projects reviewed in this chapter, as well as current research, online professional development:

- Is flexible
- Is convenient
- Is adaptable to individual differences, customization
- Creates a learning community—which can be local, national, or global

- Helps participants master technology
- Provides more choices than are available in a face-to-face workshop
- Can have specific goals
- Provides regular ongoing contact with colleagues
- Can provide regular support from an online facilitator
- Removes geographic distance
- Provides for time to reflect on and prepare assignments and postings
- Leads to thoughtful discussion
- Can be cost effective
- Allows those who are usually quiet an opportunity to participate

There are also, however, challenges that must be addressed when moving a professional development program online. Many of these challenges can be overcome with awareness and thoughtful planning. As online education becomes more and more accepted, the possibility exists that these challenges will get overlooked in planning processes. If that happens, the challenges themselves can lead to the demise of the program shortly after it is introduced.

Before getting swept into the trend of developing these online programs, the same individuals responsible for providing funding must be made aware of these challenges:

- A need for self-discipline among participants (even within cohorts)
- The lack of spontaneous conversation
- A need for participants to be resourceful
- Acknowledgment that much of the online program may rely on independent learning
- Awareness that some participants have difficulty accessing the Internet
- Reliability of local networks, particularly in public schools, is varied
- Writing is usually the sole source of communication
- Technology issues can hamper success of the program
- Participants may not be used to the lack of immediate feedback

- In most cases, little or no personal contact

When challenges such as those presented above become "make or break" issues, one solution may be to develop a hybrid approach. Programs that target specific localized audiences can plan for a certain level of face-to-face instruction that is developed to be part of the program—as opposed to leaving it up to the locations to design this on their own. This face-to-face instruction could include exercises that assist with the bonding of the cohort and reinforce the community-building aspect of the program. However, target audiences must be carefully analyzed prior to building a hybrid program or course. Some audiences do not require a hybrid approach, or it may not be geographically possible to conduct this type of delivery. However, a program that includes a complete online curriculum, as well as one that provides specific instruction for a hybrid, will likely be favored as these programs expand. Such comprehensive programs will allow those who are not involved in a cohort to complete the program independently, while those who desire a hybrid approach can be accommodated as well.

The future will also bring new types of learners into the professional development world. Young people today who are considered Millennials (those born after 1982), or the Net Generation, will soon be participants in professional development programs. This new generation of learners will have very different expectations of how online programs should be delivered. Communication models that include Instant Messaging (IM), downloading content to Personal Data Accessories (PDAs), and interactive content will be expected. Perhaps these issues are not a primary concern today, but as the Millennials mature into adulthood, programs need to be prepared to meet new expectations.

The future of online professional development seems clear as the busy schedules of working adults are likely to increase, not decrease. Having professional development programs available online will provide adults with convenient avenues for career mobility, the opportunity to enhance their current methodologies, and an opportunity for those in higher education to improve the overall teaching and learning experience.

CONCLUSION:
HARNESSING THE POWER OF INNOVATIVE TECHNOLOGY IN HIGHER EDUCATION

by Kathleen P. King and Susan C. Biro

OVERVIEW

Throughout the pages of this book we have sought to convey some of the advances, innovations, and challenges that distance education brings to educational pursuits. The experiences of the programs described herein are not always smooth successes. Instead, like the near catastrophes we have with our own desktop and laptop computers whenever deadlines loom, these distance education programs experience the complications, uncertainties—and, yes, victories of technology.

Innovative technology in higher education provides the opportunity to identify needs among our communities and learners, envision solutions, and identify the technology, resources, partnerships, and programs to make it happen. In the process, we learn that the pathway is not linear, and that as we are learning about technology along the way, we are also learning about our learners, our organizations, and *ourselves*. Working with innovative technologies to provide distance education in higher education is a dynamic and intensive process of envisioning, shaping, and discovering the future of teaching and learning and technology all at once.

THE GOOD NEWS AND THE BAD NEWS

Just how intense this experience can be was made especially vivid when my (Kathy's) first nation-wide distance education project was about to go live in 2001. Even though I am a gadget-loving, pull-it-apart techie, I was pleased that my university was in New York City and that the partner corporation was hosting the technology infrastructure from the west coast. Until ... two days before we went live, the west coast was hit by an earthquake, and, of course, it hit our web servers. Thankfully (!), though, we had been through the Code Red worm (computer virus) during that summer and the company had established a mirror website further up the coast; within about 24 hours most of the system was live. So I was able to breathe again, for the next 12 hours at least. The east coast—yes, New York City, of course—was hit by a snow blizzard and many in our pilot class of teachers relied on computers in their (New York City) schools to connect to the Internet. As I stood watching snow plows push through the streets, I realized that distance education was not eliminating my logistical problems by any means; instead, I was now susceptible to geographical conditions across the entire country. The good news that day was that we learned teachers in New York City found a way to engage in online professional development, even during a snow day!

LESSONS LEARNED AND PATTERNS OF PRACTICE

From a much larger frame we have the vantage point of being able to examine themes of practice and patterns across the topics of this book. While each chapter has provided an in-depth review of its specific topic across several programs, in this chapter we step further back and look for broader patterns. Our perspective is on lessons learned and framing principles for practice, while later in the chapter we provide a few suggestions on what appears to be future directions of distance education.

The themes that we identify in here are: Expecting the Unexpected, Unmasking the Digital Divide, Truth in Advertising about Partnerships, Making People Primary in a Technological Project, Struggling for Support, Hailing Hybrids, Evaluation as a Lifeline, and Challenges of Transformation.

Expecting the Unexpected

Among these distance education projects, unexpected events became the routine. Rather than projects proceeding through project management plans, timelines, and milestones on neat progress courses of advancement, there were dips, peaks, and u-turns. Why is this landscape so unstable? One reason is that distance education involves the fickle gods of technology, where everything that can go wrong, does go wrong. Another is that these projects have many variables of change projecting in multiple directions simultaneously: changes in technology, organizational changes, economic changes, funding and political realignments and reversals, global catastrophes, local, national, and global educational enrollment trends, and the complexities involved in working with many people.

In all, the projects depict amazing accounts of persistence, flexibility, talent, and ingenuity as educators work together to create solutions to master the changing conditions they confront daily in the world of distance education. Whether it is a project that involves placing computers at the workplace, only to discover that employees/students would not use them without support, to the collaborative projects that had to regroup when partners were lost, distance education planners, designers, administrators, and instructors quickly develop the ability to be flexible and create solutions while making it seem like it was the original plan. The excitement of distance education might not be matched in any other field of education!

Unmasking the Digital Divide

The term "digital divide" came into mass awareness in the late 1980s. In the late 1990s, the U.S. government provided several insightful reports on how masses of the population were "Falling through the 'Net'" (NTIA 1995, 1999). Our book likewise adds to this literature by not only providing additional insight into the issues of access in understanding the digital divide (i.e., the HETS project), but also the critical components of technology literacy, because even when people have access and could potentially "plug into" or "sign onto" the Internet and other technologies, what good is it if they do not know how?

Rather than limiting our definition of the digital divide to access, we need to expand it to include issues of technology awareness, understanding, and ability. Is the use and possibility of using technology even on the radar screen for people? Do they understand that technology offers potential solutions to their educational, health care, employment, political, or economic needs? Certainly our society and educational systems have a great distance to go in closing the gap on both of these dimensions of the digital divide. Distance education can provide several ways to assist in achieving this by providing varied levels and combinations of technology use.

Several of the FIPSE projects discussed demonstrate these principles, including the Connecticut Distance Learning Consortium and WECT, each of which showed the power of collaborative learning groups; the HETS projects, which used mentoring among people of color; and the WebAIM project, which educates higher education organizations and faculty in developing websites that are compatible with disability assisting software. Rather than letting technology serve as another barrier, these projects use technology to break down barriers and create new opportunities for access.

Providing Truth in Advertising about Partnerships

Some funded FIPSE comprehensive projects focused on individual institutions, but all the LAAP grants and many of the comprehensive grants provide a substantial body of experience and data about collaborations and partnerships in distance education. Many of the chapters in this book refer to different aspects of these partnerships; indeed, one entire chapter is devoted to partnerships. However, the major theme that comes ringing through each of these discussions is that collaborations and partnerships for distance learning initiatives have both benefits and drawbacks. While they enable organizations to join together to "expand their resources, reach, and possibilities" (as Chère Campbell Gibson says) collaborations are, by definition, comprised of multiple organizations, people, cultures, and processes. Thus, they are inherently complicated and ineloquently put, often "messy."

With all candidness it must be said that "in the best of times" partnerships can accomplish great achievements, advancements, glories, and camaraderie. Likewise "in the worst of times," partnerships can include strife, back biting, fiscal entanglements, and legal battles. Of course, these are both extremes, and it would appear that the usual experience is somewhere in between, and with a mixture of the positive and the negative. Partnerships are based not only on human relationships, but also on organizational relationships and processes, and this creates many levels of complexity.

Making People Primary in a Technology Project

Closely aligned with the previous theme is this one about the primacy of people; however, it is highlighted nonetheless because to people not experienced in directing or coordinating distance education programs, it sometimes appears to be an oxymoron. In various forms the question often arises, "Distance education is all about technology, so why are human relations important?"

In fact, human relations are essential in these projects: from determining the needs for programs, through their design, pilot, delivery, instruction, support, evaluation, redesign, and so forth, it is *people* who should be the focus. Technology is the vehicle to serve the needs of people. When we let technology become the focus, it seems as though the road gets very bumpy. FIPSE funding has always held as a major focus solutions for how to increase access to education, how to increase services, and increase achievement. The role of technology has been to serve these purposes, which are about people; technology is not the end, in and of itself.

The reality of this maxim is that again, distance education projects can be quite complex. This dimension has been discussed in terms of the undergirding relationships of the organizations that develop and deliver the distance learning, the partnerships, and the collaborations. When programs and processes have to be developed and articulated so that they can be communicated and flow one through another, it is about *people* communicating and understanding one other. Technology can be used to accomplish this goal, or it can be a hindrance. When, in fact, did projects learn to hang up the conference call and get on the plan for face-to-face meetings? When do they set aside the bargaining table and revisit values and goals? You will find several examples of these experiences embedded in this book.

Additionally, in an increasingly consumer-oriented learner community, distance education has to be savvy about how to serve the needs of the learners. Many of the FIPSE and LAAP projects in this book demonstrate different flexible models and paradigms that allow for variations of individual or group needs. For example, these models used different technologies, articulation agreements, and course competencies (vs. traditional credit hours) and combinations to provide alternatives for learners based on research-based understanding of their needs and instructionally sound approaches to meet those needs (e.g., JesuitNET, Western Governors, UTMB). The needs of our learners should drive us to discover how technology can be used best.

Struggling for Support

Throughout the distance education projects we can also see a theme of the need for supporting learners. Indeed, today many traditional educational programs are finding increased need for academic support among their learners compared to 10 to 15 years ago (Wirt, Choy, Provasnik, Rooney, Sen, and Tobin 2003). This challenge is even greater when the instructor and learner may be separated by time and space. The distance education projects described and analyzed in this book reveal a wide variety of strategies for providing support for distance learners. However, it is not only the "how" of providing the support, it is also the "what."

When delivering distance education, one also has to keep in mind the technological background and access of the intended audience—students. Bonk and Dennen (1999, 8) caution that "even when all is operational, students may have anxiety about this new form of instruction or exhibit low self-esteem about their technology skills in general." In my experience (Susan's) administering distance education programs for adult and traditional students, I quickly learned what the "how" and "what" of support meant for online students who had little hesitation in communicating their frustrations, concerns, and questions about this environment. The same technology that made it possible for students to engage with one another and their instructors, nearly 24/7 in an asynchronous learning format, also meant that students could (and did) engage the institution in a similar non-stop manner about their needs! It was not unusual for me and our support staff to function as Help Desk technicians, 8 hours a day, the first week of the semester as we handled phone calls, emails, and in-person visits from students who were unsure about when to begin, how to begin, and what to do first. This occurred despite our mailing, emailing, and posting information about all of these details in advance!

For our staff, it was an important lesson in understanding how support infrastructures had to be *planned*, *built*, and *in place* prior to any course going online. From those first rocky starts, though, we became flexible and creative in building support systems (including an on-campus orientation to online learning) that gradually eased our burden those first few weeks and resulted in fewer issues, higher retention rates, and more satisfied online faculty. A key piece to this improved infrastructure was a campus-wide committee that met three times over the summer to better understand distance learners and their needs before gauging the steps we needed to take as an institution to improve our online support systems.

What many FIPSE projects in this book showed is that it's possible for innovative technology to connect learners to a host of support services if these programs are envisioned, designed, and supported to do precisely that. Some examples include writing skills (the OWL project), language skills (HETS), professional mentoring (HETS), online learning needs analysis (Diagnostic Pathfinder of Iowa State University), academic advising, financial aid (SREB), and online registration (OASIS).

However, there are many choices in what technology to use to support students, and these decisions have to be made on several levels, again including access, skills, cost, and sustainability. Examples of technologies used in these projects include private chat rooms, instant messaging, posted lists of frequently-asked-questions (FAQs), threaded discussions (web-based bulletin boards), websites, telephone, webcams, and online mentoring via email to support learners in their distance education pursuits. Although some of the distance education projects had the development of innovative or comprehensive technology solutions for student support as their primary focus, most of the projects realized they needed to address these needs in some manner in order to retain students.

Hailing Hybrids

Following closely from the last few themes is hailing hybrids. Back in the 1980s it was felt that technology was the death knell for bricks-and-mortar classes, that the traditional university classrooms would be left vacant as distance education would replace the traditional classroom professor. As the years have unfolded, a different reality has emerged. Instead of an "all or none" phenomenon, we have seen a hybridized form of distance education that the early geneticist Mendel would have been proud of! For the attuned educator and organization, distance education provides the opportunity to develop innovative, flexible, and multiple-dimensional learning experiences.

Rather than being confined to one form of educational delivery, the hybrid model is a "mix-and match" variety. Compared to the 1970s forms of videoconferencing that were mostly "talking heads," today's technologies allow interactive instructional methods through many different formats. Instructional designers and instructors can design courses and programs for different learning styles, content area and learning objections, accreditation, licensing needs, and competencies using more appropriate technologies for each different aspect, rather than having to make one choice for the entire curriculum (see the following projects for examples: LADDER K–16, Oregon University System; Call Center Training, the Montana Consortium and Alcanza; Fordham University, AALPDS; and, the Competency Assessment in Distributed Education). Hybrids are one example of how we are learning to take advantage of the innovative dimensions of technology and offer a depth to distance education that provides much greater power for teaching and learning.

Evaluation as a Lifeline

The role of evaluation in the life of distance education projects cannot be missed. Indeed, as experienced program directors, we would have to say that it is the primary lifeline. An evaluator who will work closely with the project team can provide timely data, dialogue, and insight that is invaluable in guiding a project toward success.

Examples of signals that evaluators identified in these projects which helped steer the project teams included:

- "Problems related to the pace at which project decisions and activities were progressing;"

- "Technical service providers ... fail(ing) to consider the techno-logical infrastructure and expertise of their partners;" and,
- (Identifying) "disparate learners' goals and the over-estimation of learners' entering experience with technology."

Unfortunately, evaluators cannot foresee all obstacles, such as: "The bursting of the 'dot.com bubble';" or, "Two days before we went live, the west coast had an earthquake."

Again, given the current limitations of technology, human knowledge, and prescience, the value of an evaluation team that closely follows and communicates with a project team can provide a lifeline that can help the project fulfill even more than it originally envisioned.

Challenges of Transformation

The final theme we would suggest would be that there are inordinate challenges inherent to creating transformation through distance education. Indeed it seems to be a tremendous contradiction that in a field so defined and dominated by technology, and where technological change comes so quickly, organizational change comes so slowly.

Experts who have studied organizational behavior, specifically change, are well aware of this phenomenon. However, very often those of us who venture into the ring with not one but, it seems, a veritable line of these distance education tigers in front of us, are unaware of the strategies and relationships needed and the incremental pace characteristic of transformational change. This book is a wonderful compendium of persistent success; however, be sure to read carefully and remain cognizant of the challenges, barriers, and delays that may lie ahead as you seek to gain those great distance education opportunities. We are very appreciative of the stories that are shared here so we can help others build upon our experience and be validated in the paths we have walked, and sometimes stumbled.

This vantage point of looking over 50-plus distance education projects for patterns and themes of practice and experience provides the opportunity to reflect on a path that many days seems too slow. Looking across the larger span of time and scope of organizations and institutions, the change is happening. We are harnessing that wild tiger! It is through the efforts of projects such as those funded by agencies like FIPSE, along with distance education professional conferences and publications, that we realize our work in our outpost is contributing to a much greater effect in the movement. Of great excitement is that we are part of a much greater effort to accomplish this educational and sociological change, and while the end result is un-known, we are creating the future ... together.

FRAMING PRINCIPLES

To step up a level, beyond drawing together themes from among these stud-ies, is to determine framing principles that may guide distance education caution planning and practice. This section offers several such principles for the reader to consider and discuss in the planning process, including being formative, cyclical, visionary, scalable, sustainable, and supportive of life-long learning.

Formative

First, it is our intent that distance education be pursued as a formative edu-cational program planning process (Caffarella 2002, Lawler and King 2000). That is, the planning process should start from a basis of experience and data, and be continually revised based on data-gathering and improvement. This principle also emphasizes the critical role of evaluation in distance edu-cation programs. While face-to-face educational programs may provide a few weeks leeway in handling difficulties, if the servers go down, distance education teachers and learners are cut off immediately and completely. Ad-ditionally, if the formats, technologies, or instructors are not meeting the needs of the learners, they will not walk into their advisor's or dean's office, they just won't come back. Retention rates are even more difficult in dis-tance education than in traditional delivery modes. For these and many other reasons, a solid evaluation plan, frequent communication of the infor-mation, and decisions based on the information, can be the lifeblood of suc-cess for these programs.

Cyclical

Such an approach also provides for an iterative design model (King 2003). This approach allows for a project to be run in several cycles, and to be re-vised or improved based on context, participants, and needs with each rendi-tion. More than "practice makes perfect," this model provides for first, sec-ond, and third revisions! At times information may even cause a course or program to go the way of the Ford Edsel, but it is infinitely better to know this early on by trying to refine a program rapidly, than to invest resources, and compromise the success of students by not tracking the programs. Ad-ministrators of distance education programs juggle a variety of issues—everything from overseeing student registration, student support and readiness, to providing faculty training and support—all the while keeping an eye on program costs, enrollment, retention, and fit within the institution. If they could understand their programming needs within this iterative perspective, they might utilize an approach that builds on successes and makes adjustments for the variety of issues encountered along the way.

Visionary

While building on the resources and experiences of the organization, distance education is an excellent opportunity to stretch the boundaries of conventional educational programs. This point came through in these FIPSE projects, just as we have seen it highlighted many times in the literature previously. For instance, Gandolfo states that there is a "need for educators (administrators and professors) to identify a technology vision at their institutions that is consonant with their idea of what teaching and learning is all about" (Gandolfo 1998, 29). Additionally, Cantelon notes that in distance education "the site of learning is transformed from a place to a process" (Cantelon 1995, 9), and insists that distance education fits postsecondary education by satisfying the unmet needs of new students, thereby complementing colleges and universities.

What this all means for institutions of higher learning is as varied and complicated as the institutions themselves. Perhaps more than in any other venue, distance education will truly take you places you have never been. I know that as I (Kathy) start distance education projects—indeed most of my educational projects now—I am keenly aware that I have a clear view of my objectives and a distinct plan of approach, but I know that I can really, only dimly see the vision of the endpoint of a few years ahead. The excitement can be great, the challenge always substantial. Innovative technology in higher education provides the opportunity to cast a vision and shape it as you work through the process and discover new needs, pathways, and solutions.

Lifelong Learning

In an age when technology, economies, and political climates are changing rapidly, the need for lifelong learning is no longer an obtuse claim. There is incredible demand on today's learners and workers to acquire not only technical skills, but skills which foster success within rapidly changing technologies and promote problem-solving abilities. A writer in *Fortune* magazine summed it up succinctly when he noted, "In an economy when technology leadership determines the winners, education trumps everything" (Colvin

2005). At the state level, governors charged with improving student outcomes in our schools have voiced concern that global competitiveness has made U.S. students vulnerable in an economy which demands greater technological skills (Balz 2005).

The use of most innovative technologies today in creating and sustaining teaching and learning environments in higher education today requires effective self-directed learning skills for students to succeed. At the root of these skills is the realization of the importance of lifelong learning for both learners and organizations. Although access remains a key issue, as noted by several FIPSE projects here, the flexibility and portability of technology-assisted, distance education has also brought about a leveling of the educational field for many students. Such learning then provides an "unintended outcome" that is a valuable commodity in today's marketplace precisely as a result of its delivery mode: it is flexible, convenient, and portable. Distance education programs have the opportunity to build a framework of lifelong learning into their programs and help students understand, value perspective, and build these skills. By learning to plan their own learning objectives, find educational resources, budget their study time, evaluate their learning satisfaction, and make choices about their future, distance education programs incorporate into their programs' skills that will help their students succeed in a world that demands constant, independent learning.

Scalable

If you are only creating one distance education course, that is fine, but most educational institutions plan to design complete programs of study online. When several courses, teachers, and many students become involved in the experience, scalability becomes a very important principle. Scalability helps prevent institutions of higher education that are pursuing innovative technology solutions from hitting the technological ceiling!

Rather than having every course designed differently, strategies that utilize and share common features and functions can leverage design, development, and delivery resources. While registration, grading, and transcripts for 20 students is a different matter than when you have 500 or 5,000 students, it helps to consider these matters from the beginning so that systems do not have to be entirely redesigned when student number 500 wants to enroll at midnight before a class begins.

FIPSE's focus on the development and exploration of support systems and learning objects in these applications provides for innovative, context-independent, and shared resources. While the Advanced Distributed

Learning (www.adlnet.org) system has facilitated and supported one wide-spread network of shared learning resources, so can common support service design provide for scalability. Indeed, within higher education, outsourcing has become a major avenue for solving scalability issues when it comes to technological solutions. Scalability solutions that institutions may utilize can help address issues around the articulation of services, organizational, staffing, and curriculum.

Sustainable

Certainly, it is a rewarding experience to build something of great impact and to be recognized as a one-of-a-kind leader, but what legacy is it really when, if we have to leave a project, it loses momentum, or falls apart behind us? And external funding is a great opportunity to jumpstart an innovative distance education project, but unless you have the Midas touch, usually the grants will not sustain a program forever. This situation raises the issue of sustainability. By building a solid foundation within an organization and of personnel, a financial plan that replenishes expenses with diversified sources of income, and continuing improvement to account for innumerable changing conditions, your efforts and resources may be able to continue on a firm basis.

Again, the chapters of this book have explored over 50 programs that represent many years of experience in this field, and detailed examination of these areas will offer more specific direction. With these thoughts in mind, where then is the field of distance education headed, or where *should* it be headed?

WHERE DO WE GO FROM HERE?

Certainly, as we consider the simultaneous but often contradictory land-scapes of education and technology, it is no surprise that distance education is such a demanding and exciting field. Looking at the landscape of distance education it would seem that this volume provides a basis to frame our consideration for its direction. Rather than being caught up in the frenzy of the latest technological gadgetries (and it is exhilarating and tempting!), we have the opportunity to use this powerful resource and platform to address major educational and societal issues.

We would recommend the following be considered as further developments though distance education:

- Providing greater access to education for underserved populations;

- Championing lifelong learning among the general population by building greater and easier continuity and pathways among educational pursuits;
- Providing greater opportunities for technology literacy for all ages and people groups;
- Closing the achievement gap in literacy, academic study, and math, science, and technology;
- Promoting innovations to facilitate global cross-cultural communication, understanding, and appreciation;
- Developing innovative partnerships to reach greater purposes together than alone;
- Promoting understanding, strategies, and support for policy making and change across and within organizations;
- Exploring instructionally focused and innovative distance education technologies and delivery systems;
- Creating faculty development content, delivery, rewards systems, models, and theories;
- Exploring innovative distance education technologies. The Internet is only the second generation of distance education, so what will the third, fourth, and fifth generations be like? What do they hold for education and human potential?

Distance education technologies have been continually moving towards convenience and adoption. The exact scale of this movement is unknown. In 2005, it appears that the Internet is the "common currency" of distance education and for most learners' educational pursuits, although they are also using cell phones, portable music players, and multiple wireless devices for all sorts of communication.

The primary issues of instruction that surface repeatedly for us are: (1) interaction with instructor and peers, and (2) multiple instructional methods. Continuing to explore these components in distance education design can take us to places yet unknown.

Therefore, with the great challenges of being agents of change in a world that wants the status quo, distance education seems to be a tiger that is wild. However, we have tremendous technological opportunities continually opening ahead of us to address educational, social, economic, and political needs. Rather than letting the field be dominated by technology breakthroughs, we can chart a course of educational excellence and innovation.

CONCLUSION

Distance education has the potential to open wider the door to greater access and advancement for learners across their life spans. This chapter has provided an integrated overview of the extensive research offered in this book. We have brought together comprehensive themes, offering framing principles to guide distance education initiatives, and considering some of the pressing issues that need to continue or be freshly pursued. The purpose has been to provide a substantial resource of information, guidance, and controversy that will not only serve as a basis for practice and research to harness the great yet untapped potential of that "tiger" of distance education, but also stir your thoughts, consideration, conversations, initiatives, and policies to explore new areas.

When we consider the many people who cannot access education for so many different reasons, we realize that education has so many areas yet to reach. Distance education, through so many technological possibilities, has the potential to span:

- geographical boundaries,
- languages,
- learning styles,
- learning disabilities,
- physical disabilities,
- time and space limitations,
- technological limitations,
- and many more parameters.

We urge you, our colleagues, to never be satisfied with the status quo in education, but to seek out the opportunities to use every means available to advance teaching and learning. For many years, distance education has been part of this innovative and effective creative movement to discover new dimensions of teaching and learning, and we see no indication of this receding in years to come. More than ever, we need experienced, talented, visionary, and persistent educators to harness the power of this tiger. We look forward to sharing in your experiences—your successes and your challenges—for in all their many ways, they help us learn more about distance education, teaching, learning, and what it means to help others reach into their futures to realize their dreams.

FIPSE /LAAP Projects

This gallery of projects provides a description of each project as well as organizational affiliation, project director, address, telephone, fax, e-mail, and website. They are listed alphabetically by the lead organization that was awarded the FIPSE grant. More details about these projects may be retrieved from http://www.ed.gov and through the FIPSE project database, accessible at http://www.fipse.aed.org/.

ASSOCIATION OF JESUIT COLLEGES AND UNIVERSITIES: A MODEL FOR COMPETENCY-BASED DISTANCE ASSESSMENT

Project Director: Richard Vigilante
Association of Jesuit Colleges and Universities
Jesuit Distance Education Network
One Dupont Circle, Suite 405
Washington, DC 20036
Tel: 212-348-6113
Fax: 212-348-6113
E-mail: Vigilante@ajcunet.edu
URL: http://www.jesuit.net

The goal of this project was to develop and evaluate a distance assessment model using evidence-based design to identify and represent student competencies, and to embed performance and assessment tasks in online courses. The project began as a face-to-face workshop and evolved into an online workshop in order to reach more faculty across several schools. CADE (Competency Assessment in Distance Education) has since evolved further, using both online and hybrid approaches. The online workshops are delivered in eight weeks, while the hybrid workshops are a four- to five-week effort and are institution specific. Faculty leave the workshop with a full design portfolio which serves as the blueprint for a course that focuses on assessing students using parameters of expertise (e.g., novice, graduate, or expert) in a scoring rubric.

CADE requires participants to go through an evidence assessment first, and then to determine the learning objectives. The evidence analysis helps them to determine what the various tasks should be, and then to identify the appropriate technology. This unique "backward" approach wherein competencies are identified first, followed by the evidence that will indicate mastery, the required student behaviors, and the identification of necessary instructional tasks helps faculty think strategically about the design of a course.

CITY COLLEGE OF SAN FRANCISCO: NATIONAL ARTICULATION AND TRANSFER NETWORK (NATN)
Building an Alternative Pathway for Underserved Student Populations to Access Historically Black Colleges and Universities, Hispanic-Serving Institutions, and Tribal Colleges and Universities

Project Director: Ann Zinn
City College of San Francisco
50 Phelan Avenue, E200
San Francisco, CA 94112
Tel: 415-239-3303
Fax: 415-239-3918
E-mail: azinn@ccsf.org
URL: http://www.collegestepz.net/

The goal of the National Articulation and Transfer Network (NATN) is to develop a pathway for students generally underrepresented in the college population to access colleges and universities whose missions include education of minority and low-income students. The Network is made up of community and senior colleges, most of them minority-serving institutions and urban high schools. The project is large in scale. At one time the membership included 61 colleges and universities and 46 high schools.

The project has several facets, perhaps the most ambitious being the development of articulation agreements between the community colleges and senior institutions of higher education that are part of the Network. A "General Articulation Agreement" guarantees that senior institutions will admit community college students graduating with an associate's degree who meet certain conditions, such as a GPA of at least 2.5. Under study is the feasibility of an agreement that would involve the senior institutions accepting all credits earned in the general education core at a community college, and applying them to departmental and program as well as institutional requirements. The project also facilitates specific articulation agreements among institutions.

Collegestepsz.net, a website developed by the Network, makes this information available to students enrolled in participating community colleges and high schools. In addition to the information on transfer and articulation, the site leads students to a powerful array of resources to assist them in preparing for college or for transfer. A particularly interesting feature of the website is that it matches the information students provide in personal profiles with institutions that meet their criteria.

COLLEGE SUMMIT: COLLABORATIVE SOLUTION TO INCREASE COLLEGE
ACCESS FOR AND RETENTION OF LOW-INCOME YOUTH

Project Director: Kevin O'Shaughnessey
College Summit, Inc.
1763 Columbia Rd, NW
2nd Floor
Washington, DC 20009
Tel: 202-319-1763, Ext. 424
Fax: 202-319-1233
E-mail: koshaughnessey@collegesummit.org
URL: http://www.collegesummit.org

College Summit (CS) is the most extensive of these projects in terms of its scope. As of the 2004–2005 school year, the project is serving 3,600 students in 39 high schools in five locations across the country as compared to 900 students in 2002–2003. The CS protocol is designed to build low-income students' confidence that attending college is a feasible goal both academically and financially, help students identify colleges where they are likely to succeed, manage the application process, and present themselves effectively in college applications and portfolios supplementary to the application.

Initially, the program served a limited group of rising seniors who had been selected by participating high schools on factors, other than their academic records, that signaled they possessed characteristics that would enable them to be successful in higher education. These students were invited, along with teachers in their schools, to participate in four-day workshops conducted on a host college or university campus during which they worked through the CS protocol. Since 1993, 79% of the students who participated in the workshops enrolled in college, as compared to 46% of low-income students nationally (College Summit 2004, Abstract). These invitational workshops remain an important part of the CS program. However, for the 2003–2004 school year, the program was expanded to serve all seniors in participating high schools, and the approach was modified to accommodate these larger populations. While the emphasis of the CS program remains on helping students work through the steps that will help them be successful in college, it also serves as a pathway for students who are not college bound to make other post-high-school plans.

Technology is essential to the scalability of the program, and CS is now in the process of developing the technology (CSNet) that will support administration of the program as it expands. Also, with the completion of CSNet, students will have online access to the CS training modules and teachers will be able to comment on student work and track student progress online. CSNet will also provide the capability to forward student portfolios electronically to colleges and universities. With the technology in place, CS projects the program will be able to serve 55,000 students by the year 2009.

COLORADO STATE UNIVERSITY: DEVELOPING AN ONLINE CREDENTIALING SYSTEM FOR CAREER AND TECHNICAL TEACHERS

Project Director: Teresa Yohon
Room 216, Education Building
Fort Collins, CO 80523-1588
Tel: 970-491-5029
Fax: 970-491-1317
E-mail: yohon@cahs.colostate.edu
URL: http://www.coloradocredentialing.org/

Colorado State University (CSU) developed a pathway for career and technical teachers to obtain State of Colorado certification. A shortage of certified teachers trained in this field has required the state to issue emergency credentials to meet instructional needs. Once employed, constraints of time and location within the state have made it difficult for teachers to participate in the training needed for certification.

CSU and its partners, Northeastern Junior College and the Colorado Community College System, the credentialing office, addressed these problems by creating an online training and certification process. The first step in its development was the identification and validation of the competencies required for certification. Once this step was completed, content from previous courses was selected and new material necessary for students to meet each competency requirement developed and organized into instructional modules. The content for each module is delivered in a variety of formats that include narrative, links to Web-based resources, PowerPoint presentations, videotaped interviews, samples of work, and experts online. Each module also contains pre- and post-assessments. All modules have three levels of content, which means they can benefit educators interested in professional development as well as those seeking entry level certification. The use of online modules allows students to enroll anytime that is convenient for them.

The second phase of the project was the development of the Colorado Credentialing website. The website, providing both information and services, is a one-stop credentialing center for career and technical education teachers. The information concerning credentialing requirements, previously dispersed and difficult to locate, is readily available on the website. A planning tool helps credential applicants assess the training they need to meet the requirements and to develop a plan for completing the training that meets their individual needs. Once an application for certification is made, the system tracks the plan as the teacher progresses through the requirements. The website also provides links to the training modules and information concerning how teachers might develop a portfolio documenting their learning and experience that would meet some of the certification requirements.

EDUCATIONAL COMMUNICATIONS FOUNDATION: NATIONAL COMMUNITY COLLEGE ASYNCHRONOUS LEARNING NETWORK FOR THE AV INDUSTRY (AV–ALN)

Project Director: Randal A. Lemke
Educational Communications Foundation
Suite 200
11242 Waples Mill Road
Fairfax, VA 22003
Tel: 703-273-7200, ext. 324
Fax: 703-2798-8082
E-mail: rlemke@infocomm.org
URL: http://www.avaln.org

The AV–ALN is the result of a national partnership committed to educate the current and future workforce of the audiovisual communications industry. There is a labor shortage in high tech industries, and it is estimated that the United States AV communications workforce will grow by 20,000 to 30,000 new jobs each year for the next five years. Currently no higher education institution offers a program to prepare audiovisual system technicians.

In 1997, the Educational Communications Foundation, Inc.® and the International Communication Industries Association, Inc.® joined Coastline Community College, Dallas County Community College District, Metropolitan Community Colleges, Miami-Dade Community College, Monroe Community College, Northern Virginia Community College, and Portland Community College to organize the National Partnership for Workforce Development. The AV–ALN is a product of this partnership.

The AV–ALN project will develop eight courses and offer certificate and/or degree programs for the incumbent workforce and those seeking careers in the industry. To eliminate duplicative effort and expense, the partners will share the instructional design, development, and teaching of asynchronous learning courses. To facilitate student access and success; instructional, technical and academic advising systems will be provided anywhere and anytime students can participate. In this forty-month project, 1,200 student are expected to participate.

Dallas County Community College District (DCCCD) will lead the development of Internet-based courses for distribution to the partner colleges either (1) for delivery through their own servers using WEB CT, Blackboard, or Top Class platforms; or (2) for use through linkage to the DCCCD server. The courses will provide ample opportunity for the professors at the local college to modify them by adding assignments, lessons, and other resources. Laboratories will be located at AV communication dealers' offices in cities within driving distance of enrolled students. The industry partners will provide the equipment and the facility for students to perform self-guided laboratory exercises designed and supervised by the colleges. Northern Virginia Community College will serve as the lead institution for the development of learner support services that supplement the seven partners' local services.

To sustain this effort after the FIPSE funding has concluded, the colleges plan to offer these courses, certificates, or degree programs as part of their regular offerings with the number of sections dependent upon enrollment. Scaling up to serve more students will be done by increasing the number of faculty or sections in the seven partner colleges, and by adding more colleges to the partnership.

FLORIDA COMMUNITY COLLEGE AT JACKSONVILLE: CREOLE (CREATING OPTIMUM LEARNING ENVIRONMENTS)

Project Director: Kenneth Whitten
Florida Community College Jacksonville (South Campus)
11901 Beach Blvd.
Jacksonville, FL 32246
Tel: 904-646-2294
Fax: 904-646-2078
E-mail: FIPSE@fccj.edu
URL: http://www.creole-online.org/creolemain.html

The CREOLE project used online professional development as a way to facilitate faculty expertise in both the classroom and online. Four modules were developed: *Applying Teaching/Learning Research, Applying Motivation Research, Revising Traditional Lecture-based Courses to Incorporate the Internet,* and *Developing Interactive Web-based Courses.* Each module consists of several chapters written by a variety of authors.

Although FCCJ coordinated the project and developed some of the content, CREOLE also involves authors from universities and consulting organizations. CREOLE Module Four, *Developing Interactive Web-based Courses,* has been offered for professional development at FCCJ and for postgraduate credit at the University of Utah. Because the goal of the project was to address an international audience, it was developed independent of any specific course management system. The content is largely text-based and can easily be embedded in the course management system of choice.

FORDHAM UNIVERSITY:
ANYTIME ANYWHERE LEARNING PROFESSIONAL DEVELOPMENT SCHOOL

Project Director: Kathleen P. King
Fordham University
Regional Educational Technology Center
441 E. Fordham Rd., Bldg. 557, Rm. 302
Bronx, NY 10458
Tel: 718-817-3503
Fax: 718-295-4262
E-mail: kpking@fordham.edu
URL: http://www.retc.fordham.edu/aalpds/

Today's educators face new mandated standards of accountability. Teachers must implement standards-based instructional programs and measurably raise student achievement. Since most teachers have never been trained to do this, there is a growing and unmet need to prepare new and existing teachers to design and deliver standards-based instructional programs. Meanwhile, there has been an explosion of distance and virtual learning programs on the Internet. At a time when schools face severe teacher shortages and a need to improve the quality of learning provided by existing teachers, an alternative delivery model in distance learning could help resolve some of these problems.

To address these needs, this partnership developed an Anytime Anywhere Learning Professional Development School (AALPDS) model of professional development. This is a school-based, flexible, online, learning program that gives teachers practical, hands-on experience in learning about and building standards-based programs in their own local contexts. The project addresses current national standards of the National Staff Development Council (NSDC) and at the same time builds local leadership and capacity to conduct and evaluate their own school-based AAL professional development programs. Educators who enroll in this Internet-based program are members of a local school-based community of learners, and they will engage in professional collaboration, dialogue, and peer assessment virtually with remote teams. Teachers will develop, review, and share curriculum resources not only with their own school, but with their remote peers.

Project goals include the development of (1) customizable courses that prepare classroom teachers to design, develop, and implement effective programs of instruction that produce objective measurable gains in student achievement, (2) local leadership, and (3) new professional development technology tools.

Successful principles, strategies, and approaches will be disseminated via conference presentations, journal articles, listserv announcements, and an Internet discussion board for professional development exchange. The program also permits teachers to share their developed curriculum within their school, among online participants and, finally, nationwide through Classroom Connect, Inc.

The base of participating schools in AALPDS has expanded to an estimated 200. More than 1000 teachers have registered for classes since the project went live in March 2001. Among these are some centralized areas in New York City, North Carolina, and California.

GEORGETOWN UNIVERSITY: CROSSROADS ONLINE INSTITUTE

Project Director: Randall Bass
Georgetown University
Box 571113
Washington, DC 20057
Tel: 202-687-4535
Fax: 202-687-8367
E-mail: bassr@georgetown.edu
URL: http://cndls.georgetown.edu/projects/fipse/coi/apply.cfm

The Crossroads Online Institute was created to guide national cohorts of faculty through a process of reflection and redesign of their courses for technology-enhanced learning environments. The project addressed three challenges in effective online professional development: a lack of excellent faculty development models, the fact that most curriculum resources do not discuss the transformation of teaching and learning in academic fields, and the misunderstandings about hybrid teaching/technology innovations.

The core element of the Institute is a 10-week online workshop that addresses these challenges as faculty develop modules that utilize technology-enhanced pedagogies and student assessment techniques. A blog approach is used throughout the workshop so that participants can share their thoughts and ideas about each segment of the workshop. Although the workshop is delivered online to a national audience, faculty are encouraged to sign up in pairs so that face-to-face collaboration can take place as well. The culmination of the workshop is the development of an online "poster" where participants summarize their experience as it relates to the courses they teach.

GOVERNORS STATE UNIVERSITY: FOSTER PRIDE DIGITAL CURRICULUM

Project Director: Charles Nolley
Governors State University
Communications Services
University Park, IL 60466
Tel: 708-235-3975
Fax: 708-534-8956
E-mail: c-nolley@govst.edu
URL: http://www.govst.edu/

The Foster Pride Digital Curriculum project has a two-fold mission. The project first addresses the issue of training and education for foster parents. Many of these parents are confronted with logistical challenges in accessing the traditional classroom methods currently used for the required training to maintain licensure. Second, the project is also developing multiple asynchronous delivery systems to provide the current Foster Pride curriculum to homebound foster parents who need to fulfill the continuing education requirements for relicensure or seek to complete professional development sequences in specialized areas. The curriculum is used in classrooms in 18 states and four countries.

Governors State University is leading the project in partnership with the Child Welfare League of America, the Illinois Department of Children and Family Services, and child welfare agencies in six states (California, Illinois, Kentucky, Michigan, North Dakota, and Texas). Texas is pilot-testing the first modules. Preliminary reactions have been extremely positive.

The project is creating digital versions of nine modules during the grant period, each capable of delivery in a variety of formats including broadband Internet, CD-ROM with Internet components, videotape, and DVD with printed workbooks. Once the modules are completed and tested, they will be placed into national and international distribution. The resulting revenue stream will fund production of the final three modules after FIPSE funding ends.

The technology being developed for the project has broad applicability to other areas and will advance the field of distance education. The methods being developed will be replicable in several educational contexts including other underserved populations in need of skill competency credentials.

HERITAGE COLLEGE: A PREPARATION PROGRAM TO INCREASE POSTSECONDARY ACCESS FOR NATIVE AMERICAN AND LATINO POPULATIONS

Project Director: Ryan Landvoy
Heritage College
3240 Ford Road
Toppenish, WA 98948
Tel: 509-865-8630
Fax: 509-865-4469
E-mail: landvoy_r@heritage.edu
URL: http://www.heritage.edu

The Heritage College project entailed the development of pre-college courses in mathematics and English specifically designed for the particular population of Native American and Latino students the University serves. The impetus for the project was the extensive amount of remedial work that entering students from these populations required before they were ready for college level mathematics and English. What is unusual about these courses is that they were designed to be culturally relevant to the student populations.

The first phase of the project was the development of standardized assessments in mathematics and English, both of which are available in Spanish. The assessments themselves use situations and vocabulary that would be familiar to the populations to be served, thus removing some of the cultural barriers to performance. The pathway consists of online college preparation courses in mathematics and English reading, writing, and comprehension that address deficiencies identified in the assessments. The reading, writing, and comprehension course is designed to increase communication skills of both Native Americans and Hispanic students for whom English is a second language.

Assessments are conducted electronically, and the courses are delivered via the Internet in order to reach widely dispersed populations. The project uses Adaptex multimedia software, which enables the incorporation of multimedia files that are important to establishing a familiar context for students. The mathematics course utilizes film clips that use situations that Native Americans and Hispanics would commonly encounter to illustrate mathematical concepts. The English course, still in development, will also use materials that are culturally relevant.

Hispanic Educational Telecommunications System (HETS): Forging Partnerships and Networking Learners with the Virtual Learning & Support Plaza

Project Director: Nitza Hernández-López
University of Puerto Rico
Hispanic Educational Telecommunications System
P.O. Box 364984
San Juan, PR 00936-4984
Tel: 787-250-0000, ext. 2063
Fax: 787-751-1031
E-mail: n_hernandez@upr.edu
URL: http://www.hets.org/

The Hispanic Educational Telecommunications System (HETS) is the first bilingual distance learning consortium dedicated to serving the higher education needs of our fast-growing Hispanic communities. Founded in 1993, HETS comprises a membership of 22 colleges and universities in the mainland United States, Puerto Rico, and Latin America. HETS provides a greater opportunity for affiliated institutions to offer and deliver educational and training programs, courses, and conferences across distances reaching geographically distributed Hispanic communities.

Each participating institution brings to HETS its particular strength by delivering specific courses and its own diversity of program offerings that may be attractive to Hispanic students enrolled in other colleges and universities. The following are some of the program areas that HETS encourages its member institutions to collaborate in and explore:

- Sharing credit courses and academic programs among affiliated colleges and universities and other higher education institutions that wish to participate.

- Developing live, interactive video conferences with experts and distinguished lectures for students, faculty, professional groups, and other adult learners to enhance learning and promote intercultural communication.

- Developing training courses in cooperation with business, industry, and workplace within local Hispanic communities.

- Exchanging educational information and research between colleges and universities in the United States, Puerto Rico, and other Spanish speaking countries.

- Developing bilingual certification programs for teachers, including Spanish and English immersion programs.

- Training faculty and other professionals on distance learning strategies and techniques.

INDIANA STATE UNIVERSITY: VIRTUAL INSTRUCTIONAL DESIGNER: AN INTERNET-BASED FACULTY DEVELOPMENT TOOL FOR DESIGNING ONLINE INSTRUCTION

Project Director: Don Kaufman
Dean, Continuing Studies
Vincennes University
1002 N. First Street
Vincennes, IN 47591
Tel: 812-888-5343
Fax: 812-888-2054
E-mail: dkaufman@vinu.edu
URL: http://vid.vinu.edu

Indiana University, Vincennes University, and Ivy Tech State College created a partnership called DegreeLink in order to address the small proportion of students, and the overall low rate of Indiana residents aged 22 and older, who have earned associate or bachelor degrees. The partnership focused on developing and delivering anytime, anywhere online courses and programs that lead to the completion of a degree.

Faculty required instruction in the effective design of online courses in order to successfully deliver these programs. Online courses not only demand a significant level of technology expertise that may be unfamiliar to higher education faculty; they also demand knowledge and experience in the kinds of pedagogy necessary to take advantage of this dynamic learning environment.

The challenge for the partnership was to create a "just-in-time" tool rich in media and resources to help faculty transform traditional courses to asynchronous online courses. The VID includes a Faculty Needs and Skills Survey that generates a customized learning plan that makes it easy for a professor to jump into the site and get the information necessary to create an effective online course. Upon conclusion of the grant life, Indiana State University chose not to lend further support to the VID; Vincennes University offered to take ownership and has made the VID publicly available.

INDIANA UNIVERSITY–BLOOMINGTON: LEARNING TO TEACH WITH TECHNOLOGY STUDIO (LTTS)

Project Director: Thomas Duffy
Indiana University–Bloomington

School of Education
Center for Research on Learning and Technology
Education Building
201 North Rose Avenue
Bloomington, IN 47405
Tel: 812-856-8459
Fax: 812-856-8245
E-mail: duffy@indiana.edu
URL: http://www.ltts.org/

The LTTS was developed to provide standards-based individualized professional development to in-service teachers, assisting them in the integration of technology in the classroom. With almost 60 online courses in Science, Mathematics, Language Arts, and Social Studies (17 are cross-discipline), LTTS has created a comprehensive catalogue of courses that take a guided problem solving approach to teaching.

All courses follow a common methodology that culminates in a lesson plan that is inquiry based. Each LTTS course uses a unique inquiry framework that supports teachers in not only understanding issues relates to specific types of technology projects, but how to develop a project they can use in their own classroom.

The courses are self-paced, and participants may begin at any time. Participants begin with a curriculum problem, receive individual mentoring, and end with a classroom lesson plan. In addition to Indiana University, program partners include PBS TeacherLine, University of Colorado–Denver, University of Georgia, Alliant International University, and KyEducators and Kentucky Virtual University.

KANSAS STATE UNIVERSITY:
A NATIONAL MODEL FOR INTERINSTITUTIONAL POSTBACCALAUREATE DISTANCE EDUCATION PROGRAMS

Project Director: Virginia Moxley
Kansas State University
College of Human Ecology
119 Justin Hall
Manhattan, KS 66506-1401
Tel: 785-532-5500
Fax: 785-532-5504
E-mail: moxley@ksu.edu
URL: http://www.gpidea.org

Postbaccalaureate education represents the fastest-growing and most rapidly changing sector of higher education. To be competitive, universities must alter institutional policies and practices as well as programs. The Great Plains Interactive Distance Education Alliance (GPIDEA), initiated by the College of Human Sciences at the partner universities eight years ago, has collaborated to support inter-institutional graduate distance education programming.

More than 60 prominent academic leaders, representing graduate faculty, academic administrators, graduate deans, chief financial officers, registrars, continuing education directors, and national higher education leaders are engaged to revamp the policy and practice for postbaccalaureate education. A collaborative coaching method is being developed as a strategy to facilitate rapid implementation of inter-institutional programs. Project participants will be prepared to serve as "collaboration coaches" to enable emerging programs to capitalize on proven policies and practices to ramp up rapidly.

KANSAS STATE UNIVERSITY:
ADVANCING THE EFFICACY OF DIVERSE HIGHER EDUCATION ACADEMIC ALLIANCES

Project Co-Director: Virginia Moxley
Kansas State University
College of Human Ecology
119 Justin Hall
Manhattan, KS 66506
Tel: 785-532-5500
Fax: 785-532-5504
E-mail: moxley@ksu.edu
Project Co-Director: Sue Maes
Kansas State University
Educational Communications Center
128 Dole Hall
Manhattan, KS 66506
Tel: 785-532-3110
Fax: 785-532-7355
E-mail: scmaes@ksu.edu
URLs: http://www.gpidea.org; http://www.k-state.edu/iaa

The project was designed to support the implementation of multi-institutional academic programs and partnerships. Participating collaborative projects involve (1) the Community Development multidisciplinary and multi-institutional graduate programs, (2) Hispanic Educational Telecommunications System multi-institutional programs, (3) Kansas Early Childhood Higher-education Options Consortium statewide collaboration, and (4) Family and Consumer Sciences Distance Instructional Alliance financial planning program.

During Year One, the project leaders will identify and orient collaborators and document need for proposed inter-institutional programs. An Institute for Academic Alliances (IAA) will be established at Kansas State University. In Year Two, the project will secure institutional approval for multi-institutional programs, establish practices to support such programs, and formalize alliances. During Year Three, project leaders will finalize programs and admit students. Findings from the project will be disseminated.

Throughout the project, participants will receive consultation from the project staff, participate in training and planning meetings, and have access to online materials to support the development and implementation of multi-institutional programs.

KIRKWOOD COMMUNITY COLLEGE:
ENVIRONMENTAL TECHNOLOGIES ONLINE (ET ONLINE)

Project Director: Patricia Berntsen
Kirkwood Community College
HMTRI
P.O. Box 2068
Cedar Rapids, IA 52406
Tel: 319-398-5893; toll free, 800-464-6874
Fax: 319-398-1250
E-mail: pbernts@kirkwood.edu
URL: http://www.et-online.org

Environmental Technology Online (ET Online) is a new way to learn anytime, anywhere. Internet supported instruction, coupled with hands-on training and workshops provided by partner organizations across the nation, provide flexible training for workers in the hazardous material, wastewater, water, and solid waste fields. Students will register at the partnering college or institution in their area and be provided the "lecture" via the Internet.

ET Online is being developed through a grant from the U.S. Department of Education by HMTRI, Hazardous Materials Training and Research Institute, a non-profit corporation formed by the Eastern Iowa Community College District headquartered in Davenport, Iowa, and Kirkwood Community College in Cedar Rapids, Iowa. The intent is to reach students and workers who may not be able to attend training in a traditional setting, but would be able to study using the Internet.

LaGuardia Community College: eTransfer

Project Director: Paul Arcario
LaGuardia Community College/CUNY
31-10 Thomson Avenue, M400
Long Island City, NY 11101
Tel: 718-482-5405
Fax: 718-482-5443
E-mail: arcariop@lagcc.cuny.edu
URL: http://www.lagcc.cuny.edu/

LaGuardia Community College has developed a transfer preparation program that is designed to assist students in developing career goals and preparing for transfer to senior colleges. Virtual Interest Groups (VIGs) are the centerpiece of the program. These are essentially asynchronous online five-week mini-courses which lead students to explore possible career fields and issues relating to transfer. Participation in a VIG is a course requirement and is included in the course grade. The groups are led by faculty members and former LaGuardia students currently attending senior colleges.

eTransfer also has an e-portfolio component. Beginning in their first year and throughout their programs, students contribute to the development of their own e-portfolios. The portfolio is an "online locker" for students to store the information gathered in completing the VIG requirements and to refine and further reflect upon the career and transfer goals they began to formulate in this program. The plan is that students will ultimately use these portfolios, which document their learning and their academic and career goals, as supplements to their applications to senior colleges and as electronic resumes.

Miles Community College:
Bridging Health Connections in Montana

Project Director: Kathleen K. Wankel
Miles Community College
Nursing
2715 Dickinson Street
Miles City, MT 59301
Tel: 406-874-6188
Fax: 406-874-6282
E-mail: wankelk@milescc.edu
URL: http://www.milescc.edu/CampusServices/fipse/default.htm

Part of the impetus for the Texas A&M/Delmar College partnership was the need to address serious shortages in the nursing workforce. The Miles Community College program is also designed to address this shortage. The first step in the project was to develop career pathways to advancement from Certified Nursing Assistant (CNA) to Associate Degree in Nursing (AND), Licensed Practical Nurse (LPN) to AND, and AND to Bachelor of Science (BSN). A second was to provide the programs at a distance to students throughout Eastern Montana. All of the nursing courses required to move through the career pathways are available through a combination of online and videoconferencing technologies. The College offers the AND degree both onsite and via ITV at several educational partner sites. The LPN to RN program is also offered via ITV. Clinical training is provided by partner hospitals and other health care facilities.

In addition to providing clear and accessible pathways to advancement in the nursing profession, the program is reaching out to high school students to generate interest in students at this level in pursuing careers in the health professions. The College offers two courses to high school students. These are Fundamentals for Health Professions, which is an introduction to careers and issues in the health area, and the Certified Nurse Assistant (CNA) Preparatory Course. This latter course prepares students for state certification and employment in long-term care. Students earn both high school and college credits for the courses.

OREGON UNIVERSITY SYSTEM:
LINKING ASSESSMENT DATA DIRECTLY TO ENTRY REQUIREMENTS (LADDER K–16)

Oregon University System
P.O. Box 751
Portland, OR 97207
Tel: 503-725-5700
URL: http://pass.ous.edu/?id=ladderproject

The project grew out of a larger effort initiated by the state legislature in 1991 to improve student performance at the K–12 level by regular assessments of student knowledge and skills. Now that the assessments are in place, Oregon is revamping its state university admissions criteria by replacing traditional measures as the primary means of determining admissibility with assessments of student competencies or proficiencies. This change in admissions policy is scheduled to begin in 2006.

During the first stage of this project, OSU developed new college admissions standards and aligned these with the competencies required for high school graduation. The second stage, currently underway, is to align high school assessment data with college admission. The goal is to create a more transparent pathway to college admission that will enable students and parents to assess progress toward meeting admissions requirements.

On a somewhat smaller scale, a common goal of many pathways projects has been to increase the representation of minority and low-income students in higher education and to facilitate their success. While the goal of many pathways is academic remediation, there are other barriers to address. Many minority and low-income students are simply not aware that attending college is a possibility. The projects being developed focus on the importance of the student developing goals for higher education, obtaining the knowledge and skills necessary to be successful in the admissions process, and finding the right fit between the students and the college(s) where they are applying.

These programs also provide support to students in various ways as they go through the admissions or transfer process. Many minority and low-income students lack the confidence that they can be successful, and support is an important ingredient of success.

OREGON UNIVERSITY SYSTEM: ONE (OREGON NETWORK FOR EDUCATORS)

Oregon University System
P.O. Box 3175
Eugene, OR 97403-0175
Tel: 541-346-5700
Fax: 541-346-5764
URL: http://OregonONE.org

OregonONE is an initiative to establish a virtual postsecondary consortium in the state. Funded with a three-year grant in 1998, the Oregon Network for Education (ONE) developed a one-stop website with a searchable database of distance education courses, certificate/degree programs, and other information for students interested in electronic delivery modes. Nine Oregon community colleges, eight Oregon universities, and four independent higher education institutions participated in ONE, with several K–12 providers of distance education courses joining in 2002. Among the perceived advantages of having information consolidated at a common site were an increase in student access to quality courses, a reduction of course duplication across institutions, and useful information and cost-effective services to faculty and staff. The project was also seen as a means of facilitating planning among distance education staffs and policymakers.

Central to ONE was Common Course Marketplace (CCM). An inter-institutional committee of faculty reviewed the concept, identified critical barriers to advancing a CCM, and suggested approaches for resolving them. Other committees addressed CCM concepts from disciplinary perspectives (math/sciences, liberal arts/social studies, writing) or from career/degree articulation pathways (nursing, agriculture, liberal studies, teacher education, business).

As a result, the LAAP resources were directed toward 13 demonstration projects that advanced practice and policy in other areas. These included a gap analyses in the fields of math, writing, and gender studies; studies on staffing for new distance education needs; academic residence policies; and the development of distance education minors which could be used in different degree programs and shared across multiple campuses.

OREGON UNIVERSITY SYSTEM:
SECOND GENERATION UNIVERSITY SYSTEM DISTANCE EDUCATION MODEL VIA PUBLIC/PRIVATE PARTNERSHIPS

Oregon University System
P.O. Box 3175
Eugene, OR 97403-0175
Tel: 541-346-5700
Fax: 541-346-5764
URL: http://www.ous.edu/dist-learn/

For more than a decade, the eight universities of the Oregon University System (OUS) had offered degrees using the state's "first-generation" satellite interactive video network. Seeking to expedite the transition to delivery over high-speed broadband terrestrial Internet (the "second generation"), OUS received a LAAP grant for the "Second Generation Distance Education Partnership Project." The goals of the project were to:

- Conduct collaborative planning and policy development among the eight institutions and its distance education partners;
- Balance interactivity, cost, and flexibility;
- Develop high quality, interactive courses;
- Find new ways of packaging courses, programs, and services;
- Improve quality and accountability in university distance education programs;
- Create new opportunities for underserved learners; and
- Improve support services for both students and faculty.

The centerpiece of the project was the redesign of 238 courses from 20 programs across the state, preparing them for the "second generation" of delivery systems. More broadly, however, OUS sought a model that would address all salient elements of the model. As noted in the chapter on policy, this involved issuing broad policy guidance on 53 policy areas within five general categories.

Oregon University System: The PK–16 Digital Learning Environment

Oregon University System
Office of Academic Affairs
P.O. Box 3175
1431 Johnson Lane
Eugene, OR 97403-0175
Tel: 541-346-5799; toll free, 800-961-7277
Fax: 541-346-5764
URL: http://pass.ous.edu/

One of the challenges of the state of Oregon in implementing the plan to assess student performance at various points in K–12. education was the need to train teachers to evaluate student proficiencies. A digital learning environment was developed to meet this need. The learning environment has three parts: a training laboratory where teachers can learn about teaching and assessment in a competency-based environment, a scoring laboratory where teachers review and assess student work, and a "calibration" laboratory where teachers can compare their judgments of student work with that of their colleagues' throughout the state.

The training is critical to developing a level of commonality among teacher judgments such that colleges can confidently rely on their evaluations in making admissions decisions. The Digital Learning Environment makes the training readily available to all teachers in the state, a task that would be almost impossible without the technical solution the Oregon University System devised.

Prince George's Community College: Quality Matters — Inter-Institutional Quality Assurance in Online Learning

Project Director: Mary Wells
Prince George's Community College
301 Largo Road, A-206
Largo, MD 20774-2199
Tel: 301-386-7582
Fax: 301-386-7568
E-mail: mwells@pgcc.edu
URL: http://www.pgcc.edu/index.html

Recognizing that a concern with quality is a primary barrier to the sharing of courses between institutions, Prince George's Community College in Maryland took the lead in "Quality Matters," a project designed to certify the quality of online courses and course components. The key was to establish a set of objective standards for identifying and demonstrating quality. This rubric encompassed eight categories of standards:

- Course overview and introduction
- Learning objectives (competencies)
- Resources and materials
- Learner interaction
- Course technology
- Learner support
- Assessment and measurement
- ADA compliance

The other critical success factors were (1) training faculty to conduct the course reviews so that other faculty would perceive that the quality had been assessed by peers, and (2) providing training and instructional design support to faculty. Nineteen institutions from Maryland and eight other states have participated in the Quality Matters consortium. To date, Quality Matters has reviewed 14 courses and certified 65 peer course reviewers. The Maryland Distance Learning Association (MDLA) recognized Quality Matters as the Best Distance Learning Program for 2005.

Puget Sound Educational Service District: | Early Literacy Outreach Project

Project Director: Anne Quinn
Puget Sound Educational Service District
400 SW 152nd Street
Burien, WA 98166
Tel: 206-439-6910, ext. 3943
Fax: 206-439-6942
E-mail: aquinn@psesd.org
URL: http://www.earlyliteracy.psesd.org

The Early Literacy Outreach Project (ELOP) addresses barriers faced by early childhood educators, such as course fees, timing of offerings during the day, course length, and schedule, by focusing on creating partnerships throughout the region to offer training, resource connections, and opportunities to learn more about early literacy development of children. With support from a diverse group of local, state, and regional partners, the Early Literacy Outreach Project makes these courses available using a variety of formats and media, including web-based, cable television, and self-paced learning modules.

To support and promote these courses, ELOP created an interactive website that provides course descriptions along with a variety of shorter learning opportunities, resources, highlights from the field, discussion boards, and articles written by local experts on early literacy. Each course can use a variety of distance learning tools to create specialized models that facilitate participation by different student learning groups.

RIVERSIDE COMMUNITY COLLEGE:
PROFESSIONAL DEVELOPMENT FOR NEW FACULTY: 4FACULTY.ORG

Project Director: Kristina Kauffman
Riverside Community College Districts
Office of Faculty Affairs
4800 Magnolia Avenue
Riverside, CA 92506
Tel: 951-222-8257
Fax: 951-328-3590
E-mail: kristina.kauffman@rcc.edu
URL: http://4faculty.org/

The 4faculty.org project was developed by Riverside Community College (RCC) as a way to improve the quality of first-time faculty teaching and also to involve adjunct faculty more fully into the campus community. RCC formed a collaborative partnership with eleven other California community colleges due to the dramatic increase in adjunct faculty across the California Community College System. Courses cover basic information from how to develop a syllabus to understanding copyright in a digital world.

Although the modules were originally designed for adjunct faculty, today they target all community college faculty. The courses follow the D.R.E.A.M. system, created by Riverside for this project. Lessons include Discover, Read, Explore, Apply, and Measure sections, which take the user from introduction through assessment. Because 4faculty.org runs on software independent of an outside course management system, other colleges can easily become partners by adding content that is specific to their colleges. This allows all partners to experience a level of ownership in the project. Feedback from participants has been highly positive and the membership now includes 41 California community colleges.

SOUTHERN REGIONAL EDUCATION BOARD:
ESTABLISHING THE SREB DISTANCE LEARNING POLICY LABORATORY

Project Director: Bruce Chaloux
Southern Regional Education Board

592 Tenth Street, NW
Atlanta, GA 30318
Tel: 404-875-9211
Fax: 404-872-1477
E-mail: bruce.chaloux@sreb.org
URL: http://www.electroniccampus.org/

Due to increasing enrollments and activity in e-learning, the Southern Regional Education Board (SREB) created the Distance Learning Policy Laboratory in 1999. The Laboratory was intended as a vehicle for assessing, developing, and promoting policies that encourage distance learning in the South. Partners included commissions, boards, and consortia from Alabama, Arkansas, Delaware, Florida, Georgia, Kentucky, Louisiana, Maryland, Missouri, North Carolina, Oklahoma, South Carolina, Tennessee, Texas, Virginia, and West Virginia.

The perceived need for the Lab arose of SREB's success with its *Electronic Campus*, a regional marketplace of more than 5,000 electronic courses and 250 degree programs from more than 375 colleges and universities. Each of the seven Policy Lab committees was asked to focus on four outcomes:

- Policy goals and recommendations for regional/state policy changes;
- Policy guidelines and principles that support distance learning;
- Illustrative practices, which are exemplary or promising models, strategies, and approaches; and
- Pilot projects aimed at initiating, supporting, or encouraging change.

Through its network of state partners, SREB has had varied influence in changing policies within each state and institution. In the case of federal financial aid policy, about which it expressed "a sense of urgency," SREB could only offer itself as a source of information and as a voice. SREB has also pushed only so far on the issue of a common price for electronic courses. Still, the Lab has made progress in bringing down the walls that bar students from an open academic marketplace, and has served a valuable purpose by convening the parties and serving as an advocate for change.

TEXAS A&M–CORPUS CHRISTI: ELECTRONIC LEARNING IN NURSING EDUCATION (ELINE)

Project Director: Claudia Johnston
Texas A&M University–Corpus Christi
6300 Ocean Drive

Corpus Christi, TX 78412
Tel: 361-825-2712
Fax: 361-825-2496
E-mail: johnston@falcon.tamucc.edu
URL: http://www.eline.tamucc.edu/

The e-Line nursing education program developed by Texas A&M and Delmar College was designed to remove barriers, enabling students to complete an entire Associate Degree in Nursing (AND) or Bachelor of Science degree (BSN) curriculum online and at their own pace. The clinical component of the program is provided in locations convenient for the students by preceptors who are required to complete extensive online training.

Developing the online nursing curriculum required working around a host of obstacles posed by the traditional organization of education in courses and terms. A first step was to move from a content oriented curriculum to one based on the nursing competencies as defined by the Board of Nurse Examiners for the State of Texas. The second was to develop instructional modules that provide students with the knowledge and skills needed to achieve the competencies and to organize the modules into courses. Project staff describe this process as unpacking the nursing curricula at the two schools to their "basic competencies," and repacking them into the existing course numbers for "purposes of crediting and transcripting" (eLine, *FY2003 Annual Report*, 4).

Offering the curriculum in modules provides considerable flexibility to students in completing their work. Students can move through the program as quickly as they are able to complete the modules, or if the time they have for study is limited, they can stretch the work out over a longer period of time as long as they complete the program within four years, an accreditation requirement. The program structure also allows a student to stop out during a semester and still retain credit for any modules completed.

Another advantage of the program is that it enables a more efficient articulation between the AND and BSN. Students do not have to repeat modules they completed while enrolled in the AND program if they choose to continue on to a BSN degree. Conversely, students enrolled in the BSN program who decide to transfer to the AND program do not have to repeat modules they completed as BSN students. The information concerning the modules required to complete each program is available on the eLine website so that students can plan their course of study.

University of Maryland College Park: Consortium for ITS Training and Education

Project Director: Kathleen Frankle
University of Maryland
Center for Advanced Transportation Technology
Building #806, Ste. 3103
College Park, MD 20742
Tel: 410-414-2925
Fax: 301-403-4591
E-mail: kfrankle@umd.edu
URL: http://www.citeconsortium.org/

The purpose of the Consortium for ITS Training and Education (CITE) is to create an integrated advanced transportation training and education program. The program, based on a consortium of universities, is open to anyone pursuing a career in advanced transportation. Instruction offered through CITE may include graduate and undergraduate level courses, as well as skill-based training and technology transfer. In addition to its educational responsibilities, CITE will facilitate networking and communication among universities and other CITE members.

CITE objectives include coordinating the creation of new advanced transportation courseware using distance learning, developing and maintaining curricula based on the needs of government and industry, functioning as a clearinghouse, fostering relationships among organizations, and supporting member efforts to offer comprehensive advanced transportation training and education programs.

University of Minnesota–Twin Cities: University of Minnesota School Technology Leadership Initiative (STLI)

Project Director: Scott McLeod
University of Minnesota
EDPA, 330 Wulling Hall
86 Pleasant Street SE
Tel: 612-626-0768
Fax: 612-624-0377
E-mail: mcleod@umn.edu
URL: http://www.umn.edu/~mcleod

The goal of this hybrid K–12 professional development project is to address the nationwide shortage of school administrators who can effectively facilitate the implementation of technology in schools and school districts. Fifteen one-credit hour courses (eight online, six on campus, one independent study) were developed to address the International Society for Technology in Education (ISTE) National Educational Technology Standards for Administrators (NETS-A). Students may take all 15 courses and receive a School Technology Leadership graduate certificate from the University of Minnesota, or they may choose to take individual courses (on a space available basis) to meet their needs.

Online courses include a customized Flash interface to facilitate online guest speakers. In addition, STLI has created lessons, teaching activities, reviews, decision-making guides, and comparison charts to help teachers and administrators deal with technology issues in schools. Through a partnership with Microsoft, they have developed self-contained electronic lesson plans. The project includes other corporate and educational partners, which makes STLI an outstanding resource for K–12 technology leadership.

WGBH NATIONAL CENTER FOR ACCESSIBLE MEDIA (NCAM): SPECIFICATIONS FOR ACCESSIBLE LEARNING TECHNOLOGIES (SALT)

Project Director: Madeleine Rothberg
WGBH Educational Foundation
WGBH National Center for Accessible Media
125 Western Avenue
Boston, MA 02134
Tel: 617-300-2492
Fax: 617-300-1035
E-mail: madeleine_rothberg@wgbh.org
URL: http://ncam.wgbh.org/salt/index.html

The SALT project is working with IMS Global Learning Consortium members and experts on distance learning and accessibility to develop and promote open access technical specifications for accessibility of software applications for the e-learning industry. Through IMS, an Accessibility Project Group has been formed. The group is one of the many IMS Project Groups working on developing specifications for e-learning.

Goals of the SALT Project include fostering collaboration among international players in the online learning field which has resulted in a set of guidelines to educate the e-learning community about the challenges that people with disabilities face in accessing online education, and to provide solutions and resources to solve these challenges.

IMS Global Learning Consortium supports the adoption and use of learning technology worldwide. IMS is a non-profit organization that includes more than 50 contributing members and affiliates who come from every sector of the global e-learning community. They include hardware and software vendors, educational institutions, publishers, government agencies, systems integrators, multimedia content providers, and other consortia. The Consortium provides a neutral forum in which members with competing business interests and different decision-making criteria collaborate to satisfy real-world requirements for interoperability and re-use.

During each cycle of specification development, the IMS Accessibility Group will develop specific goals for the scope of work that will occur during that cycle. These documents are not in the public domain; however, the results of the group's work will be publicly available on the IMS website.

RELEVANT RESOURCES ARRANGED BY TOPIC[1]

ORGANIZATIONAL

Policy Resources

AMERICAN ASSOCIATION OF UNIVERSITY PROFESSORS. 1999. *Statement on distance education.*
Statement of principles guiding distance education adopted by AAUP. Url: http://www.aaup.org/statements/Redbook/StDistEd.HTM.

AMERICAN COUNCIL ON EDUCATION. 2000. *Developing a distance learning policy for 21st century learning.*
Primer on issues institutions confront in planning distance education. Url: http://www.acenet.edu/washington/distance_ed/2000/03march/distance_ed.html.

KING, J.W., G.C. NUGENT, E.B. RUSSELL, J. EICH, AND D.D. LACY. 2000. *Policy frameworks for distance education: Implications for decisions makers.*
Model policy analysis framework for distance education. Url: http://www.westga.edu/~distance/king32.htm.

MARYLAND ONLINE. CONSORTIUM OF 19 COMMUNITY COLLEGES /SENIOR INSTITUTIONS.
Project to develop a process and replicable pathway to certify quality in online learning projects. Inter-institution quality assurance in online learning. Url: http://www.qualitymatters.org.

OLINGER, D., C. BARONE, AND B. HAWKINS. 2003. *Distributed education and its challenges: an overview.* AMERICAN COUNCIL ON EDUCATION AND EDUCAUSE.
First report in the ACE/EDUCAUSE series, Distributed Education: Challenges, Choices, and a New Environment. Identifies significant issues associated with

1   Note: Online sites are accurate as of August 2005, when last accessed.

distributed education and suggests a series of questions to help institutional leaders establish and validate their options. Url: http://www.educause.edu/policy.

OREGON STATE SYSTEM OF HIGHER EDUCATION. 1994. *Education unbounded: a vision of public higher education serving Oregon in 2010.*
Progress/status report on distance education policy. Url: http://www.ous.edu/dist-learn/dist-pol.htm.

OREGON NETWORK EDUCATION, DISTANCE EDUCATION POLICIES, PRINCIPLES AND GUIDELINES.
List of websites related to distance education policy. Url: http://oregonone-org/DEpolicy.htm.

WESTERN INTERSTATE COMMISSION ON HIGHER EDUCATION. 2005. *Policy analysis and research.*
Url: http://www.wiche.edu/Policy/index.asp.

PROVIDERS — PROGRAMS — EXEMPLARY PARTNERSHIPS

BERGE, Z. (ED.). 2000. *Sustaining distance training: Integrating learning technologies into the fabric of the enterprise.* SAN FRANCISCO: JOSSEY BASS.
Descriptions of how 20 well-known organizations and businesses have employed technology to develop successful distance workforce training programs.

THE EARLY COLLEGE HIGH SCHOOL INITIATIVE AND THE MIDDLE COLLEGE CONSORTIUM.
Early and middle college high schools are pathways to college degree completion for the low-income high school age student. They offer a restructured high school curriculum that provides the opportunity for students to earn up to two years of college credit while still in high school. Url: http://www.earlycolleges.org/Index.html and http://www.lagcc.cuny.edu/mcnc/.

FIELDSTONE ALLIANCE.
Formerly Wilder Research Center. Offers consulting, training, network development, demonstration projects, and capacity building for nonprofits and their communities. Url: http://www.fieldstonealliance.org.

MOXLEY, V.M., AND S.C. MAES. 2003. THE GREAT PLAINS INTERACTIVE DISTANCE EDUCATION ALLIANCE. *Continuing Higher Education Review Consortium* 67.
National model for inter-institutional alliance offering online graduate programs. Url: http://www.gpidea.org/alliance/ResourceCenter/UCEAarticle.pdf.

WESTERN COOPERATIVE FOR EDUCATIONAL TELECOMMUNICATIONS (WCET), BOULDER, CO.
Western interstate state commission for higher education. Url: http://www.wcet.info/consulting/.

PROFESSIONAL DEVELOPMENT RESOURCES

CHARALAMBOS, V., AND G.V. GLASS (EDS.). 2002. ONLINE PROFESSIONAL DEVELOPMENT FOR TEACHERS. *Current perspectives in applied information technologies.* GREENWICH, CT: INFORMATION AGE.

THE CONNECTED TEACHER. ANYWHERE, ANYTIME LEARNING MEETS PROFESSIONAL DEVELOPMENT. *American School Board Journal* SUPPLEMENT. ELECTRONIC SCHOOL.
Url: www.electronic-school.com.

EISENHOWER NATIONAL CLEARINGHOUSE FOR MATH AND SCIENCE EDUCATION. 2002. IS ONLINE PROFESSIONAL DEVELOPMENT FOR YOU? *ENC Focus* 9(4).
Url: www.enc.org.

NATIONAL CENTER TO IMPROVE PRACTICE. 2001. A ROUNDTABLE DISCUSSION ABOUT ONLINE PROFESSIONAL DEVELOPMENT. *Mosaic* 3(1).
Url: http://main.edc.org/mosaic.

NATIONAL TECHNOLOGY PREPARATION NETWORK CONFERENCE. 2005. WEB-BASED PROFESSIONAL DEVELOPMENT STRATEGIES.
Programs and projects to prepare students for technology future. Url: http://www.cord.org.

WEKSEL, T., L. KRUGER, R. GARBETT, AND G. MACKLEN. 2002. THE FUTURE IS NOW: USING ONLINE COURSES FOR PROFESSIONAL DEVELOPMENT. *National Association of School Psychologists Communiqué* 31(3).
Internet metaphors: library, support group, diary, and classroom. Url: www.nasponline.org.

HIGHER EDUCATION RESOURCES

ACHIEVE, INC. 2004. *Ready or not: creating a high school that counts* [ELECTRONIC VERSION].
The goal of the project described in this publication was to improve the level of performance of high school graduates through restructuring the system of assessment and the requirements for graduation around the knowledge and skills

needed for success in college or the workforce. Url:
http://www.achieve.org/dstore.nsf/Lookup/ADPreport/$file/ADPreport.pdf.

ADELMAN, C. 2004. *Principal indicators of student academic histories in postsecondary education, 1972–2000.* [ELECTRONIC VERSION] WASHINGTON, DC: U.S. DEPARTMENT OF EDUCATION.
Cliff Adelman's research and analysis of patterns of college attendance are helpful in understanding both the extent of the problem of access and the reasons why many students are not successful in making the transition to college and completing. Url:
http://www.ed.gov.rschstat/research/pubs/prinindicat/prinindicat.pdf.

AMERICAN ASSOCIATION OF COMMUNITY COLLEGES. 2004. *Improving access to the baccalaureate* [ELECTRONIC VERSION]. WASHINGTON, DC: COMMUNITY COLLEGE PRESS.
A joint publication of the American Association of Community Colleges and American Association of State Colleges and Universities, this report explores the barriers that inhibit transfer from community colleges to state colleges and universities and provides recommendations for changes in both policies and practice. Url: http://www.pathtocollege.org (Lumina_Rpt_AACC.pdf).

COUNCIL FOR ADULT AND EXPERIENTIAL LEARNING. *CAEL and DOL healthcare lattice program.*
This report describes a Council for Adult and Experiential Learning (CAEL) project, which is designed to address shortages in the nursing workforce. Their healthcare "lattice" program is designed for current hospital employees and provides a pathway for hospital employees to complete a CNA program, the LPN, and, ultimately, an RN program. Url: www.cael.org/healthcare.htm.

Journal of Hispanic Education, 3(2). 2004.
This issue of the *Journal of Hispanic Higher Education* contains several articles dealing with access of Hispanic students to higher education. Url:
http://jhh.sagepub.com/content/vol3/issue2/.

McDONOUGH, P. [ELECTRONIC VERSION]. 2004. *The school-to-college transition: Challenges and prospects.* WASHINGTON, DC: AMERICAN COUNCIL ON EDUCATION.
Volume in the continuing series *Informed practice: synthesis of higher education research for campus leaders*. Url:
http://www.acenet.edu/bookstore/pdf/2004_IPTransitions.pdf.

NATIONAL POSTSECONDARY EDUCATION COOPERATIVE [ELECTRONIC VERSION]. 2004. *How does technology affect access in postsecondary education? What do we really know?* (NPEC 2004-851), PREPARED BY RONALD PHIPPS FOR THE NATIONAL

Postsecondary Education Cooperative Working Group on Access-Technology. Washington, DC.
This publication consists of a compilation and analysis of recent research concerning the extent to which distance education has increased access to postsecondary education, the barriers to increased access, and the effectiveness of the technology based education. Url: http://nces.ed.gov/pubs2004/2004831.pdf.

Other Resources

The College Board.
The College Board sponsors research and publishes reports relating to college access. Url: http://www.collegeboard.com/prof/index.html.

Relevant Organizations

A*DEC – American Distance Education Consortium.
State and land grant institutions providing distance education and services through information technology. Url: http://www.adec.edu/.

Distance Education Clearinghouse.
Url: http://www.uwex.edu/disted/.

EDUCAUSE/National Learning Infrastructure Initiative (NLII).
Advancing higher education's intelligent use of information technology. Url: http://www.educause.edu/nlii/.

United States Distance Learning Association.
Url: http://www.usdla.org.

INSTRUCTIONAL

Instructional Effectiveness

Abel, R. 2005. *Internet supported learning study. Achieving success in internet-supported learning in higher education: case studies illuminate success factors, challenges, and future directions.* Alliance for Higher Education Competitiveness.
A study by Abel from the Alliance for Higher Education Competitiveness that identifies key institutional characteristics necessary for promoting successful online learning, noting aspects such as commitment, focus on quality rather (rather than quantity) and that provide solid commitment to technology and learning support. Url: http://www.a-hec.org/e-learning_study.html.

BELL, P., AND P. REDDY. 2004. *Rural areas and the Internet.* PEW INTERNET AND AMERICAN LIFE PROJECT. WASHINGTON, DC: THE PEW FOUNDATION. Url: http://www.pewinternet.org/pdfs/PIP_Rural_Report.pdf.

BROWN, A.R., AND B.D. VOLTZ. 2005. ELEMENTS OF EFFECTIVE E-LEARNING DESIGN. *International Review of Research in Open and Distance Learning.*
Article addresses effective design and development of cost effective, high quality materials, that maintains a focus on the activities in which learners need to engage, the context those activities require, and the impact the learning might yield. Url: http://www.irrodl.org/content/v6.1/brown_voltz.html.

PERRY, B., AND M. EDWARDS. 2005. EXEMPLARY ONLINE EDUCATORS: CREATING A COMMUNITY OF INQUIRY. *Turkish Online Journal of Distance Education* 6(2).
Qualitative study that explores what makes some online educators more effective than others. The authors identify the essential aspect of online learning-centered instruction that challenges students and faculty by promoting a model in which faculty share and learn with students. Url: http://tojde.anadolu.edu.tr/tojde18/articles/article6.htm.

SHIH, J. 2004. A PEDAGOGICAL DESIGN STRATEGY FOR EFFECTIVE TECHNOLOGY-BASED LEARNING: iLEARN MODEL. *International Journal of Instructional Technology and Distance Learning* 1(8).
The approach Ju-Ling Shih takes in this article uses an architecture model that integrates activities and technologies that encourage and depend upon increasing learner responsibility. Url: http://itdl.org/Journal/Aug_04/article06.htm.

YOUNG, L.D. 2003. BRIDGING THEORY AND PRACTICE: DEVELOPING GUIDELINES TO FACILITATE THE DESIGN OF COMPUTER-BASED LEARNING ENVIRONMENTS. *Canadian Journal of Learning and Technology* 29(3).
Young proposes principles for guiding the creation of effective online learning, including social negotiation, cognitive responsibility, and authentic contexts. Url: http://www.cjlt.ca/content/vol29.3/cjlt29-3_art4.html.

Student Support Resources

ANDERSON, T. 2004. PRACTICE GUIDED BY RESEARCH IN PROVIDING EFFECTIVE STUDENT SUPPORT SERVICES. *EDEN Research Workshop and International Conference.*
European Distance Education Network. Argues need for sustained research. Url: http://www.change.co.nz/docs/eden/Anderson.pdf.

BRIGHAM, D.E. 2001. CONVERTING STUDENT SUPPORT SERVICES TO ONLINE DELIVERY. *International Review of Research in Open and Distance Learning.*
Url: http://www.irrodl.org/content/v1.2/regents.html.

BURNETT, D.J. 2002. BEST PRACTICES AND PROCESS INNOVATION MODELS AND TRENDS. *Innovation in student services: planning for models blending high touch/high tech.* SOCIETY FOR COLLEGE AND UNIVERSITY PLANNING.
Url: http://www.scup.org/studentservices/iss-1.pdf.

COX, D.H. 2001. ONLINE STUDENT SERVICES SELF-ASSESSMENT TOOL. *Austin Community College Instructional Resources & Technology.*
Url:
http://irt.austincc.edu/presentations/2003/aacc/McRaeOnlineStudentServices.pdf.

DUNLAP, J.C., AND S. LUDWIG-HARDMAN. 2003. LEARNER SUPPORT SERVICES FOR ONLINE STUDENTS: SCAFFOLDING FOR SUCCESS. *International Review of Research in Open and Distance Learning.*
Url: http://www.irrodl.org/content/v4.1/dunlap.html.

KRETOVICS, M. 2003. ROLE OF STUDENT AFFAIRS IN DISTANCE EDUCATION: CYBER-SERVICES OR VIRTUAL COMMUNITIES. *Online Journal of Distance Education Administration.*
Url: http://www.westga.edu/%7Edistance/ojdla/fall63/kretovics63.html.

MEYERS, P., AND H. OSTASH. 2004. PUTTING THE PIECES TOGETHER: COMPREHENSIVE ONLINE SUPPORT SERVICES. *Ijournal: Insight Into Student Services.*
Url: http://www.ijournal.us/issue_08/ij_issue08_MeyersAndOstash_01.htm.

RYAN, Y. 2001. THE PROVISION OF LEARNER SUPPORT SERVICES ONLINE. IN *The changing faces of virtual education*, EDITED BY G. FARRELL. VANCOUVER, BC: COMMONWEALTH OF LEARNING.
Url: http://www.col.org/virtualed/virtual2pdfs/V2_chapter5.pdf.

STOERGER, S. *Examples of online student support initiatives.*
Provides examples of services provided by institutions for distance learners that reflect the realm of possibilities in online student services. Url: http://www.web-miner.com/desupport.htm.

WESTERN COOPERATIVE FOR EDUCATIONAL TELECOMMUNICATIONS. 2005. *Beyond the administrative core: creating web-based student services for online learners project* [PROJECTS]. BOULDER, CO: WESTERN COOPERATIVE FOR EDUCATIONAL TELECOMMUNICAITONS.
Url: http://www.wcet.info/projects/laap/index.asp.

RELEVANT PUBLICATIONS

HORRIGAN, J., AND L. RAINIE. 2002 . *Getting serious online.* PEW INTERNET AND AMERICAN LIFE PROJECT. WASHINGTON, DC: THE PEW FOUNDATION.
Survey of Internet use. Url:
http://www.pewtrusts.com/pdf/vf_pew_internet_serious.pdf.

LENHART, A. 2003. *The ever-shifting Internet population: a new look at Internet access and the digital divide.* PEW INTERNET AND AMERICAN LIFE PROJECT. WASHINGTON, DC: THE PEW FOUNDATION.
Patterns of non Internet users. Url:
http://www.pewinternet.org/pdfs/PIP_Shifting_Net_Pop_Report.pdf.

NATIONAL TELECOMMUNICATIONS AND INFORMATION ADMINISTRATION (NTIA). 2000. *Falling through the Net: toward digital inclusion.* WASHINGTON, DC: U.S. GOVERNMENT PRINTING OFFICE.
Url: http://search.ntia.doc.gov/pdf/fttn00.pdf.

NATIONAL TELECOMMUNICATIONS AND INFORMATION ADMINISTRATION (NTIA). 2002. *A nation online: how Americans are expanding their use of the Internet.*
Survey of 57,000 households and 137,000 individuals. Url:
http://www.ntia.doc.gov/ntiahome/dn/html/anationonline2.htm.

U.S. CONGRESS, OFFICE OF TECHNOLOGY ASSESSMENT. 1995. *Telecommunications technology and Native Americans: Opportunities and challenges,* OTA-ITC-621. WASHINGTON, DC: U.S. GOVERNMENT PRINTING OFFICE.
Url: http://www.wws.princeton.edu/~ota/disk1/1995/9542_html.

WARSCHAUER, M. 2002. RECONCEPTUALIZING THE DIGITAL DIVIDE. *First Monday,* 7(7).
Suggests alternative conceptual framework of social inclusion rather than digital divide. Url: http://www.firstmonday.dk/issues/issue7_7/warschauer.

PALLOFF, R. M., AND K. PRATT. 1999. *Building learning communities in cyberspace: effective strategies for the online classroom.* SAN FRANCISCO: JOSSEY-BASS.

PREECE, J. 2000. *Online communities: designing usability and supporting sociability.* SUSSEX, UK: WILEY & SONS.

GENERAL RESOURCES

OPEN SOURCE SOFTWARE INITIATIVE.
Url: http://www.opensource.org/

TAPPED IN.

Online workplace for education professionals from SRI's Center for Teaching in Learning. Url: http://tappedin.org/tappedin.

THE TEACHING LEARNING & TECHNOLOGY (TLT) GROUP.

Support organization to improve teaching and learning with technology. Url: http://www.tltgroup.org/.

VIRTUAL INSTRUCTIONAL DESIGNER.

Principles of instructional design. Url: http://www.e-learningcentre.co.uk/eclipse/Resources/isd.htm.

WEBAIM – WEB ACCESSIBILITY IN MIND.

Potential of WWW for people with disabilities and how faculty and web designers address their needs. Url: http://www.webaim.org/.

RELEVANT CONFERENCES

ANNUAL CONFERENCE ON DISTANCE TEACHING AND LEARNING.

Website has streaming media keynotes and years of proceedings. Url: http://www.uwex.edu/disted/conference/.

EDUCAUSE ANNUAL CONFERENCE.

Resources on teaching and learning with instructional technology. Url: http://www.educause.edu/Browse/645?parent_id=107.

NATIONAL UNIVERSITY TELECOMMUNICATIONS NETWORK (NUTN) ANNUAL CONFERENCE.

Advancing higher education through technology and distance learning. Benchmarking for quality. Url: http://www.nutn.org/.

WESTERN COOPERATIVE FOR EDUCATION TELECOMMUNICATION (WCET).

Url: http://www.wcet.info.

REFERENCES

Introduction

Kathleen P. King

Alexander, B. 2004. Going nomadic: Mobile learning in higher education. *EDUCAUSE Review* 39(5):28–35. Url: http://www.educause.edu/ir/library/pdf/erm0451.pdf.

Blumenstyk, G. 2001. Temple U. shuts down for-profit distance education company. *The Chronicle of Higher Education* 47(45):A29.

Boettcher, J. 2004. Are we there yet? *Campus Technology.* Url: http://www.campus-technology.com/article.asp?id=10203.

Cahoon, B. (ed.). 1998. *Adult learning and the Internet.* New Directions for Adult and Continuing Education, vol. 78. San Francisco: Jossey-Bass.

Cantelon, J. E. 1995. The evolution and advantages of distance education. In *Facilitating distance education,* edited by M. H. Rossman and M. E. Rossman. New Directions for Higher Education, vol. 67. San Francisco: Jossey-Bass.

Carr, S. 2001. Is anyone making money in distance education? *The Chronicle of Higher Education* 47(23):A41.

Desanctis, G., and B. Sheppard. 1997. Bridging distance, time, and culture in executive MBA education. *Journal of Education for Business* 74(3): 157–161.

Foster, A. 2005. Technology: Keeping networks safe is administrators' dominant worry. *The Chronicle of Higher Education* 51(18): A10.

Green K. 2004. Tech budgets get some relief. *The Campus Computing Project.* Url: http://www.campuscomputing.net/summaries/2004/.

Hodgins, W., and M. Conner. 2000. Everything you ever wanted to know about learning standards but were afraid to ask. *LineZine: Learning in the New Economy.* Url: http://www.linezine.com/2.1/features/wheyewtkls.htm.

Holmberg, B. 1986. *Growth and structure of distance education.* Wolfeboro, NH: Croom Helm.

King, K. P. 2001. Playing out the realities of web-based bulletin boards: Enhancing face-to-face learning. *New Horizons in Adult Education* 15(1): 3–9.

King, K. P. 2002. Testing the waters for distance education in adult education programs. *PAACE Journal of Lifelong Learning* 11: 11–24.

King, K. P. 2005. Distance education. In *Encyclopedia of adult education,* edited by L. English. London: Palgrave.

Moore, M., and G. Kearsley. 1996. *Distance education: A systems view.* Belmont, CA: Wadsworth.

Northrup, P., and B. Harrison. 2005. *Learning on demand: Using the PDA for mobile course delivery.* Paper presented at the 21ˢᵗ Annual Conference on Distance Teaching and Learning, Madison, WI. Url: http://www.uwex.edu/disted/con ference/ Resource_library

Palloff, R. M., and K. Pratt. 1999. *Building learning communities in cyberspace.* San Francisco: Jossey-Bass.

Shih, Y. E. 2005. *Apply mobile technology in foreign language learning.* Paper presented at the 21ˢᵗ Annual Conference on Distance Teaching and Learning, Madison, WI. Url: http://www.uwex.edu/disted/conference/Resource_library.

Tozman, R. 2004. Another new paradigm for instructional design. *Learning Circuits.* Url: http://www.learningcircuits.org/2004/nov2004/tozman.htm.

Wallace, R. M. 2003. Online learning in higher education: A review of research on interactions among teachers and students. *Education, Communication, and Information* 3(2): 241–280.

CHAPTER ONE

The Pivotal Role of Policy in Distance Education

Harvey Blustain

American Association of University Professors. 1999. *Statement on distance education.* Url: http://www.aaup.org/statements/Redbook/StDistEd.HTM.

American Council on Education. 2003. *Developing a distance learning policy for 21ˢᵗ century learning.* Url: http://www.acenet.edu/washington/distance_ed/2000/03 march/distance_ed.html.

Educause. n.d. *Educause policy initiatives.* Url: http://www.educause.edu/policy.

King, J. W., G. C. Nugent, E. B. Russell, J. Eich, and D. D. Lacy. 2000. *Policy frameworks for distance education: Implications for decisions makers.* Url: http://www.westga.edu/~distance/king32.htm.

Moxley, V. M., and S. C. Maes. 2003. The Great Plains interactive distance education alliance. *Continuing Higher Education Review* 67:1-10. Url: http://www.gpidea.org/alliance/ResourceCenter/UCEAarticle.pdf.

Oregon University System. 2001. *OUS distance education policy guidelines.* Url: http://www.ous.edu/dist-learn/DEguidelines2001.htm.

Timpane, P., and L. White, L. 1998. *Higher education and school reform.* San Francisco: Jossey-Bass.

Western Interstate Commission on Higher Education. n.d. *Policy analysis and research.* Url: http://www.wiche.edu/Policy.

CHAPTER TWO

Extending the Reach of Distance Education Through Partnerships

RAYMOND J. LEWIS

American Council on Education. 2003. *Developing a distance learning policy for 21ˢᵗ century learning.* Url: http://www.acenet.edu/washington/distance_ed/2000/03march/distance_ed.html.

Bear, L. L., and A. H. Duin. 2004. *Exploring success indicators for partnerships.* Washington, DC: Fund for the Improvement to Postsecondary Education.

Eckel, P., B. Affolter-Caine, and M. Green. 2003. *New times, new strategies: Curricular joint ventures.* Washington, DC: American Council on Education.

Eckel, P., M. Hartley, and B. Affolter-Caine. 2004. *Cooperating to compete: A campus leaders' guide to developing curricular partnerships and joint programs.* Washington, DC: American Council on Education.

Hilderbrand, D., and B. McLeod. 2003. A model for collaboration in multi-institutional graduate programs. *Council of Graduate Schools Communicator* 36(2):9.

Kanter, R. M. 1994. Collaborative advantage: The art of alliances. *Harvard Business Review* 72(4): 96–108.

Mattessich, P. D., M. Murray-Close, and B. A. Monsey. 2004. *Collaboration: What makes it work.* St. Paul, MN: Wilder Foundation.

Merrill-Sands, D., and B. Sheridan. 1996. *Developing and managing collaborative alliances: Lessons from a review of the literature.* Boston: Simmons Institute for Leadership and Change, Organizational Change Briefing Note No. 3.

Moxley, V. M., and S. C. Maes. 2003. The Great Plains interactive distance education alliance. *Continuing Higher Education Review* 67:1–10.

CHAPTER THREE

Using Distance Education to Increase Higher Education Opportunities

MARIANNE R. PHELPS

Cavanagh, S. 2004. Barriers to college: Lack of preparation vs. financial need. *Education Week* 23(19): 1–13.

College Summit. 2004. Results and awards.
Url: http://www.collegesummit.org/resves.htm.

National Center for Educational Statistics. 2002. Student effort and educational progress—completions.
Url: http://nces.ed.gov/programs/coe/2002/section3/indicator25.asp.

National Center for Educational Statistics. 1995. Event, status, and cohort dropout rates. Url: http://nces.ed.gov/pubs/dp95/97473.asp.

Orfield, G., D. Losen, J. Wald, and C. Swanson. 2004 *Losing our future: How minority youth are being left behind by the graduation rate crisis*. Cambridge, MA: The Civil Rights Project at Harvard University.
Url: http://www.Urban.org/UploadedPDF/4109036_LosingOurFuture.pdf.

Rudolph, F. 1962. *The American college and university, a history*. New York: Knopf.

Venezia, A., M. W. Kirst, and A. I. Antonio. 2003. Fix K-16 disconnections, or betray the college dream: Excerpted from "Betraying the college dream," a policy report by the Bridge Project. *Education Digest* 68(9): 34–39.

CHAPTER FOUR

New Perspectives on Instructional Effectiveness Through Distance Education

GARY BROWN

Alldredge, J. R., and Brown, G. 2006. *Association of course performance with student beliefs: An analysis by gender and instructional software environment*. Proceedings of the Statistics Education Research Journal and European Research in Mathematics Conference, 5(1): 64–77.

Anonymous. 2002. *Lessons learned from FIPSE projects III*.
Url: http://www.ed.gov/about/offices/list/ope/fipse/lessons3/index.html.

Bransford, J. D., R. D. Sherwood, T. S. Hasselbring, C. K. Kinzer, and S. M. Williams. 1990. *Anchored instruction: Why we need it and how technology can help*. New York: Atheneum.

Brown, G., C. Myers, and S. Roy. 2003. Formal course design and the student learning experience. *Journal of Asynchronous Learning Networks* 7(3).
Url: http://www.aln.org/publications/jaln/v7n3/v7n3_myers.asp.

Ehrmann, S. 1999. What outcomes assessment misses. *Architecture for Change: Information as Foundation*. Washington, DC: American Association for Higher Education.

Henderson, T., and G. Brown. 1999. A cost/benefit analysis of three technology development strategies in higher education using the Flashlight Economic Model. In *Modeling resource use in teaching and learning with technology*, edited by S. Ehrmann and J. H. Milam.. Washington, DC: American Association for Higher Education.

House, E. R. 1993. *Professional evaluation: Social impact and political consequences*. Newbury Park, CA: Sage.

Phipps, R., and J. Merisotis. 1999. *What's the difference? A review of contemporary research on the effectiveness of distance learning in higher education.* A Report from The Institute for Higher Education Policy. Url: http://www.ihep.com/PUB.htm.

Schutte, J. 1997. *Virtual teaching in higher education: The new intellectual superhighway or just another traffic jam?* Url: http://www.csun.edu/sociology/virexp.htm.

Wiggens, G. P. 1993. *Assessing student performance: Exploring the purpose and limits of testing.* San Francisco: Jossey-Bass.

Worthen, B. R., J. R. Sanders, and J. L. Fitzpatrick. 1997. *Program evaluation: Alternative approaches and practical guidelines.* New York: Longman.

Zemsky, R., and W. F. Massy. 2004. *Thwarted innovation: What happened to e-learning and why.* The Learning Alliance at the University of Pennsylvania. Url: http://www.thelearningalliance.info/WeatherStation.html.

Chapter Five

New Challenges, New Solutions for Supporting Distance Education Students

Julie Porosky Hamlin

Chaloux, B., and J. Mingle. 2002. *Technology can extend access to postsecondary education: An action agenda for the South.* Atlanta, GA: Southern Regional Education Board.

Connecticut Distance Learning Consortium. 2004. *Year 2 final report. Supporting online learners: A statewide approach to quality academic services.* Url: http://www.ctdlc.org.

Sachs, S. G. 2003. *Instructional support services best practices.* Northern Virginia Community College.

Shea, P. 2002. Peering into the future of Web-based services for online learners. *Educational Pathways.* Url: http://www.edpath.com/wcet.htm.

Sloan-C Consortium. 2004. *Effective practices.* Url: http://www.sloan-c.org/effective/SortByStudentSat.asp.

Twigg, C. A. 2003. *Expanding access to learning: The role of virtual universities.* Troy, NY: Center for Academic Transformation.

Western Cooperative for Educational Telecommunications. 2003. *Beyond the administrative core: Creating Web-based student services for online learners.* Url: http://www.wcet.info.

Western Cooperative for Educational Telecommunications. 2005. *Electronic delivery of student services.* Url: http://www.wcet.info/community/index.php?s=0b89a422fa7c5af154bb9312362390e4andact=SFandf=.

CHAPTER 6

Increasing Equity: Seeking Mainstream Advantages for All

CHERE CAMPBELL GIBSON

Bell, P., and P. Reddy. 2004. Rural areas and the Internet. Pew Internet and American Life Project. Washington DC: The Pew Foundation.

Carranza, S. 2004. *Reach Out/Alcanza Project for migrant farm workers and their families.* LAAP Final Report to the Fund for the Improvement to Postsecondary Education. Url: http://alcanza.uwsa.edu and http://reachout.uwsa.edu.

Courtnage, L. 2004. Information technology across the miles. LAAP Final Report to the Fund for the Improvement to Postsecondary Education. See also Url: http://it.rocky.edu.

Dhanarajan, G. 1997. *Globalization, competitiveness and open and distance education: Reflections on quality assurance.* Paper presented at the Asian Association of Open Universities 11th Annual Conference, Malaysia. Url: http://www.col.org/speeches/aaou11th.htm.

Dick, W., L. Carey, and J. Carey. 2001. *The systematic design of instruction,* 5th ed. New York: Addison-Wesley Educational Publishers.

Gibson, C. (ed.). 1998. *Distance learners in higher education: Institutional responses for quality outcomes.* Madison, WI: Atwood Publishing.

Gunawardena, C., P. Wilson, and A. Nolla. 2003. Culture and online education. In *Handbook of distance learning*, edited by M. Moore and B. Mahwah, NJ: Lawrence Erlbaum Associates.

Hernandez, N. 2003. *Forging partnerships and networking learners with the HETS virtual learning and support plaza.* LAAP Final Report to the Fund for the Improvement to Postsecondary Education. See also Url: http://www.virtualplaza.org.

Klein, S., R. Bugarin, R. Beltranen, and E. McArthur. 2004. *Language minorities and their educational and labor market indictors—Recent trends* 6(1, 2). National Center for Educational Statistics (NCES 2004-009). Url: http://nces.ed.gov/programs/quarterly/vol_6/1_2/7_2.asp.

Mehan, H., A. Datnow, E. Bratton, C. Tellez, D. Friedlaender, and T. Ngo. 1992. *Untracking and college enrollment.* Research Report 4, San Diego, CA: National Center for Research on Cultural Diversity and Second Language Learning. Url: http://www.ncela.gwu.edu/pubs/ncrcdsll/rr4/.

Mulhausen, P. 2004. *An innovative web-based educational program for health care workers in long-term care facilities.* LAAP Report to the Fund for the Improvement to Postsecondary Education.
See also Url: http://www.medicine.uiowa.edu/igec/laap/index.html.

National Center for Educational Statistics. 1995. *Event, status and cohort dropout rates.* Url: http://nces.ed.gov/pubs/dp95/97473-2.asp.

National Center for Educational Statistics. 2000. *Postsecondary students with disabilities: Enrollment, services and persistence.*
Url: http://nces.ed.gov/pubs2000/2000092.pdf.

National Center for Educational Statistics. 2002. *Student effort and educational progress – completions.*
Url: http://nces.ed.gov/programs/coe/2002/section3/indicator25.asp.

O'Brien, C. 2003. *Project CONNECT.* LAAP Final Report to the Fund for the Improvement to Postsecondary Education. See also Url: http://www.pbs.org/literacy/esl.

Pew. 2001. *More online doing more.* Pew Internet project – Tracking report.
Url: http://www.pewinternet.org/report_display.asp?r=30.

Swanson, C. 2004. *A statistical portrait of public high school graduation, class of 2001.*
Url: http://www.urban.org/url.cfm?ID=410934 .

United States Department of Agriculture. 2003. *Race and ethnicity in rural America: Educational attainment.*
Url: http://www.ers.usda.gov/Briefing/RaceAndEthnic/education.htm.

Warschauer, M. 2002. Reconceptualizing the digital divide. *First Monday* 7(7).
Url: http://www.firstmonday.dk/issues/issue7_7/warschauer.

Willard, M. J. 2003. *The development of Anytime/Anywhere model of call center training for individuals with disabilities.* LAAP Report to the Fund for the Improvement to Postsecondary Education. Url: http://www.nticampus.org.

CHAPTER SEVEN

No Time to Spare: Technology Assisted Professional Development

DARCY W. HARDY

Baumgardner, G. 2000. *Strategies for effective online education.* New York: Forbes Custom Publishing.

Cooper, C., and J. Boyd. 1998. Creating sustained professional growth through collaborative reflection. In *Professional development for cooperative learning: Issues and approaches*, edited by C. M. Brody and N. Davidson. Albany NY: State University of New York Press.

Cyrs, T. E. 1997. Competence in teaching at a distance. In *Teaching and learning at a distance: What it takes to effectively design, deliver, and evaluate programs*, edited by T. E. Cyrs. New Directions for Adult and Continuing Education, vol. 71. San Francisco: Jossey-Bass.

Gaff, J. G. 1975. *Toward faculty renewal. Advances in faculty, instructional, and organizational development.* San Francisco: Jossey-Bass.

Gandolfo, A. 1998. Brave new world? The challenge of technology to time-honored pedagogies and traditional structures. In *The impact of technology on faculty development, life, and work*, edited by K. H. Gillespie. New Directions for Adult and Continuing Education, vol. 76. San Francisco: Jossey-Bass.

CHAPTER 8

Conclusion: Harnessing the Power of Innnovative Technology in Higher Education

KATHLEEN P. KING AND SUSAN C. BIRO

Balz, D. 2005. 45 states target graduation rates. *The Washington Post* July 18: A3.

Bonk, C. J., and V. Dennen. 1999. Teaching on the web: With a little help from my pedagogical friends. *Journal of Computing in Higher Education* 11(1): 3–28.

Caffarella, R. S. 2002. *Planning programs for adult learners: A practical guide for educators, trainers, and staff developers*, 2nd ed.. San Francisco: Jossey Bass.

Cantelon, J. E. 1995. The evolution and advantages of distance education. In *Facilitating distance education*, edited by M. H. Rossman and M. E. Rossman. New Directions for Higher Education, vol. 67. San Francisco: Jossey-Bass.

Colvin, G. 2005. The 97-pound weakling? *Fortune* 152(2): 70–82.

Gandolfo, A. 1998. Brave new world? The challenge of technology to time-honored pedagogies and traditional structures. In *The impact of technology on faculty development, life, and work*, edited by K. H. Gillespie. New Directions for Adult and Continuing Education, vol. 76. San Francisco: Jossey-Bass.

King, K. P. 2003. *Keeping pace with technology: Educational technology that transforms. Vol. Two: The challenge and promise for higher education faculty*. Cresskill, NJ: Hampton Press.

Lawler, P. A., and K. P. King. 2000. *Planning for effective faculty development: Using adult learning strategies*. Malabar, FL: Krieger.

National Telecommunications and Information Administration (NTIA). 1999. *Falling through the net: Defining the digital divide*. Washington, DC: NTIA. Url: http://www.ntia.doc.gov/ntiahome/fttn99/contents.html.

National Telecommunications and Information Administration (NTIA). 1995. *Falling through the net: A survey of the "Have Nots" in rural and urban America*. Washington, DC: NTIA.
Url: http://www.ntia.doc.gov/ntiahome/fallingthru.html.

Wirt, J., S. Choy, S, Provasnik, P. Rooney, A. Sen, and R. Tobin, R. 2003. *The condition of education 2003* (NCES 2003-067). Washington, DC: National Center for Education Statistics.
Url: http://nces.ed.gov/pubsearch/pubsinfo.asp?pubid=2003067.

ABOUT THE AUTHORS

Susan C. Biro is a researcher and professional developer at Fordham University's Regional Educational Technology Center (RETC). An experienced administrator, she has extensive knowledge in implementing professional development that supports faculty who teach with technology. Before coming to Fordham, Dr. Biro was the director of distance learning at University College, Widener University, where she oversaw the delivery of distance learning courses and degree-completion programs to a part-time adult student population. These responsibilities included providing online student support, and Dr. Biro led a campus-wide implementation team of administrators and academic support staff in improving online student services. She was also responsible for designing and delivering professional development to adjunct faculty across disciplines, including supporting the use of technology in traditional, online, and hybrid formats.

As an adult educator, Dr. Biro has taught in a variety of settings including community college, workplace training initiatives, and a correctional facility. Her research interests have focused on professional development for faculty who teach in a distance learning format, with a special interest in the needs of adjunct faculty. Dr. Biro has presented at state, regional, and national academic conferences on issues related to distance learning program development, student support for distance learning initiatives, faculty development (both full-time and adjunct), and professional development that supports faculty who teach online. Her most recent publication is titled *Preparing Faculty to Teach Online: A Successful Collaboration*, co-authored with T. J. O'Tanyi and D. Harp Ziegenfuss (2004–2005).

Susan received her Ed.D. in Higher Education from Widener University, Chester, PA. She also has a M.Ed. in adult education from Widener University, and a B.A. in journalism from Delaware State University, Dover. In addition, she serves as assistant editor and copy editor of *Perspectives: The New York Journal of Adult Learning*.

Harvey Blustain is President of Act IV Consulting, Inc., a firm dedicated to helping higher education institutions address their business and organizational challenges. His services include organizational assessment and development, planning, and market research.

Harvey's career has included positions in academia, international development, market research, corporate consulting, and entrepreneurial start-ups. For the past ten years Harvey has focused on higher education as President of Act IV Consulting and, prior to that, as a Director in the Price Waterhouse Coopers National Higher Education Consulting Practice. Among his recent clients are Tufts University, Boston University, Brandeis University, Connecticut College, and the University of Massachusetts.

Harvey has consulted extensively with numerous corporations in the areas of change management and organizational effectiveness. His clients have been in a range of industries including information technology, telecommunications, healthcare and insurance, manufacturing, financial services, agriculture, and government. He has held management positions at EDS and Coopers & Lybrand/PwC. His international experience spans work in western and eastern Europe, South Asia, the Caribbean, Mexico, Africa and the Middle East.

Harvey received his B.A. from New York University and his M.Phil. and Ph.D. in anthropology from Yale University. His doctoral work was based on two years of research in northern Nepal, where he studied politics and ritual in a Hindu and Muslim village. A postdoctoral position at Cornell's Center for International Studies included three years of research on natural resource management in Jamaica. He taught at the University of Kentucky. He has over three dozen professional publications, and his articles have appeared in the NACUBO *Business Officer*, EduCause *Cause/Effect*, and AGB *Trusteeship*. He has spoken to a variety of higher education audiences, including NACUBO, EACUBO, CACUBO, CAUSE, the Department of Education, and the Council of Independent Colleges.

Gary Brown directs the Center for Teaching, Learning, and Technology at Washington State University. Gary has written and presented extensively on undergraduate learning, assessment, and technology. He is a leader on WSU's FIPSE-funded critical thinking project, and in collaboration with the National Learning Infrastructure Initiative, Coalition for Networked institutions, and the Teaching, Learning, and Technology Group, the Transformative Assessment Project.

He has worked with a variety of professional associations on the assessment of the costs and outcomes of educational technologies and, with CTLT colleagues, was the recipient in 2002 and 2003 for the NUTN award for best research on course design and faculty motivation for using technology to enhance instruction.

He has been a National Learning Communities fellow as well as lead facilitator of the EDUCAUSE New Academy project. Gary directs the CTLT Silhouette Project, which hosts Flashlight Online for TLT-Group and is currently involved in the Better Teaching through Assessment (BeTA) project. He has served on the Washington State Governor's Task Force presaging the establishment of a statewide Digital Learning Commons. His current work includes assessing projects and activities to reflect instructional priorities, the impact and costs of course design, and assessing the efficacy of various assessment strategies.

Vicki S. Freeman is currently the Project Director of the Clinical Laboratory Sciences Accessibility project, and the Partners and Ladders Project. In the past 5 years, she has successfully lead the FIPSE LAAP WebCLS Project and the LEAP Project. Prior to coming to UTMB, she was Co-Project Director of the Rural Education Program with the Division of CLS at the University of Nebraska Medical Center in Omaha.

She completed her doctoral degree in Community and Human Resources, with dissertation work in the area of delivery methods, learning styles, and outcomes for distance medical technology students. Dr. Freeman has authored and co-authored several computer assisted instructional programs, developed a test bank system, and developed and delivered course materials via the Internet. She is active in presenting workshops and other programs at the national level. Her bibliography includes papers on web-based curriculum, CAI, learning styles, distance learning, and reports from interdisciplinary research projects.

Chère Campbell Gibson is Professor Emeritus in the School of Human Ecology and in the Graduate Program in Continuing and Vocational Education at the University of Wisconsin–Madison, and has taught credit courses related to the adult distance learner, instructional design for distance learning and issues in distance education, among others. Video, audio, and computer-conferencing are routinely incorporated as part of these learning experiences.

Chère is equally committed to providing non-credit opportunities for professionals to learn more about distance education and training. The Certificate of Professional Development in Distance Education, which she founded, and the Annual Conference on Distance Teaching and Learning, which she chaired for many years, exemplify her commitment to continuing professional education in our field. Her research focuses on learners and learning at a distance with a specific emphasis on persistence and learner support. Her recent research includes work on cognition and group dynamics in computer mediated conferencing, and the impact of wireless Internet on learners and learning at tribal colleges.

Currently, she is evaluating the use of the Internet on education of migrant families as well as providing professional development via the Internet to teach higher education professionals to develop educational programs to help learners with disabilities transition to college. An author of numerous research articles on teaching and learning at a distance, she recently edited *Distance Learners in Higher Education: Institutional Responses for Quality Outcomes*.

Joan Krejci Griggs is currently the National Training Officer for the National Archives and Records Administration (NARA) in Washington. She directs NARA's records management training for the Federal government and serves on a working group for the Office of Personnel and Management (OPM) to develop quality standards and procedures for online training in the Federal government.

Prior to her position at NARA, Dr. Griggs was a Program Officer for eight years with the Fund for the Improvement of Postsecondary Education (FIPSE), the U.S. Department of Education. There she coordinated the Fund's primary grant vehicle, The Comprehensive Program; was on the team that designed and managed the Learning Anytime Anywhere Partnerships grant program, and served as an evaluation specialist for FIPSE programs. Her tenure with FIPSE included monitoring many of the innovative projects applying new technologies to education.

Dr. Griggs has also held administrative positions in continuing higher education at the University of Maryland; among other posts, she directed a research institute at the University of Maryland University College, studying adult learners, assessment, and distance learning in higher education. Prior to this work, she initiated and managed continuing education programs at Union College, Schenectady, New York, and The State University of New York: Albany.

She co-authored *Effectiveness and Efficiency in Higher Education for Adults: A Guide for Fostering Learning* and has presented at numerous professional conferences in the areas of assessment in higher education; the professional development of working adults; education and training program development; and the dissemination of innovation. Her doctorate from SUNY Albany is in program development and evaluation.

Julie Porosky Hamlin is Executive Director of MarylandOnLine, an inter-segmental consortium of Maryland colleges and universities engaged in collaborations in online learning. Previously, she served with the University of Maryland University College (UMUC) and with the University System of Maryland central office. At UMUC, Dr. Hamlin began as a faculty member in the university's overseas programs and progressed to Vice President for Statewide Programs and then to Senior Vice President.

Throughout her career, Dr. Hamlin has developed expertise in adult students, accreditation, online learning, regional extension centers, programs for military communities, inter-institutional alliances, reengineering of institutional processes, international programs, leadership training, faculty development, and assessment of learning outcomes. She has made a number of presentations on these topics. Dr. Hamlin has served on several accreditation teams and participates in ACE's evaluations of collegiate programs on military installations. She holds a Ph.D. in higher education from the University of Maryland, and bachelor's and master's degrees in English from the University of Arizona.

Darcy W. Hardy is Assistant Vice Chancellor and Director of the UT TeleCampus, the virtual university of the University of Texas System that supports online delivery of system-wide collaborative academic programs from UT institutions. The UT TeleCampus serves as a portal for students and faculty to access courses, programs, and virtually all services necessary for success when teaching and learning online.

Darcy received her Ph.D. in Instructional Technology from the University of Texas at Austin in 1992. She was a founding member and is a past president of the Texas Distance Learning Association (TxDLA) and has served two separate terms on the TxDLA Board of Directors. Currently, she serves as President of the United States Distance Learning Association (USDLA), where she has been a member of the Board of Directors since 1999. She is the immediate past chair of the Texas Higher Education Coordinating Board Distance Education Advisory Council and has previously served on the Texas Association for Educational Technology Board of Directors. She is the past chair of the University Continuing Education (UCEA) Division of Educational Telecommunications. From 2001–2003, Dr. Hardy served as the onsite host for the Institute for Managing and Developing e-Learning (MDE), presented annually by the Western Cooperative for Educational Telecommunications (WCET). She is also a member of the WCET Steering Committee, representing the Southern Caucus.

Darcy received the 2003 Gayle B. Childs Award from UCEA for exemplary long-term leadership, scholarship, and applied contributions to the field of continuing and distance learning. In 1998, she received the UCEA Nofflet Williams Up-and-Coming Leadership Award and the TXDLA Don Foshee Leadership Award. Other honors include the 2000 UCEA Charles Wedemeyer Publication Award as a co-author of *Teaching at a Distance: A Handbook for Instructors*. Under her direction, the UT TeleCampus has been honored with over a dozen regional and national awards from such organizations as USDLA, UCEA, and the International Association of Business Communicators for courses, programming, communications, and faculty excellence. The UT TeleCampus has been recognized nationally as a model for multi-campus, collaborative online programming.

Kathleen P. King is a Professor and Director of Fordham University's Regional Educational Technology Center (RETC), and Program Director of the M.S. in Adult Education and Human Resource Development at Fordham's Graduate School of Education. She coordinates several grants that provide professional development of teachers in educational technology and also non-technology content areas. These include New York City Department of Education Title IID grants and a US Department of Education FIPSE/LAAP grant that serves teachers across the nation via online technologies, Anytime Anywhere Learning Professional Development School (AALPDS). The RETC serves as a dynamic base for many initiatives in professional development services, partnerships, and research.

She has planned, designed, conducted, and researched faculty and staff development in educational technology for K–12 schools, higher education institutions, and other organizations. Her background is distinct in that although she is an educator and academic, she also has been a "techie" as a private computer consultant for hardware and software purchasing and troubleshooting and training for many years.

Dr. King has authored and co-authored six books, including *Bringing Transformative Learning to Life* (2005), *Keeping Pace with Technology* (2002, 2003); a co-authored book, *A Model for Planning for Effective Faculty Development*; and a co-edited volume: *New Perspectives on Designing and Implementing Professional Development of Teachers of Adults.* In addition, she is founding editor of *Perspectives: The New York Journal of Adult Learning.* In addition, she has published several conference proceedings, 8 book chapters, and over 60 articles and papers. Her grant writing has resulted in over $16 million in external funding and contracts for the University during the past 8 years.

Dr. King is a frequent presenter and keynoter at local, national and international research and professional conferences on the topics of faculty development, transformative learning, and educational technology. Her research has been widely recognized through refereed presentations at conferences including ACHE, AERA, AERC, International Learning Conference, Professional and Organizational Development Conference, and Sloan E-Learning Conference. She earned her B.A. at Brown University, her M.A.. at Columbia International, and her M.Ed. and Ed.D. at Widener University.

Raymond J. Lewis has more than 25 years experience in higher education and distance learning as a program officer for the Fund for the Improvement of Postsecondary Education (FIPSE), as director of Oregon's statewide distance learning network (Oregon ED-Net), and as a higher education consultant. He is Director of the educational consulting firm Connections Associates based in Portland, Oregon, and a Senior Advisor with WCET Consulting in Boulder, Colorado.

Currently, he is external evaluator for three FIPSE projects: the Hispanic Educational Telecommunications System's (HETS) Virtual Plaza project, the Puget Sound ESD'S Early Childhood Education Outreach Education Project, and Kansas State University's Academic Alliances Project. He was also the evaluator on two FIPSE projects that had no-cost extensions and ended in 2004—Montana State University's BATE project, and CONAHEC's electronic portal project.

As part of WCET Consulting, he recently worked with the Hispanic Association of Colleges and Universities (HACU) in their planning effort to establish a Hispanic Virtual Learning Market space. In addition to a focus on collaborative distance learning projects, Ray also has a strong interest in the delivery of higher education services in the international arena. He is the former director of Oregon ED-NET, a statewide educational telecommunications network. As a consultant to WICHE in the mid-1980s, he wrote the concept paper that led to the creation of WCET. He has a Ph.D. in political science from Syracuse University.

Marianne R. Phelps is a higher education consultant in the areas of distance education, accreditation, and institutional assessment, working with individual institutions and educational organizations. She is also an adjunct faculty member at

Walden University. Dr. Phelps has significant experience in university administration and academic policy, having held a number of posts at George Washington University, including University Planning Officer and Associate Provost.

Between 1993 and 2001, she was employed by the U.S. Department of Education in several capacities, most recently as Special Assistant to the Assistant Secretary for Postsecondary Education, where she was responsible for the Distance Education Demonstration Program. Other positions held were Chief of Staff to the Assistant Secretary and Director of the Institutional Participation and Oversight Service. For her work in reengineering the Oversight Service, she received the Secretary of Education's Executive Management award. Prior to her work at the Department, she served as Vice President of the Council on Postsecondary Accreditation. Dr. Phelps holds a bachelors degree from the University of Michigan and two masters degrees from the University of Wisconsin. She earned M.Phil. and Ph.D. degrees at George Washington University.

Index